Every Warrior Has His Own Song

Alan B. Walker

iUniverse, Inc.
New York Bloomington

Every Warrior Has His Own Song

iUniverse books may be ordered through booksellers or by contacting:

iUniverse
1663 Liberty Drive
Bloomington, IN 47403
www.iuniverse.com
1-800-Authors (1-800-288-4677)

Because of the dynamic nature of the Internet, any Web addresses or links contained in this book may have changed since publication and may no longer be valid.

ISBN: 978-1-4502-5220-1 (sc)
ISBN: 978-1-4502-5219-5 (dj)
ISBN: 978-1-4502-5217-1 (ebk)

Library of Congress Control Number: 2010912019

Printed in the United States of America

iUniverse rev. date: 10/25/2010

Contents

To the Hatchett family—past, present, and future

Introduction

When I first started this project, it was my intention to make this story a novel, but as I delved deeper into the history, I knew that this was a true story that needed to be told. In my research, I found my great-great-great-grandfather's name, He-Is-Always-There. It was exciting to go back that far, into history and have a connection. This book is titled *Every Warrior Has His Own Song*, to honor William Hatchett, the only warrior to have received a warrior song in my family.

The Winnebago people are patriotic and fiercely loyal to this country and the land of their ancestors. This is evidenced by the way they show respect to the returning veterans of any war. The meaning of a Ho-Chunk warrior is 'to see your enemy and kill him.' Only a veteran with combat experience can feather a young Indian maiden with an eagle feather. This is done in the great circle at the powwow. The only way a woman can wear an eagle feather is if it was given to her by a warrior.

Every Warrior Has His Own Song is my story of my family and the Ho-Chunk/Winnebago nation—the hardships they endured being forced to move by the U.S. government and finally being placed in northeast Nebraska, on a small reservation.

No one living today knows how the reservation affected the lives of our ancestors, being placed on a strange land, not having the ability to travel or live where their ancestors are buried! Placing the Ho-Chunks on a reservation and treating them like a defeated tribe broke many a warrior's spirits. No longer could they provide food and lodging for their families; they had to depend on the government for monthly rations of food, blankets, and medical attention.

The Ho-Chunk warriors told many stories about World War II and some of the great things that our Winnebagos had done while in service. As I grew older, I knew that I wanted to be a warrior and wondered if I had the right stuff. *Every Warrior Has His Own Song* ends with my story of being in Vietnam.

A tattoo on a Marine reads, "To really live you must nearly die." Only those that were in the bush that have survived the gore of a firefight or lived through the charging of NVA soldiers in full battle dress, throwing grenades and spitting lead from an AK-47, will know what it means.

The Marine recruiter asked me what kind of a job I would like to do in the Corps. "I want to be a grunt in Vietnam," was my answer. Like my great-great-grandfather, I wanted to serve my country. To write my part of this story, it had to be lived.

Alan B. Walker
Xu Kagle Gle (Buffaloes Sitting in a Circle)

Chapter 1

The Treaty of 1832

Author's note: The name Cloud is not the true family name. It wasn't until after 1865 that Hatchett appears on any government document. Cloud is a fictitious name that I chose to use in my writing. Later in life, William Cloud would change his name to Hatchett after he proved himself in battle; only then was he allowed to change his name.

On a sweltering day in late summer of 1832, my great-great-grandfather William Cloud Ku-nu (firstborn son) was born in an earthen lodge somewhere in the territory of Wisconsin. This was part of the Ho-Chunk Nation that consumed the southern portion of the present state of Wisconsin, the northern part of Illinois, and the eastern edges of Iowa and Minnesota. Fish and game were plentiful. Corn, squash, and other plants were grown easily on this fertile land. The nation traded with the wild rice people from the north.

This was where William Cloud took his first faltering steps and spoke his first words of the Ho-Chunk language; it was there that he was strapped on to a cradle board and placed on his mother's back. (Indian women carried their young this way because it freed their hands and gave them more mobility.)

William was one of the first Indians to have a white man's name. His mother (*Na-Nee*), Descending Eagle, and father (*Jda-Gee*), E-jah-nic-nah-ke-gah (He-Is-Always- There), did not follow the Ho-Chunk tradition when they named him William, nor would they consider

1

having his name changed later in life. This was a trend that other Native Americans would follow. The white man (*Mi-Xa-da*) did have an influence on their culture. As he advanced into Indian country, bringing with him the white man's religion, he insisted the Indian customs of native prayer, fasting, and medicine lodges were evil, and the Indian people were heathens "without a god." Soon after William was born, his father gave him his Indian name of Ho-Bo-Sinch-Gah, which means "Wind Blow." Only his family would call him by his Indian name; the Indian agents didn't like to hear people called by their Indian names— they wanted to hear the proper English names.

"As long as I can remember, we have been at war with the white man or our brother Indians, and now we are gathered here, and soon our chiefs will sign a piece of paper, and all will change forever," William's father, He-Is-Always-There, told his family. "I hear that they want to move us to what they call the Neutral Ground, land given to us for signing a treaty; I don't know how long we will live in peace or how long we will be at the Neutral Ground. We have lived in this area a long time, and this is our hunting ground. Now they want us to leave here and give us a small piece of land that will be our home."

"The government wants to sell us our own land and make it sound like we are getting something great, and we will be watched like mad dogs. They say we can't cross the river and go east, can't go west or north to our old homes."

In a treaty signed on September 15, 1832, the chiefs gave away the land of their ancestors; in return, the Ho-Chunks were given the Neutral Ground a strip of land forty miles wide established for the Sauk and Fox, to keep the warring Sioux out of their land.

The government troops came in and moved a village of Ho-Chunks to the Neutral Ground, but within two weeks, the villagers were back at their old lodges in the Wisconsin territory. The U.S. government had promised the villagers wagons, horses, and supplies to see them through until regular supplies could be established at the Neutral Ground, but the Indians brought the supplies back with them. Two years after, the treaty was signed. It appeared that nothing had changed. It was a joke that if you wanted rations, you had to go to the Neutral Ground to get them. (Rations consisted of beef or pork—mostly bacon—flour, corn, sometimes coffee, sugar, and beans. This was given to the head of the household. Rations also included clothing and blankets when they were available.)

When William Cloud was two years old, he was walking and learning the Ho-Chunk language, and his mother told him stories about how he would grow up to be a good son, a loyal father, and maybe a warrior. But his father felt differently about William. He wondered where they would end up. He sensed their time was very short on this land. True, the government had tried to move some of the Indians, and it failed; but He-Is-Always-There knew the time would come when they would just put bayonets to the Ho-Chunks' backs and tell them to march.

In September of 1837, the government interpreters asked to hold council with the leaders of the tribe, but they came at a time when the leaders were away; and the sub-chiefs, not the chiefs, were the ones in attendance. The interpreters warned the sub-chiefs that evil things were about to befall them, but if they signed a certain piece of paper, everything would be taken care of, and all would be safe.

The sub-chiefs talked about it for a while, and they agreed that it would be all right for them to sign the government paper, thinking that they were doing a good thing for their people. Little did they know that they had just signed away the last piece of their land in the Wisconsin Territory. Now nothing could stop the government from forcibly removing the Winnebagos from their homeland.

It took another three years before the government started the removal of the Ho-Chunks from their land. Rumors filled the villages about bluecoats coming, but they were just that—rumors. What did come were the *Y-Sapes* (Black Robes), the white man's religious men. The Indians didn't know this, but the government had given permission to any religious group that wanted to teach the red men about God. Because there was no longer a reservation in the Wisconsin territory, the government called it "open land occupied by Indians."

The Y-Sapes settled in the larger Indian villages, and soon churches and other buildings built of wood planks with floors and windows went up. More white people came into the villages. Most of the Indians had never seen European buildings.

If anything good came from the Y-Sapes' arrival, it was the tinker who traded with the Indians. In his inventory, he carried cast-iron cookware, canvas for lighter tents, modern hand tools, steel hunting knives, boots and shoes, plus much more, which he traded for skins, money, and anything of value. It was strange how the tinker could travel in and out of Indian Territory without any problems. The word was put out by the women of the tribes to leave him alone: "We like what he has to trade." The tinker's goods made life better for the Indians.

The Ho-Chunks went about their normal way of life, not knowing when the bluecoats would ride into the villages and round them up and take them off. In fact, some of the western villages had already been moved onto the Neutral Ground. On February 10, 1840, the order was given to General Henry Atkinson to round up all of the Ho-Chunks and force them into the Neutral Ground. But to the dismay of the army, many Ho-Chunks once again crossed back into Wisconsin. This would go on now for many weeks. The Cloud village was one of the last to be moved, and by that time, the army's nerves had been worn very thin. "They took no prisoners." When anyone fell out, the commanding officers would say, "Let them go; we'll send out a detail later to pick up the stragglers."

The detail, however, turned out to be a death squad. All stragglers were shot and left to rot.

The Indians didn't have many horses. A few had Shoonks (dogs) to help with the load, so the rest of their belongings had to be lugged or packed on their backs. William was eight years old; his parents kept telling him to stay close and to keep up with them. "Why?" he asked, wanting to know.

"You see that bluecoat over there on that horse?" asked his mother, pointing.

William nodded. He saw several mounted soldiers.

"Well, if you fall behind, those bluecoats will shoot you, and there is nothing that we can do about it."

Hearing that, William stepped faster to keep up with his mother. The forced march was about 150 miles as the crow flies. They made it in five days, and it was the bluecoats who fell out in the end. The Ho-Chunks showed those white soldiers that they could handle a little walk in the forest. It's not known how many Indians were lost or shot on these marches.

Their last stop was Fort Atkinson in Iowa, a large complex with high wooden walls where the bluecoats lived. From there, they were assigned to villages in the Neutral Ground. These were typical white man–run villages, where different clans were all mixed together, not at all the way a Ho-Chunk village was set up. That was taken care of after the bluecoats left. After a few months, things settled down, and life returned to normal.

Movement within the Neutral Ground was allowed, but Indians were not allowed to wander outside of the Neutral Ground. The adventurous young members—the future Ho-Chunk warriors in training—moved to the western edge of the Neutral Ground, where the bluecoats chose not to go because one of them had seen a Sioux war party nearby.

The Neutral Ground was a mass of land approximately 165 miles long by forty miles wide and ran on an angle to the southwest. Its western boundary was the Des Moines River. The Fort Atkinson area was quite hilly, with deep ravines and many small creeks and streams, some of which dried up in the middle of the summer. Moving west in the Neutral Ground, the land turned into prairie, mostly flat with some rolling hills. During the time of the Winnebagos' stay in the Neutral Ground, most if not all of this land was virgin soil, with plenty of fish and game and plenty of material to make a lodge.

Most of the activity was around the fort, and many villages sprang up around the fort because it was close to the ration building. This was not good, because the bootleggers and the Y-Sapes could enter these villages easily, and the government did not want to deal with drunken Indians.

William's family moved into the interior of the Neutral Ground. He-is-Always- There didn't like the bluecoats, and he didn't trust the Indian agents, and he didn't like being told by the Y-Sapes that his beliefs were wrong. His discovery of the perfect lodge and longhouse (sometimes called Snake Lodge) site came one day when He-Is-Always-There was following a game trail that topped a wooded hill and zigzagged down into a large valley. He looked over the site and realized that if he made the longhouse in the north portion of the valley, the natural sidewalls of the valley would help muffle the sound of the drum. He hurried back to his family's temporary quarters and told his wife, and the next day, the Cloud family was off. They didn't tell anyone of their find, because they knew that some of the tribal members were telling agents where different people lived in return for extra rations. It was the agents' job to know the whereabouts of all of the Indians.

He-Is-Always-There stopped to ask two of his brothers, Tall De Cora and John Rise Up, to follow them later. John Rise Up stayed behind at the old lodge while the family moved out of the camp, and when all was clear, he followed them. This was done to make sure that no one saw them leave. The Cloud family followed the game trail into the valley; there was only one way in and one way out. Tall De Cora stayed on the game trail and waited for John Rise Up, and soon the two medicine lodge brothers came down the side of the hill. John Rise Up was carrying a new ax, and they all marveled at it.

"I see that you have been trading with the tinker," Tall De Cora said. "Does it fit your hands?"

"Of course it does. It may be a little small, but it will get the job done."

"I thought that you just traded for pot and pans," said He-Is-Always-There and they all laughed.

The first project was to build a lodge for the family with the opening facing to the east. Everyone helped, and it took only a few hours to have a dwelling with a fire pit, sleeping mats, a seating area, and a vent hole for the smoke to exit the lodge. The next day, they started on the longhouse.

Not far from the lodge was a good-sized stream. William and his father went down and looked for turtles; they had to be very quiet, and they saw two snappers sunning themselves on the mud bank. The two hunters came prepared; they each carried a net. He-Is-Always-There pointed at a turtle for William to catch. He-Is-Always-There counted in silence with his fingers, and on three, the two men jumped the slumbering turtles. In seconds, the two hard shells were on their way to the lodge for supper. Every part of a turtle had a use, so it was a good day. Before night fell, He-Is-Always-There had tied their government rations up in a tree so the critters couldn't get to them. There were still a few items that needed to be built in the lodge, such as a storage area for blankets and cold-weather clothes and a safe area for the rations.

The next morning, before any clearing or cutting began; He-Is-Always-There blessed the area and gave an offering of tobacco to the spirits. When this was done, the medicine lodge brothers talked about the size of the new lodge. They decided to build it in the center of the clearing with room to add on to the back side. The lodge opening faced to the east like all of the Ho-Chunk dwellings. This would be a small lodge with one fire pit. The longhouse was the meeting place for the medicine people, an exclusive group that members had to be invited to join. In days gone by, some of longhouses had had as many as fifteen fire pits in them.

"It would be nice to get some of that white man canvas to put on the top," said John Rise Up.

"Hmm," was Tall De Cora's only reply.

"It would make our work easier," admitted He-Is-Always-There. "But I don't know if putting something made by a white man on this medicine lodge is a good thing to do."

They all agreed, and they kept working. It would take three more days to finish the longhouse, and its location was kept a secret. Only members knew the location of the new snake lodge.

As more and more of the traditional Indians moved away from the fort and found their clan sites, the Indians that were left were really the hang-around-the-fort Indians. Some of them had become very pitiful—drunks and beggars and others who didn't want to do anything but wait for their rations.

"It is strange how our people have changed from being a proud and strong nation to this," He-Is-Always-There said. "Some of these Indians are still members of the longhouse, and they know better than to live like this."

On ration day, He-Is-Always-There refused to talk to the Indians who hung around the fort. "When you become a Ho-Chunk again, you can come and talk to me," he would tell them when they tried to start up a conversation. Some became very upset, while others understood and just moved on.

After two years in the Neutral Ground, most of the Ho-Chunks had settled in and came to consider the territory their new home, but not all. Many didn't trust the Indian agent. One of those Indians was He-Is-Always-There. He didn't like the treatment of the Ho-Chunks. "Our men grow fat and lazy because there is little for them to do," he told anyone who would listen to him. "Some of them like to get drunk and act very stupid. They talk about the old days and how great they were. I think that their spirit is broken, and all they have left is old memories. We wait each month for our rations, and when they come, we are all happy until the food runs out. Some of our warrior's still hunt and snare game for us. Some of them try to keep the old ways and live away from the modern Indians, and then there are the hang-around-the-fort Indians. Our medicine men are called liars by the Y-Sapes. Our way of life is soon coming to an end."

He-Is-Always-There understood that the white man had changed their way of life. No longer could an Indian roam the plains or hunt along the Rock River. That was no longer their land. Some of the members would accept the change, but others would have a hard time adjusting. Not all of the tribe lived in the Neutral Ground. Some still lived in Wisconsin and northern Illinois. A few whom the government had somehow missed were scattered along the Wisconsin and Mississippi rivers, still living the Ho-Chunk way. Those who were able to carry on without any government intervention called themselves "freemen."

The white man's religion was brought into the neutral country by missionaries who got permission from the U.S. government to "teach the Indian children the word of God."

The Ho-Chunks did not like the Y-Sape people. They tried to take over the young people and rule them with hard words and big clubs. Most of the elders hid the children as soon as they saw the Y-Sape people coming into their camps. There was no rule that said Indians had to go to the white man's church, but the missionaries made it hard on the parents who didn't send their offspring to school and church.

As far as William was concerned, this white man's religion was a game—a game of hide and not getting caught. The Black Robes could not be everywhere, after all, and they couldn't run as fast as he and the other young bucks could. But if you were slow and got snagged by them, you had to pay the price. You had to sit for hours on a hard bench—sitting up straight, not slouching or nodding off to sleep, because if you did, you would get rapped up the side of your head with a long wooden pole that one of the deacons carried around. The deacon's job, as William saw it, was to control noisy, sleepy, or unruly kids.

First the preacher would talk in English, and then the Indian interpreter would speak it in the Ho-Chunk language. It was long and boring, but the children had to listen to them talk about how they needed these religious people and how they would be saved by them and how they had come to save the red man from his destruction. The white man's religion insisted its words and teachings were the only way and that the rituals of the Indians were wrong. You could not get into heaven if you listened to the old medicine men, they insisted.

William found this kind of talk confusing. Was this the only way? What about the way of the ancestors, which had been taught to his parents and his parents' parents? How could it be wrong all of a sudden? The words of the missionaries did not move him. He might nod his head in agreement, but it didn't mean anything to him. It was just a way to get the Y-Sapes to shut up and let him go home.

"The Y-Sapes can talk and place us underwater and say more words, but these words mean nothing to us!" One elder warrior noted, "You can run a horse into the stream and say words, but it means nothing to the horse. They talk of salvation and that their way is the only way to the spirit world. What do they know about our spirit world? Our ancestors were here long before the white man. Our medicine men could talk with the spirit world. It was said that we should have used medicine on the first white man, but no! Said our leaders, 'Let the white men come into our lodge; he comes in peace.' He came with one hand out and the other with a piece of our Mother Earth and calling it his home! This is the way it has been and will be for our next generation and theirs; they can put me underwater and mumble a few words and say that I am saved, but it means nothing to me. I am a Ho-Chunk warrior. My power comes from me and the warriors that I ride with. When you choose to become a Ho-Chunk warrior, you choose to die. This has been passed down from generation to generation."

Others who had gathered to listen agreed with him, and some of the young children could only stop and stare at the old warrior and wonder how he could say all of those words and not get into trouble. The Y-Sapes didn't like the Indians to talk about the old ways or to put them down the way he had. Maybe when you reached a certain age, you could talk that way, and nothing would happen to you; or maybe the old man simply didn't care.

One day a Y-Sape approached William's mother, Descending Eagle, and asked her if her child had been baptized. "No," she said. "Why? Has yours been baptized?"

"I am a priest," he responded angrily. "We do not marry and have children like the rest of the world."

"That's a pity."

That made the priest even madder. "I am trying to save your child, and you're having fun with me," he shouted.

"We do not need your kind here," Descending Eagle said, looking the priest squarely in the eyes. "We believe in Mah-oonah. He is our god, and we do not need statues or to be put underwater and claim to be saved. We know right from wrong. We have lived this way long before your kind ever came here. Out of my way, priest!"

"You will go to hell for saying that."

"Then we will meet again!"

William smiled. He knew that the Cloud family came from a strong medicine background, and the white man's talk of God did not scare them at all. "Only those who are not strong medicine people will fall to the Y-Sapes," his father always told him.

To William, life in the Neutral Ground was agreeable for the most part. The government did provide rations and blankets for the winter. Many lodges were built, but he knew the teaching of the Indian ways had to be done in secret because the agent and the Y-Sapes didn't want this practice to continue. A few times when they learned of a meeting, he had seen them disrupt it and send everyone home. There was talk of building a school for the children in the Neutral Ground, but that's all it was.

William was pleased that once the Ho-Chunks were established in the Neutral Ground, they continued to have their four feasts. His favorite was the winter feast, which was the longest. This feast took two weeks. The first week was the harvesting of the meat, with the tanning and preparation of the skins. Then came the actual feast; it went on for a whole week, with short days and long nights until it was finished. If there was anyone who didn't get full, it was his fault.

Another ceremony William liked was the Ho-Chunks' Scalp Dance. At the Scalp Dance, a young man could learn a lot about how the scalp was taken; it was good just to sit and listen to the owner of many scalps talk.

William loved the storytelling too. One cold and snowy night, members of William's family met at his *Chu-wee*'s (aunt's) lodge. She was a storyteller. She knew many stories—some of them were true and some of them not. Once inside her lodge, William and his friends talked and laughed until one of the members stood up and said, "It's time to hear from my sister. She has many things that she wants to tell us. Maybe we should be quiet for a while and let her talk."

Everyone stopped talking.

"For you who don't know me, I am called Whispers in the Wind, and I am glad to see so many of my relatives here tonight. This first story that I will tell you is about a young warrior, so listen, and maybe you will learn something."

She began her story, telling about a group of Ho-Chunk warriors. One warrior was a young brave, and this was his first war party. He tried to act normal, but you could tell that he was very excited. One of the older warriors told him to stay in the back of the group to watch and learn. The young brave agreed, but he had no intention of staying in the rear. He wanted some action. He wanted his uncle to write a song about him and his bravery. He wanted to pick the prettiest woman and make her his wife, because he was going to become a great warrior.

As the party came closer to the enemy, they passed the word to dismount; they would work their way into the enemy camp on foot. Things were working well for the Ho-Chunk war party. Soon they would spring the attack, but as they got ready to move, the young warrior leapt out in front of the others and rushed into the enemy camp. The young brave saw his enemy, and he killed him. That made him a Ho-Chunk warrior, but he had acted too soon. Before he could strike again, a dozen arrows from the trees hit him in the back. As he lay dying on the ground, he remembered that the older warrior had told him to stay in the back and watch.

"It's too bad that this young warrior had to die, but he died from his own foolishness. He should have waited and watched as he was told. Trying to make a name for yourself is not the way of the Ho-Chunk warrior," said the storyteller. "If you wish to be a successful warrior, you must first know your enemy, know how he gets himself ready for battle, know when he sleeps and eats, and know his strengths and weaknesses. Don't rush in just because he is there. So I tell you, young people, don't rush into everything just because it's there. Learn first, and then make smart decisions. Don't get your shirts full of arrows."

William thought about the young brave and how foolish he had been. This would never happen to him! He would never do anything so stupid. He would first learn how to fight and steal his way into an enemy camp.

Another storyteller stood up and started a new story about three white men who came into the Ho-Chunk Nation; they were fur trappers. Many years before, the three had stolen, raped, and finally killed the young daughter of a powerful medicine man. They left the body in a shallow grave and tried to cover it up with leaves and dead branches from the trees.

The name of the medicine man was Young Prophet. He knew where his daughter was, and his medicine told him where to look. When Young Prophet brought back his daughter to the village, there was much crying and mourning, for she was a beautiful young girl and well liked. Many members of the tribe wanted to go after the three, but Young Prophet said, "No! I will take care of this."

Young Prophet was asked one day by the leader of the young men to let him and a few of his braves go after these whites, but again, the medicine man told them no. "I will avenge my daughter's death."

The medicine man went into the timbers and was gone for a many days. When he returned to the village, he said nothing to anyone. They knew that he had spoken with the spirit world. Young Prophet and his family were still in mourning. This went on for a long time, maybe two years or more. Then one day Young Prophet announced that he and his family were no longer in mourning. That night the spirits came to him and showed him that they had found the three white men that killed his daughter, and they told of how they met their own deaths.

A few days later, Young Prophet called for a council, and he told the story. He started out slowly so everyone could hear the story. The three white men had ridden for many days until they reached the foothills of the Rocky Mountains. One day when the three were on the open prairie, riding in the high prairie grass, the sun was bright and high in the sky, and a light breeze swept the tall prairie grass back and forth.

Birds flew overhead, and in the distance, a flock of buzzards soared in the sky, looking or waiting for their next meal. Then all of a sudden, an ear-piercing death shrill came out of the blue, the horses bolted, and the pack mule threw off his load and galloped off into the distance.

One of the trappers looked into the sky, only to see a horrifying sight; a creature from hell was swooping down on the terrified men. Drool ran from its razor-sharp teeth. Its mouth was wide open, with horrifying screams coming from it. The men could hardly hold on to their mounts, but before they could dismount or pull out rifles, the creature had grabbed one of the men. Its long curled talons plunged into the helpless man. Three of the talons went right through his upper torso. The beast of prey was so close that the other two could see the yellow on the aged talons.

The grass whipped and was laid flat in the strong downdrafts of the ancient man-eating creature. As the helpless victim screamed and tried to wiggle free, his face was wrenched with pain. His eyes were as large as silver dollars. Higher and higher the bird flew with its victim; they went north to a mountain range. The helpless trapper moved less and less. His body was drenched in blood, the ground was red with his blood, and even his horse had blood dripping from the saddle.

The two remaining trappers just stood in shock and terror. What was this thing? Where did it come from? Both of the men were white as sheets and shaking so badly that they could hardly stay in their saddles, so they galloped off to the nearest tree line, hoping that it wouldn't return. When they finally reached the tree line, the horses were just about ready to collapse. Still shaken and very terrified, they dismounted and quickly ran to the trees, thinking that the large bird couldn't get at them in the thick trees. What they had just witnessed was a sight that no other human had ever seen before. Nothing could have been so horrible as this evil thing from hell. Had they invaded its hunting grounds? Whatever it was, they made plans to get out of this area as quickly as possible!

The plan was to move at night and stay close to the tree line so in case it came back, they could run into the trees. This plan seemed to work. They had been on the move for six nights, and they hadn't seen any sign of it. Early one morning, the two stopped for the night when the moon was full in the western sky. They had stayed close to the trees and a small creek ran through the tree line. One of the trappers went down to get some water and wash up.

As he bent over, the demon from hell let out a murderous scream, swooped down, and grabbed him, thrusting its steel-like talons into the trapper's head. The man was twisting and turning, trying to get to his knife, but he couldn't reach it. The large winged reptile with one swift movement clutched its victim straight up from the creek. Wiggling and squirming, the white man was still trying to reach his knife. The thumb like talon had sliced right into the back of the trapper's head. Still wiggling and screaming, again, this victim was carried off in the same direction as the last one, north into the Rocky Mountains.

The last trapper knew that he was next. Shaking and crying, he couldn't control himself, or his bodily functions he was sick to his stomach, he fell down, crying and shaking, and he even tried to praying to God. The poor soul cried himself to sleep, only to have nightmares that woke him up. He was so scared that he couldn't even sit up in the daylight. He thought about shooting himself but couldn't get the courage to do it. He put his pistol up to his head but could not pull the trigger. Somehow this sick man wanted to go to the mountains where the large bird had carried his two friends. This would mean traveling back over the same ground that they had just covered in the last six nights.

Maybe he was crazy; maybe he wanted to get it over with. Now it didn't seem to make any difference if he traveled at night or in the day light. He did make it over to the mountains, always looking up into the sky. Finally, on the seventh day, he came across a bald mountain where all of the trees and grass were gone except for three large naked pines. All of the branches were gone; the trees were without bark and came to a needle point at the top. What he saw made him sick to his stomach. His two friends were impaled on two different pines. The sight was disgusting and sickening; buzzards were landing and lunching on the two corpses. He knew that the third pine was for him. What would he do? Where could he go? How could he get away from this demon? Who would even believe his story?

Now the thought of killing himself was very strong in him, but still he just couldn't do it. Riding at night again and staying close to the tree line, he made it back to a small town on the outskirts of the prairie.

This little town was the last stop for the freight wagons. His plan was to go east as far as St. Louis, where he thought, nothing could get him, in the big city. The open freight wagon couldn't move fast enough for him. Every now and then, he looked into the sky, and sometimes he would just start to tremble and shake uncontrollably. The driver would ask him if he was okay. "Do you need a drink?"

His reply was always the same: "I just need to get home." He made it back to the Missouri River and took a boat down to St. Louis. He had heard that the Indian spirits could not cross water, so if he could make it to St. Louis, he would live on the east side of the Mississippi River.

Once on the Missouri River steamboat, he stayed in his cabin the whole trip. Some of the other passengers thought maybe he was sick, so they stayed away from him. He was sick. He had terrible nightmares, and they were always the same: the creature didn't kill him; instead, it took him to the bald mountain and dropped him alive on the third naked pine. He could feel himself free-falling, and when he glanced down, he could see the sharp naked pine waiting for its sacrificial human. He would wake up screaming and violently thrashing about, his bed wet with sweat and urine.

The steamboat couldn't go fast enough, but it finally made port at St. Louis. It was his luck that he ran into some of his old friends. They got him a job and a place to live, but he never told anyone about the killing of the young Indian girl and the naked pines on a bald mountain.

His second year in St. Louis, he even started to go to church, thinking maybe this would help him with his past and get rid of his bad dreams and help put it all behind him. One night he went to a prayer meeting. When it was his turn to say a prayer, he asked for forgiveness of the killing of the Indian girl a long time ago, but he made it sound as though his friends did this terrible deed. After the meeting, some of the church people wanted to hear more about the young girl's death. He told them of how they had kidnapped her, raped her, and then killed her out on the prairie and left her in a shallow grave. Then he went on to tell them about the monster from hell and how it had come out of the sky and swooped up his two partners and how it had carried them off and dropped them onto the naked pines on the bald mountain.

Some of the members thought it made a good story, but others didn't believe him at all. Some even wondered about the killing of the young Indian girl. "Maybe this guy was just trying to impress us," they said.

Others said, "Maybe he was out in the mountains too long."

Well, no matter, they agreed it made for an interesting evening. As the trapper left the church building and started to walk down the street, a powerful downdraft hit the people, and a bloodcurdling scream filled the air, and now the third killer was in the death talons of the great monster! Higher and higher, the human prey was taken; his body wrenched with pain, blood squirting all over the place. As fast as the monster hit, it was gone.

The people stood in awe, and some of the women fainted. A creature from hell here in St. Louis! People couldn't believe what had just happened. They called the police and told of the monster and how it took one of their members away in the air. No one was found that night, but the next day, the body of the third killer was impaled on the church spiral of the steeple.

When the old storyteller finished, she turned to the group. "Never kill anyone, only in a battle, and never lie. You must always tell the truth. And never steal from a medicine man."

The younger ones just sat there with their mouths open, too scared to move. William wondered whether his father could do this, because he too was a medicine man. But he didn't want to know. No one wanted to leave the lodge that night. When William got back to his lodge, he asked his father about the last story and how the three men were killed. "Is this possible?"

His father's reply was, "The power of some medicine men is very strong."

One night William asked his father if he was a Ho-Chunk warrior.

"It's in our clan that we become warriors, but not everyone in the nation has that right, and not everyone in the clan wants to become a Ho-Chunk warrior," said He-Is- Always-There.

He-Is-Always-There was a powerful medicine man. It was said that his medicine was good, and this helped him in battle. Other warriors would ask him for help. Some would want to know about the spirit world, because they knew that soon they would join their ancestors. The wise medicine man would tell those who wanted to know about their future, "When you became a Ho-Chunk warrior, you chose to die, so why do you even ask?"

When they heard those words, they were ashamed that they had asked the question about dying.

A few weeks later, a meeting was held in the longhouse. These meetings were illegal. The government called them "secret meetings." The government thought the reason for holding a secret meeting was to make plans for a war party, to break out of the Neutral Ground, or some other kind of move against the government or white settlers. William was asked to attend this meeting.

This was a big event in a young boy's life, to sit in on a meeting in the longhouse. William hoped that he could stay awake through the long meeting, yet he was very excited about being invited. Other young boys were in the longhouse when William walked in. He thought maybe this was how you got into the Ho-Chunk warrior society. It was a long meeting, and still nothing was said about the young boys at the meeting.

Finally, He-Is-Always-There got up to speak. "You, young boys who were asked to be here today, I have news for you. Some of it is good, and some of it is not so good to hear. You have been asked to sit here and listen to us; we have talked about a lot of things—some from the past, some for today, and some we will see in the future. You young boys someday will carry on all of the tribe's traditions, ways of life, and some of you will become warriors in our society. It is said that if you choose to become a warrior, you choose to die—this is true. Even as we speak right now, there is talk of moving the Ho-Chunk Nation. As warriors, we must be ready for war at any time. I don't know how much of a battle we will have. We don't even have any weapons, and the government won't let us even have a bow, but it is our tradition to have a warrior society.

"We were warriors long before we were farmers or raised pigs. This is what the government would like us to be, pig farmers. We, as your elders, will tell you everything about our society and teach you things that will be useful someday. I do not know if our nation will ever hold a war council again, since peace has been made with all of the tribes in the Midwest, as the white man calls it. We have all signed treaties and were promised land, land that was once ours in the first place, but the great white father said that we could live in peace and not have to be moved ever again!

"This land they call the Neutral Ground was given to us because we signed away our Mother Earth on the Wisconsin and Rock rivers and other lands, which we no longer can walk on, and now they talk of moving us again. I do not know where our nation will be in the next generation. But I do know this—where our ancestors are buried, we can never be buried there."

In the days that followed the meeting in the longhouse, "young men," as they were called now, were sent into the woods with an elder of the warrior society. They were gone most of the day. They had to be careful not to draw attention to themselves, so they moved in small groups, most of the time leaving their lodges in groups of two or maybe three.

Stories were told of how a warrior should act and be responsible to the war chief, always following orders. "We have warriors that will follow the war chief to death if it comes to that," and "Do not act like the young warrior that was killed because he thought he knew better," they were told.

It was fun at first; it seemed as if there was always something new to learn every day, and it was exciting to have a secret that they could never tell the Y-Sapes. Yes, they were in training to become warriors, and one of the first rules that a young warrior had to learn was to never tell a secret to anyone, because once a secret was told, it was not a secret anymore. One of the warriors was none other than the war chief, Chief Little Priest. He had the young men meet him at the western edge of the Neutral Ground. "Here is where I saw a Sioux war party only last year," he told them. "But they didn't see me because I used my knowledge of camouflage, and that is what you will learn here today."

Every ear tuned in.

The chief went on to tell them that sometimes a wise man just sits and watches and does nothing. "You can learn much about your enemy that way, and to do that, you must know how to hide yet be able to see him without him seeing you." The war chief showed the young men how to use Mother Earth and how important it was not to use anything the white man had made, because it stuck out too much. The enemy could see anything made by the white people.

The young men were there for a week. They had to provide food for themselves, cook it without any smoke from the fire, and cover their tracks to make everything look natural. Some days they had nothing to eat. They were told that in battle, they might go many days without food or water. "This too is part of your training, so prepare your bodies well. What you learn here will stay with you for the rest of your lives," said Chief Little Priest. "Use your knowledge well."

On their final day, all of them had to go and hide. "Use Mother Earth and hide well; if I can find you, so can your enemies," said Chief Little Priest.

Some of the young men hid in the trees, others in the water, and still others in the thick timbers. William chose to dig a hole and cover himself with tree branches and natural soil from a spot off the main trail where he could see anyone coming without being seen himself. Years ago, his father had told him that was how you caught birds of prey—by concealing yourself well and using some bait.

On their walk back to the village, each had a spring in his step and a new cockiness. The young men had learned much that week. Soon they would learn how to use a war club, hatchet, and knife. The young men would train more in the weeks to come.

Again, they had to be careful about moving about in the woods, because some of their own people worked for the Indian agent. These were mostly the drunks, the real hang-around-the-fort Indians, who were paid by the agent—but in whiskey instead of money. The young men continued their training, and only a handful of Ho-Chunks knew about the new warriors.

All they needed now was a war!

When William was eleven years old, smallpox swept through the Ho-Chunk village, killing 1,500 members of the tribe, including William's father. With her husband dead, William's mother moved in with her parents. William could feel the hurt that his mother felt, and he also understood that things had changed in his life. And it would only get worse. Things would never be like the old days. Life would never be the same for any native living in the Neutral Ground. The government had rounded up all of the Ho-Chunk Indians and put them there. Those who had sneaked off and lived in Wisconsin were turned in by the white people for bounty, and this action alerted the warrior society.

Young William liked to hear the storyteller's talk about the old ways and how good things were, trading with the wild rice people from the North. They told stories about young men of the tribe trying to buy a bride, offering anything of value, some even offering services. In those days, horses were scarce, so if a young warrior offered up his horse, then that meant he really wanted that woman and was willing to give anything for her.

Life at his grandfather's lodge was peaceful. By this time, William knew most of the medicine songs from the medicine lodge. His grandfather too was a medicine man in the Ho-Chunk Nation. Sometimes his grandfather would be gone for several days, and when he came home, he would be very tired. At those times, William was told to stay outside.

By 1840, all of the Ho-Chunk members had been ordered to move to the Neutral Ground. Still, three years later, some of the Indians managed to make it out of the Neutral Ground and venture back to their old villages. When they did, they found white settlers on their land. The new landowners then told the army, and the runaway Ho-Chunks were rounded up and taken back to the Neutral Ground, sometimes in shackles. William listened to those who were brought back, telling of beatings by the soldiers and being dragged when they couldn't keep up. Some reported the white man had cleared their land, burned the villages to the ground. William was shocked to hear that in some instances, a white man's house stood where a Ho-Chunk lodge had been. The white man had fenced in the land, put a plow to Mother Earth, and put dams on the creeks and small streams. "It will never again be the way it was," one Ho-Chunk elder told William. "It is now the white man's land. He has contaminated Mother Earth. Now she is a slave to the white man."

This was the army's way of teaching the Indians not to leave the Neutral Ground. It seemed to William that with nowhere to go, the Ho-Chunks were at the mercy of the U.S. government.

Chapter 2

The Treaty of 1846

"Keep up or get left behind!" the soldier shouted. "No stragglers!"

Fourteen-year-old William looked up to see the bluecoat pushing one of his Chu-wees who had fallen far behind the rest of the group. William turned around and hurried to help her; but the bluecoat, seeing what he was up to, pulled his horse in front of him.

The warrior and the bluecoat locked eyes, and the soldier tried to stare William into submission.

"Get out of the way," William told him through clenched teeth. "Or I will drag you off that nag and use you for a *sheench* (ass) wipe!"

The white soldier knew he had pushed this young buck too far, and he backed off. William went to help his Chu-wee. He took her bundle and helped her to catch up with the rest.

"*Chu-shgay* (nephew), I am so glad you came back to help me! I wasn't ready to meet Mah-oonah just yet."

William just smiled and stayed by his Chu-wee's side for the rest of the day.

It was 1846, and the Ho-Chunks had signed another treaty of cessions, giving up their land in northeast Iowa for land along the Long Prairie, Watab, and Crow Wing rivers north of St. Cloud, Minnesota. Once the treaty was signed in Washington, the move to Minnesota had started. It was late fall, and the 240-mile-long trip was hard, even for people with little or nothing. It seemed to William that the army liked to bring anguish to the red man, to make life miserable for him.

He was especially worried about his grandparents, who were getting old and seemed to be troubled both physically and emotionally by the journey.

"If I should fall back," his *Cho-ka* (grandfather) told him that night when the march had stopped for the day, "don't come after me. I don't want to see you get into any trouble. I heard what you did today for your Chu-wee, and that was good. She has a family and has many years on this earth, but I am an old man who has seen too much lately, and I don't know if I will like living in Minnesota. It's not my home. My medicine bundle has already been taken care of. In fact, I don't have it anymore; it is in safe hands."

William was the man in his family now; it was up to him to get all of them to their new home in the St. Cloud area of Minnesota.

This too was part of being a Ho-Chunk warrior—taking care of your family and others in the tribe. Descending Eagle was up early the next day, and she made sure that her family got enough food for the long walk. When William told her about his conversation the night before with his Cho-ka and about the old man's wishes if he should fall behind, Descending Eagle didn't say anything. As she looked off in the direction that they would travel that day, tears came to her eyes. Then she turned and walked away from her son. The thought of her father just lying on the side of the trail dying was too much for her; she needed some time by herself.

The industrious Indians who had been in the Neutral Ground lost everything that they had worked for, including large herds of horses and cattle that they had to leave behind. "You can only take what you can carry," was the order. This was gravy for the Indian agent and his cronies. All the livestock, crops, and whatever else was left behind were found money for them. Most of the booty would be sold to the new white landowners who were streaming into the area. William and other members of the snake lodge burned down the lodge and destroyed anything that they couldn't carry, burying some of the heavier items in a deep hole.

This was the first time William saw how his people were treated by the white soldiers through the eyes of a warrior. He remembered the soldiers being so mean when they had moved there a few years ago, the yelling and cussing, and it was no different this time. The bluecoats treated the Indians very badly while they were on the move. Many of the young Indian boys talked about becoming warriors and they would make changes. They wouldn't take the beatings and abuse from any Mi-Xa-da soldier. William completely agreed with them, but he knew it was not up to the young warriors to make war. That decision would come from all of the chiefs.

Chief Little Priest had his hands full with these young warriors. In the evening, he told them to be patient. This was not the time to make war. All they had to do was to look around and see who had all of the rifles—the white soldiers. If anyone started anything at that moment, the soldiers would kill off a lot of the Ho-Chunk women and children just because they could, and they would enjoy it.

It took eight days to make the 240-mile trip. Once they got there, there was nothing, even though the army had said that rations would be there waiting for them. In the dark of night, some Winnebagos left and went back to Wisconsin, and some followed the Mississippi River to their old villages on the river. Most were never seen again. No one knew if any of these Ho-Chunks actually made it to their final destination.

"I will not see the sunset; it's my time," the old medicine man told his wife shortly after arriving in Minnesota. "By this afternoon, I will see our old home in Wisconsin, where I will be happy, but I will be sad because you will not be with me."

The old woman just stared at him. She knew that some of the medicine men foretold their deaths. Later that day, he was gone. He wanted to be laid in a secret place, and this was not a friendly place; he knew that the Rat Eater (*Ojibwa*) was close and might rob a grave of a medicine man.

Life in Minnesota was hard at first, but there was more to explore and do. There was a lot of timber to hunt in and rivers to fish. A young man could learn much from a seasoned hunter and warrior. William was taught advanced concealment—the use of vegetation for camouflage—and how to determine what end of a war club to use and how to shoot on a full gallop and hit what he was aiming at. It took time, but he mastered it all.

With his knowledge of living off the land and surviving in a hostile country, William was ready to become a Ho-Chunk warrior. Now all he needed was a war to prove how much of a man he was, how much of a warrior he would be. The enemy didn't make any difference. It could be the Sioux or the smelly bluecoats. In fact, he would prefer the Mi-Xa-da soldiers. It was time to pay them back for all the injustices that they had committed against the Ho-Chunks. It was time for war.

Other young warriors felt the same way. It was time to become men. It was time to kill the enemy, take scalps, and have your uncle make a war song about you and your bravery, have warriors dance to your song as others sang. It was time to tell of your actions on the battlefield, tell others how it felt to kill the enemy. If you were lucky enough to get wounded, you could show them the scar and tell them how you got it. It would be your time, your time to give an eagle feather to your niece and tell of how you earned the right to do this honor. This was the Ho-Chunk tradition from a long time ago, and it was still honored in the present.

William wanted a strong warrior name—one that would put fear in his enemy, one that would be remembered for a long time, a name that would be in the tribe for generations to come. He was good with a rifle, but his second-best weapon was the hatchet. He would change his name to William Hatchett.

The tribe was still in the St. Cloud area of Minnesota when William turned twenty, and the thought of becoming a warrior looked less and less likely every year. Members of the tribe had learned to plow and plant, raise animals, and trade with the townspeople. Even white men didn't carry guns around anymore. It had become easy for an Indian to get a gun now. You just had to work for farmers, get paid, and then purchase a weapon. Those Indians who were aggressive and energetic did very well. They worked hard and bought items that made life easier for them and their families.

It was hard for a young traditional man to live like this, not being able to go where he wanted to. William longed for the old days, when Ho-Chunks in a hunting party would follow the herds for days, kill what they needed, return to camp and at night, sit around the fire, and tell stories of the hunt.

This was not living; this was what the white man did!

There was nothing exciting—just the same old thing day after day, working in the fields from sunup to sundown and then coming home and then repeating this the next day. Now instead of the Y-Sapes, they had to listen to the Lutherans tell them how they should send their young kids and young adults to church, that all of the Ho-Chunks needed to be saved and that their way was the only way! Strange how many different gods the white man had. The Y-Sapes' god in the Neutral Ground was the only one who could get Ho-Chunks into the spiritual world. Now the Lutherans told them that their god was the one and not to listen to anyone else's. The Lutherans set up a school and forced as many young children as they could find to go to school to learn English and the "word of God." *The Lutherans were no different from the Y-Sapes,* thought William. *They push their ideas onto our children, cut their hair, and make them wear white man's clothes and shoes.* He saw a group of Ho-Chunk children walking to school one day all dressed up in white man's clothes, but they all had brown faces and hands.

One of the good things about the St. Cloud area was that the women could get cast-iron frying pans and other cooking utensils, and this made meals taste better. The tinkers would always come out to the reservation to trade and sell their wares. William traded for a steel-edged hatchet and a hunting knife. There was plenty of game in the timber, and William bought some traps from the tinker and learned how to tan pelts for money. It was good to be in the timbers and camp on the swift waters. Sometimes he would be gone for days, often with other members of his clan. The feeling of being alone with nature, with Mother Earth the smell of fresh mushrooms in the spring, picking wild onions for the soup, and just being away from the white man's plowed fields made him feel good.

It was during such times that William would think about the old story told by the elders of the society, about a war party looking for the enemy. Some members of the party could tell how many were in the enemy camp just by the smell of the smoke from their fire. William wondered how they could do that; they must have good medicine, he thought. In the tribe, there were still storytellers, and William enjoyed going to hear them. Sometimes they would tell a funny story, and everyone got a good laugh out of it.

In late February 1855, William returned home from hunting and trapping. It had been a good hunt, with plenty of meat for the rest of the winter and pelts to work on so he wouldn't get too bored. William had traded some of his game for maple syrup on his way home from the hunt, and he knew his mother would like this treat. Some of the tribal members had maple trees on their allotments and sold or traded the syrup in the winter.

When William entered the lodge, he announced that they had plenty of meat and sweet syrup to last the rest of the winter, but his words were greeted by silence. His mother was just sitting by the fire, watching the flames dance into the air. The chiefs had signed another treaty with the government, she told him, and that they had to move again.

"Where?" William asked.

"To Blue Earth River," was all she said. Word had spread all over the Winnebago tribe and in town that the Indians were moving. The move was on every white man's lips. Even though it was in the middle of winter, the white people were dancing in the streets of St. Cloud.

"We licked 'em, fair and square," one said.

"We didn't even fire a shot," said another.

"Look at them run! Run, you red Indians, run all the way to Blue Earth!" shouted a bearded man.

William now understood how things stood with the Indians and the white man. Many of the tribal members—who had tilled the soil for nine years, developing good farm land—no longer had anything; they couldn't even take their equipment with them. William thought about the old stories told by the elders and how they had traveled from the St. Cloud area to Blue Earth, even before there was a St. Cloud and Blue Earth, and thought nothing of it, because all of it was Ho-Chunk land. This new uprooting was like a death sentence. People were crying. Children were told to pack what they could carry. In fact, the Ho-Chunk tribe had become so dependent on the government that they didn't even have shoonks that could pull a travois anymore.

The day of the great move was bitter cold, but nothing was going to stop the army from moving the redskins out of St. Cloud! A few townspeople came out to say good-bye. Some of them even cried and gave the Indians small bundles of food and blankets. This would be a sad journey. William wondered how this could happen. The Indian agent kept telling the tribe that the Blue Earth River area would be their "permanent home." But what did that mean, a "permanent home"? William remembered the time when his father said, "I don't know where our nation will be in a generation. But I know that it will not be here!"

It was a slow trip to Blue Earth River. It was bitter cold. There were few rations. It was hard to get a good night's sleep on the icy ground. Some of the members tried to go back in the middle of the night, and a few were brought back and beaten, but most of the runaways were never seen again. As the crow flies, it was 160 miles to Blue Earth; it took the Ho-Chunk Nation about a week to get to their "permanent home."

What they found was more snow and cold weather. The army set up some tents, but it was not enough for all of them. The government made good on the rations, and finally, the army brought more tents, but it was still a hard life. Most of the cast-iron cookware had been left behind because they were too heavy to carry, so cooking was difficult, to say the least. But Ho-Chunk women could cook with very little, and soon everyone was full for the first time in a long time.

As the chief and elders looked around and made plans on how to settle into their new home, William and some of the other young warriors talked about how they should live between the white man and the tribe, keeping the white man away from the rest of the tribe. The thought of the white men and women dancing in St. Cloud because the Indians had to leave made William very angry. Even some of the white men that he knew and traded with had been happy to see them go. But in the end, it would be the chief and elders who had the final word on who could live here or who could live close to the white man's farm.

Some of the elders said that Blue Earth was a good hunting area and years ago, they had killed plenty of game there.

It was good to hear some of the old stories and better to have some of the old warriors still with them. An old warrior named Walking Smoke told William to set up his lodge on the river, close to where a small creek joined the river. Words of wisdom could always be used when one was trying to set up a new lodge. "You can catch a lot of fish right here, I know—I have done it before," said Walking Smoke. "This place is good for trapping too. I know because I have done it before."

Spring came early that year, and that was good for everyone. Some of the people tried to plant corn. Without tools, it was hard, but they managed to get some corn in. That first year on the Blue Earth River was rough; there was very little to work with, and some of the elderly passed on into the spirit world, not knowing where to call home, afraid that their spirits would wander the earth, not knowing where to rest.

William called his lodge on the river and creek Cloud Creek Lodge. This place gave him the solitude to practice his medicine, have a sweat lodge, and hold meetings in his longhouse. Sometimes William would go deep into the forest to fast and prayed for a day that he would have a vision. It finally happened during one of his fasts. On that day, William saw an endless prairie. He was riding along when he saw twenty Sioux warriors coming at him at a full gallop. As they got closer, they readied their bows and rifles. They came closer and closer.

Then out of the sky came the hideous screaming demon from the storyteller's tale. It grabbed all of the war party. They tried to stop, and some of the horses fell down in fear. The look on their faces William would never forget. The fear and terror could be seen through their war paint. To have all twenty of them scooped up and taken away in one swipe, this was unbelievable!

As the giant bird carried the war party away, he could see some of them try to stab the monster. Some of them lay helpless, already dead from the tight squeeze. Some of the horses were falling to the ground, but none of the Sioux warriors fell to the ground. William watched until he could no longer see the giant anymore; it moved to the north, just as it had in the story. After catching his breath and watching the giant with its prey fly north into the mountains, the only thing that William thought was, *this demon didn't hurt me. It came to help me. Do I have the power?* He wondered, *this must be my strongest medicine. With such a creature on my side, nothing can harm me.*

William told only his uncle about his vision. His reply was that William must have good medicine and for him to use it wisely, or it could come back to hurt him and his family. "You have no need to tell anyone else of this vision, because some of them would say you made it up from the storyteller's story. Maybe Young Prophet was sending his help to you in your time of need."

That evening after the meal, William went outside for a short walk, and he stopped and sat down under a large cottonwood tree. He could hear the wind moving through the leaves of the tree, and then he leaned back and thought of his vision. In his vision, the demon looked right at him, but it left him alone; it made no attempt to pick him up, and when it flew away, the downward motion of its wings made the sand and dust fly. It was such a powerful and large beast, yet it picked up his enemy as a woman would pick up a sewing needle, very carefully and very precisely.

In 1857, William was twenty-five and had been living on the Blue Earth River for two years. It was a good life, meaning that they had no Y-Sapes coming into their camp, trying to teach their young about their white god. For the most part, the Ho-Chunk Nation was left alone in their new "permanent home." That summer while he was trading furs, meat, fish and others goods, William met a woman from the village. At first she was just a woman wanting to buy some fish and a tanned hide. He didn't think anything of it, because he did this all of the time, and the people who knew of him would seek him out when he came to the village to trade.

"You are William Cloud?"

"Yes, I am. What I can do for you?"

"I need some fresh fish and a tanned hide; I want to make a *Ma-Ka* bag (medicine bag) out of it."

"This will make a good bag for you. It's a black squirrel. And here is the fish I caught this morning."

"How come I have never seen you before?"

"Because you never needed what I have, that's why."

"Perhaps will I see you again?"

"If you look hard enough, you will find me."

What a strange answer, she thought. Now her curiosity was up, and she wanted to know more about this man who lived by the river and called his lodge the Cloud Creek Lodge.

"Does the Cloud Creek Lodge have women to take care of it?"

"No, I take care of my own lodge." Now William was interested, and he was looking over the woman who was asking all of the questions. "Why do you want to know about me and my lodge?"

"Well, you must get lonesome out there all day and all night by yourself."

"I never thought about it. I just go about my work. Why do you want to know about me?"

"Maybe you should come over to my *Day-ga*'s lodge, and we could talk."

"Hmm, I'll see about that."

Alice Whirling Thunder came from a proud family. Her father had died in the Black Hawk War, and she was raised by her Day-ga Herman Whirling Thunder. So it was clear that William had to deal with Day-ga Herman when he went courting. The first time William met Day-ga Herman, he knew that he was not a soft man; his stare was like a knife going through his body. "You came here to ask for my niece?"

"Yes."

"Well, what can you give her, and what can you give me for my princess?"

"I can give her a lodge on the river, plenty of food, and warmth in the winter. I am a good provider."

"Well, good provider, I will need more than a lodge on the river and food."

William thought for a minute. "I offer you a mountain lion pelt, a dugout canoe, plenty of food for you and your family, and protection from raiding tribes."

"William Cloud, we have not had any raiding parties here on the Blue Earth since we got here."

"That is true, but we have the Santee Sioux as our neighbor to the southwest of us, and they can't be trusted."

"So you say, and are you a Ho-Chunk warrior, William Cloud?"

"Yes, I am. I have sat and listened to many a warrior, and I live and practice the traditional way of the Ho-Chunks; I belong to the medicine lodge."

"Come back next week, good provider, and I will give you my answer."

"I will be back," was William's reply.

William left the Whirling Thunder's lodge, thinking about Day-ga Herman. What a hard man to deal with! But one should not think of counting gifts when he is courting his future wife and mother of his children. *If this old man wants more, then he will get it!* Finally, it was time to meet with Day-ga Herman again.

"So you have come back, good provider," Day-ga Herman said when William returned. "And what do you have to offer me today?"

Silent for a long time, William finally replied, "I can give you the pelts, a canoe, meat for the lodge, protection, and a horse."

This raised the old man's eye brows a little. "Where will you get a horse?"

"I have ways of getting things."

"You come back with all of the things that we talked about, and you will have a bride."

The horse would be the hardest item to get on his list, but he had a plan, and he knew of a young colt that was for sale. The next day, William went to see about the young colt; it was green, but with some work, it would be all right. The owner was a white man who lived off the reservation and had dealt with Indians before.

"William Cloud, what can I do for you today?"

"I want to buy the young green colt."

"Well, William, it will cost you plenty."

"How much is plenty?"

The old man knew that the Indians didn't have much money, so he bartered with them for things he needed. "William, I need fresh meat all winter long, good pan size fish, and plenty of different kinds of pelts to trade with."

"I will have the first buck ready by this afternoon and fish by the end of the week."

"It's a deal, William."

As William led the young colt away, he had a smile on his face. The hard part was over; now came the working part of his contract. William had provided many families with fresh meat through the past winters, and now he needed a favor from those families. He first met with Joe Eagle. Then he talked with Henry Baker, and finally, he met with Walking Soldier. They borrowed a long cross saw and extra axes, and soon they were on their way to William's lodge, where they stopped to eat a quick meal of rabbit and day-old fry bread.

"I hope the rabbit and *Wy-skop* (bread) will be enough for you, because we have a lot of work to do in a few short days." He took the working party to the base of a tall and thick cottonwood tree. "You are looking at a new canoe; I will need this completed by next week."

The men just looked at him in amazement. Within an hour, the mighty giant was lying on the ground, being trimmed and cut into canoe length. The men worked until darkness and called it a day.

"I will see all of you here tomorrow."

A few grunts of yes, then the tired men went home. In two days, the canoe was shaped and dug out, but it still needed more work on it, more chopping and burning to make it slice through the water easily. William had been running his fishing lines while the canoe was being made.

Finally, it was time to waterproof the craft, so the men turned the canoe over and started to rub it down with animal fat.

Joe Eagle said, "Bear grease works the best, if we had some"

"I don't have any bear traps. They cost too much. This will have to do, and I hope that Day-ga Herman pulls it out of the water every night."

"What do you mean *Day-ga Herman?*" asked Walking Soldier.

"This will be his canoe."

They all looked at him, puzzled.

"Why do you have to make him a canoe?" asked Joe Eagle.

"Well, I made a deal with him. I need what he has, so I am trading things for her." William knew that he let it slip out when he said "her."

Now the men were really on him. "What 'her' are you talking about?" asked Walking Soldier.

"Did I say 'her'?" replied William.

"You know you did," said Walking Soldier.

"What I met to say was …" William couldn't finish the sentence because he was starting to blush.

"Look at him! He's turning red like some of the white men when they are out in the sun too long," said Henry Baker.

"Look at him, look at him, an Indian with a red face!"

Now the boys were really teasing him. Finally, Henry Baker said, "How much do you have to offer Herman?"

"One horse, one canoe, fresh meat and fish, and protection from the Santee Sioux."

"She must be worth it," said Joe Eagle,

"When do you plan to get married?" asked Walking Soldier.

"Just as soon as I can get this canoe finished," William said.

By the end of the week, the working party had moved everything over to Day-ga Herman's lodge; William went up to the opening and announced that he was here to see Day-ga Herman.

Day-ga Herman came outside and looked in amazement at the gifts that William and his friends had brought to his lodge. Herman looked over the pelts; he ran his hands through the fur, and he said nothing. "Hmm," he said, looking at the young colt, "it could use some more work."

"But he is young and has a long life ahead of him."

"Maybe so, maybe so," admitted Day-ga Herman. He moved over to the canoe, looking inside and feeling the outside of the craft and asked, "Will it float?"

"Of course it will float and move across the water very swiftly."

"I will need some fresh meat by tomorrow. If you can do that, then, William Cloud, you have a new bride."

Alice was standing in the opening of the lodge and heard everything. She gave William a quick glance when her uncle said "you have a new bride." On the walk back to William's lodge, the teasing and joking began again. Henry Baker was walking quite a ways behind the rest of the men. He wanted to have some room between himself and William.

"Hey, Henry, what are you doing back there?" asked Joe Eagle.

Henry pointed at William and said, "Trying to make baby."

Everyone just laughed, and then the three of them said in a loud voice, "Trying to make baby!"

The wedding was a large feast attended by many clan members. Children were running around and playing. There was a lot of teasing and laughter coming from both sides of the family, as well as friends wishing the newlywed couple good luck. "Be strong in your marriage. You will need strength when hard times come your way, and they will come," said Day-ga Herman.

"Remember that you two will help build the next generation of the tribe. Someday you will be called on to do many things, so be ready to help and fight if need be," said Ed Swift Wing.

The teasing continued even as the last of them left the Cloud lodge. "They may not come out until spring. That's how young married couples are."

"Soon we will see a little Cloud running around here; let's hope that it's a Thunder Cloud."

Finally alone after a long day, the newlywed couple moved into their lodge. William was nervous, as he had never seen a naked woman before, let alone made love to one. They were both very awkward, embarrassed to be naked in front of each other. William had heard stories from his friends about how babies were made. His friends talked as if they did it all the time, but he knew that they were just lying.

Finally, they dropped their last pieces of clothing. From the glow of the fire, Alice could see William. She knew that this was the time, and she was ready to accept her husband. It was time. It was right!

The weeks turned to months. William kept his promise to Day-ga Herman; he saw that his family was kept in fresh meat and fish. Then one day, Alice asked William to come into the lodge, that she had something to show him. When William entered the lodge, she was just sitting there. "What do you want to show me?"

"A while back while eating a squash, I think I swallowed a squash seed."

"So? I do it all the time."

"Yeah, but this one is different. I think it's growing inside of me."

"How can that be, and how do you know?"

"Well, I know it; look here and see." She lifted her shirt and showed him her stomach. It was large.

At first William thought it was true. "Will it make you sick?" he asked in a worried voice.

"I think in a few more months, it will come out."

Still William didn't know what she was talking about. "How do you know this?"

"Because my Chu-wee said this is how long it takes to make a baby."

Now he understood the story of the squash seed. A big smile came across William's face. *A little Cloud is in the making*, he thought. "I wonder what we will name the baby."

"We have plenty of time to pick a name."

And Alice wasn't lying. Little Louis Cloud arrived in a few months. This was a good time to be living on the Blue Earth reservation. It was peaceful, and the government made good on giving the supplies to the Indians on a timely basis.

"We will need to tell the agent that we have another mouth to feed," said William.

"He won't eat much; I will provide most of his meals," said Alice, smiling.

William couldn't wait to tell his hunting friends about his new *Kunu* (firstborn son). He had an Indian name already picked out for him, and when Louis got a little older, he would hold a naming feast for him and give him his name. It was a good time in the William Cloud lodge. It was a good time to be Indian; they had finally found or at least had been given a "permanent home" by the government.

But there were a few of the Ho-Chunks who didn't agree with the rest of the tribe and wanted to be recognized as more than just an Indian. This new kind of person had a white man for a father and an Indian for a mother. The new breed of Indians or half-breeds, as they liked to be called, wanted to live among the white men and to be free, free from the reservation and its backward people. Some of the breeds even looked like white people. It was okay for a white man to take an Indian woman for a wife, but if an Indian man took a white woman for a wife, he would be killed. This was the unspoken law, and everyone knew it.

"Why would someone want to live like a white man, when they were raised with us?" William asked Walking Smoke.

"When people want to be something that they aren't, they will endure great pain and suffer a lot just to be like that; maybe its better that the half-breeds move in with the white people. I don't trust them. Could you trust them in a battle against the white man?"

William shook his head no.

The half-breeds stayed in Minnesota and would become white men, so they thought, but the white people didn't want them either. They were tolerated, and that was it. They were at the low end of the pecking order. They gave up all their rights to any rations or gifts from the government. Later, when some of them wanted to go back to being an Indian, the government said, "No, you are white." They found out that it wasn't easy being a white man or a half-breed.

Knights of the Forest were sending out raiding parties at night to raise hell with the Ho-Chunk people, who had no way of protecting themselves against the raids. The Knights of the Forest was to Indians what the KKK would be to blacks. The tribe had no weapons to use, and if they shot and killed or wounded one of the riders, the Indians were hanged.

It was all the young warriors could do not to engage these white men. "I would love to pull one of those riders off his mount and beat the hell out of him," William mumbled.

"We could throw his body into the river, and no one would know what happened to him," his friend suggested.

"I have a better idea," William said. He organized some of the young warriors to stand on the road at night when the Knights were out riding. "This will show them we are prepared to stand and fight."

At first the Knight Riders ignored them and laughed as they rode by.

"The time has come to do more than just stand in the road," William announced. They began stretching ropes across the road about one foot above the ground to force white men's horses to stumble. In a few days, the Indians could tell who some of the night riders were, because their horses would be lame and the riders would have bruises, cuts, and scrapes on their faces.

"Now we know. They are local farmers who want our land," William said, "cowards who use scare tactics to terrorize us in the darkness of the night."

The young braves talked about paying back the Knights. William listened to the talk of getting even. But what could they do? They hardly had any weapons and no horses. Just the thought of riding in a war party caused goose bumps to run up his back.

"When you choose to be a warrior, you choose to die." This was spoken by Little Elk, the leader of the young men, the warriors. Little Elk knew that a war with the whites would be murderous to his braves and to the nation, because the white man's army would stop at nothing. It would be a complete annihilation of the Ho-Chunk tribe, but the thoughts and talk were still there. He told his warriors to keep their skills sharp and to keep their heads and bodies in shape and not to drink the white man's whiskey because someday they would ride into battle and need all of their senses.

During the winter of 1862, the Santee Sioux went on the warpath in the southern part of Minnesota because the government had been holding or selling their rations, and the Santee were starving. One of the traders at the agency told the Santees to eat grass if they were hungry. He was the hero for the day, with his clever quote. But this did not settle anything. It only added fuel to a hot fire. Nothing was said about the crooked deals and the lack of annuity payments that were supposed to be made to the starving Indians.

Chief Little Crow of the Santee Sioux asked the Winnebagos if they would help in their efforts. The Ho-Chunk war chiefs met and decided not to go on the warpath with their brothers, the Santees. This did not sit well with the Santee Sioux.

Theirs was a short and violent war in which they killed all of the white settlers in the southern part of Minnesota. They took food, blankets, and winter clothes anything of value in their raids. Many white farmers lost their lives, cattle, and everything that they had worked for. It was a brutal uprising.

The Dakota warriors hated the white man and his army, and they took no prisoners; anybody who was white was a target. The army had to work fast to settle this uprising, and it was a hard thing to do because the Civil War was going in the East, and just about all of the money set aside for the Bureau of Indian Affairs was going to support the Civil War. The army got help from the military from the Dakotas and from Colonel Henry Sibley, who reached Fort Ridgely with 1,500 troops. This put down the Santee Sioux uprising.

Chief Little Crow and many of his warriors went on trial for murder, rape, and various other charges. The repercussions of the war had a great effect on the Winnebagos. From the governor's office down to the drunk on the street, everyone wanted the Winnebagos and the Santees out of Minnesota.

On February 21, 1863, the Blue Earth reservation was sold by the government. The editor of the *Mankato Record* launched a campaign against the Indians in Minnesota; he fired up his readers by publishing such articles as "Exterminate the Savages or Remove Them from Civilization."

Chapter 3

Life in the Dakotas

"Take only what you can carry," the soldiers ordered.

It was May 1863, and it was the same old story: move or get a bayonet in the back-side. The new destination was a reservation in the Dakota Territory and some 1,945 Ho-Chunks were making the trek. The Ho-Chunk people were used to fertile land to raise crops and thick timbers to hunt, and they had heard stories of the dry and arid grasslands of the Dakotas. It was hard to give up what they had established on the Blue Earth. Worse yet, they were about to discover that the government wanted to use the Ho-Chunk tribe as a buffer between the peaceful Indians and the warring Sioux tribes of the Dakotas.

William helped the Cloud family pack what little they could on what was another very sad day for all of the tribal members. They had lived on the Blue Earth reservation for eight years, and it had been a period of peace for the nation. Now they were being driven off their land again, just because the Santee Sioux had started an uprising. The Ho-Chunks' Chief Little Priest had told the army that in December of 1861, the Santee chief, Wabasha, had asked the Ho-Chunks to join them in the uprising, and the Ho-Chunks had refused. His words fell on deaf ears.

"I will tell all of you now," the nervous young lieutenant began, "you must bring in all of your family members. If any are left behind, they will be killed. We don't want to do this, but we will if we have to."

William Cloud and his family watched as their lodge went up in smoke. William turned and left his family to set the longhouse on fire, for only he could do this. The trip on foot to the Mississippi was 175 miles; this would take the ragtag tribe six days to make.

A few of the cocky soldiers fixed their bayonets. "I might stick me a redskin today," one sneered.

The movement was slow, and even though the army tried to move the Indians along at a faster pace, the people would not move any faster; it was very hard for them to move across the land that had been their so-called permanent home. As they passed the different family lodges, one could hear soft cries coming from the masses. It was a sad sight.

One of the older members of the tribe just stopped and sat down. "I am not moving anymore," said the old Indian. "You will have to kill me, white man." He was left sitting in the middle of the road, and that evening, the lieutenant sent a patrol out to kill the old man. But when the army patrol got there, he was gone. They had no idea where he went, so they just told the lieutenant that they got the job done. The old warrior knew that his time had come to pass on into the spirit world, but he wanted to do it his way. He left the trail and moved farther into the timbers. There he found a large oak tree and made his deathbed under it. As he prepared himself to meet his ancestors, he pulled the old army blanket up and over his head and sang the warrior song that had been given to him many years ago by his Day-ga. The song told of his bravery in the face of his enemy and how he became a Ho-Chunk warrior that day. He sang the song over and over again until he was gone.

A few nights later, when they made camp, several members of the tribe slipped out of the camp; but what they didn't know was that the lieutenant had anticipated an escape, so his men were ready. Soon the shooting began, but the soldiers were bad shots, and they only wounded two Indians. Some got past the ambush, but most ran back to the camp. In the morning, the soldiers came around looking for wounded Indians but found none. Some of the warriors called out, "Bad shots!" This really made the white soldiers mad, and the tribe paid for that remark, as the army pushed the Ho-Chunk tribe hard that day, and in fact, they made it all the way to Fort Snelling.

Louis made most of the walk on his own, but he had to be carried the last few miles by his father. The future of the tribe looked very dismal. The old people knew that their time would be sooner than they had planned, as their treatment by the white soldiers was very harsh and brutal. One young brave pulled a bluecoat off his mount when the soldier struck the warrior's mother. Within minutes, the soldier was screaming for help, and other soldiers came to his aid. The young lieutenant wanted the Indian who had attacked his man brought forward and charged.

"Forget it," the commanding officer said. "Where we are sending these poor redskins will be punishment enough."

The Ho-Chunk Nation arrived at Fort Snelling on the Mississippi on May 10, 1863, and stayed there for three days, while they waited for the steamboats to come up river and pick them up.

Many members of the nation had seen steamboats before but had never been on one. The steamboats *Canada* and the *Davenport* were made to carry sixty-five to seventy people. One boat packed in eight hundred, while the smaller one took over four hundred Ho-Chunks on as human freight. The trip was horrible, to say the least, and not only because of the condition, but because of the scenery too.

As the steamboat churned down the mighty river, different members pointed and stared at clearings on the riverbank "We set up our summer village there many moons ago," they said softly. "And now it's a white man's farm." Others would point out an old village site that was now a pasture for cows and pigs. Tears rolled down their cheeks when they saw a setting where an old campsite or a hunting lodge had once stood. There was much crying as someone would say, "That's where my parents are buried!" Family members who were buried along the river shore had their final farewell from the living as the steamboat pushed farther south.

"They move us off our land and call it progress. I fear that we will soon run out of room, and then what will happen to us?" asked the old warrior Walking Smoke. "We pulled many a fish from our mother river, and now we are leaving this land forever. I have heard that in Dakota Territory, corn will not grow because it is too dry. I hear that the grass is very tall; some say a small horse can get lost in it. Why are we being treated like this? All we want to do is to live."

William agreed with Walking Smoke, and he knew only too well what the old warrior was talking about. "Louis, at one time, all of this was Ho-Chunk land," he explained to his son. "We fished and hunted this land for a long time. I was born over to the east and north of here, not far from where we are now. Then it was called the Ho-Chunk Nation. My father is buried over there, to the west in what used to be called the Neutral Ground. I will never see this land again."

Louis couldn't understand why there was much sorrow. He found it fun riding on the steamboats and watching the shore go by. Many years later, he would come to understand the hardship that was happening around him on that day.

The army knew that if one Indian had the chance to run away, he would, and others would follow. Steamboats were a much easier way of moving Indians west than over land. The army soldiers stationed on the very top level of the steamboat constantly looked into the river and behind the boat, checking for Indians who jumped overboard. Their orders were to shoot to kill.

At night when the guards couldn't see that well, some of the Ho-Chunks jumped overboard and swam for the east side of the river. When William heard what some of them had done, he wondered how they would survive when they had no home to go to. The white man had taken all of their lands on both sides of the river.

One morning, as William was standing outside of the cabins, he looked up and saw an eagle falling from the sky. It fell into the water behind the steamboat and went under with the current. He thought, *This is how the Ho-Chunk Nation's lives are today. Once we flew with the eagles, but now we don't even swim with the fish; we will just go under, and no one will ever care.*

They were only given food once a day, and the water was stale, so many became sick. More members jumped overboard. Still the steamboat kept churning downstream. They passed Rock Island, where they had signed the treaty back in 1832, giving them the Neutral Ground. Traveling farther down the great river, some of the older members could recognize areas where they once held council with the Sauk, Fox, and other tribes.

Finally, they made it to Hannibal, Missouri. Once the steamboats docked, the Indians were driven like cattle to the stockyards, where they had to wait until all of the steamboats arrived from Fort Snelling. The stockyards smelled, and it was hard to get any rest. By now the townspeople had gathered around the holding pens and were getting a good eyeful of the ragged Winnebagos. There was laughter and ethnic jokes directed at them, but there was no more fight left in the Winnebagos; the dead among them were loaded onto wagons and taken away, their families standing with their heads hung low and crying to themselves as they watched the wagons leave. Even when you have nothing, you still have your dignity and pride. It was unworthy of a warrior to cry in the open, so the men folk just stood there and said nothing.

"What a pitiful bunch of Indians these Winnebagos are," one of the men in the crowd said.

"They don't look so tough to me," said another.

"Well, they are going out to join their brothers, the Sioux Indians."

From the stockyard, they were taken to the train. When the train lurched forward, everyone fell to the back of the car, tripping and falling on one another. They hadn't eaten all day and had no idea when they would get fed again. Finally, when the train had to stop for water, some provisions were given out, and they were allowed to get off the train briefly. There were still a lot of sick members in the tribe; some were so sick that they couldn't get off the train, or they didn't want to. Every move was watched by armed soldiers. Some of the townspeople came to see the Indians; most of them were just curious, but some poked fun at the miserable Indians as they waited for the engine to load up with water and wood.

The next day, the train pulled into St. Joseph, Missouri. This town was friendlier. As they waited for steamers coming up from St. Louis, some of the townspeople gave food and other items to the tired and ragged Indians. The army moved the tribe to the outskirts of town and set up a perimeter around them. Rations were brought in, and everyone had a something to eat, and it felt good to sleep on the ground and stretch out. There were several campfires in the perimeter, so people gathered around the fire and talked; most had no idea of where they were. More of the sick died that night. The army said just to leave them, and they would be taken care of them. The next morning, a wagon came around, and soldiers threw the bodies on the wagon as if they were loading wood. There would be no four-day and four-night wakes for these Ho-Chunks; they would have to find their way to the spirit world as best as they could. It was a disgrace to the living the way the army treated their dead. The dead were taken to the town cemetery, where a large hole was dug, and the bodies were thrown into the pit and covered up. There were no final words over these first Americans.

The next day, the steamer *Westwind* and other steamboats came into port and picked up the Winnebago nation for their final trip up the Missouri River to Fort Thompson in the Dakotas. Many of the townspeople had come down to the river port to see the red men. Some of the white people just looked, but others teased and made fun of the worn out bunch of Indians. William could only wonder how many white people there were, because they were all over the place, with all of them having children and all looking the same.

The soldiers pushed and shoved the Indians forward. "Get in there, you worthless redskin," one yelled.

"Soon enough, you will have all the room you need with your brothers, the Sioux," said another bluecoat.

After much pushing and crowding, the steamboats were loaded, and the caravan started the journey north. The land was very flat. Occasionally, the bluffs would join the river; then they would fade away. Very few trees were on this prairie, but there were a few cottonwood trees along the river and a few willows, and the tall prairie grass waved in the wind. This river trip was approximately 385 miles.

North of Fort Omaha, the bluffs touched the river again. Sometimes they were straight up, casting an afternoon shadow over the steamboats, making them look small; and other times, they looked as if they literally rolled off the river and formed large hills. Going up the Missouri River, they would pass their future home, but few knew it then.

Most of the Ho-Chunks had never been this far west. The river was smaller, but it was swifter than the Mississippi. The land looked very flat, and the grass was all sunburned, William was certain that nothing could grow here, and the word was that the Dakotas were even worse than this.

Before they passed the Omaha Reservation, the war chief, Little Priest, held a meeting with some of his most trusted braves. Little Priest had been to the Omaha Reservation before, and he knew the chiefs there. He instructed two of his men to slip overboard when they got to the Omaha Reservation and ask the chiefs if they could buy the northern part of their reservation.

When a big thunderstorm hit that night, they all considered it a good sign, because the storm would help conceal the warriors slipping off the boat and swimming to shore. The two braves were strong swimmers, and once ashore, they made their way west to the Omaha village. They were greeted with suspicion and taken to the chiefs. When asked by the chiefs what they were doing so far from their home, the braves told them of how their people had been taken off the Blue Earth reservation and were presently being shipped by boat and train north into Sioux country, which was to be the new home of the Ho-Chunk Nation.

"Why did they move the tribe off the Blue Earth?" asked one of the chiefs.

"Because the Santee Sioux Indians went on the warpath and started to kill the white farmers in the area, and the white man blamed all of the Indians and forced all of us out of Minnesota. We did not take part in the uprising, but we were blamed for it anyway. We lost many of our families and friends. Some were killed by the soldiers, some ran away, others jumped overboard and swam for the Wisconsin shore, and others that were not good swimmers just sank."

"And why are you here now?"

"Our chief, Chief Little Priest, wants to know if you will sell the northern part of your reservation to us. We have money from the sale of the Blue Earth reservation. It's in trust with the government," one of the braves explained.

"We will think about this tonight, and we will give you an answer in the morning. You must be tired. We have made a place for you, and we have made food for you."

The next day, the two braves were told to come to the council lodge.

"We have made up our minds," the chief told them. "We will sell the Ho-Chunks the northern part of our reservation. However, it's a hostile area, and you will have your hands full with the Sioux," he said. "No Omahas live there anymore because Sioux war parties have stolen our horses, killed our livestock, and kidnapped the women and children."

The warriors greeted those words with smiles, ready to take on the Sioux if it meant acquiring better land.

"We will give you enough supplies to get you up to Fort Thompson," the chief told them. "You will have to be on the lookout all the time, because there are many Sioux war parties around, and they would love to have a Ho-Chunk scalp on their lodge. Give my regards to Chief Little Priest, *A-ho.*"

The steamboat kept on a northern course. It made a stop at Sioux City, Iowa, where they took on firewood and more supplies. The large bluffs gradually gave way to the flat land of the Dakotas. *Our people will die here in this land*, William thought.

The two warriors left the safety of the Omaha nation, accompanied by four Omaha scouts, as far as the reservation border. "It would be better if you stay close to the river," the scouts advised them. "You can make better time if you go across the land, but there are many Sioux war parties out there."

Hearing this, the two warriors kept the Missouri River in sight all of the way to Fort Thomson. They made good time and camped out there, waiting for the steamboats to pull in. On June 8, 1863, a hot and humid day, the caravan of streamers made landing at Fort Thompson, Dakota Territory. One by one, the Winnebagos left the boat, under the watchful eye of the bluecoats.

As the Indians passed by, they were counted. This count would later be inflated to make it look as though more had survived the trip when the report finally reached Washington. With all of the commotion going on at the dock, nobody paid much attention to the two riders who had crossed the river and entered the fort area. They dismounted and walked over to Chief Little Priest and told him the good news.

It was desolate prairie land. A few cottonwoods grew along the banks of the Missouri River, but the grass was turning brown, and it was only June. The wind kicked up large clouds of dust, and the ground was hard. It looked like it hadn't rained in weeks.

The superintendent of Indian affairs was there to meet the Winnebagos. The Indians were told to gather around him because he had something very important to tell them. "Here," he said, "you can become good farmers and learn how to live off the land. You can also become civilized human beings—just like me and the rest of the white population!" He smiled hopefully.

That's a white man's dream, William thought to himself. *Our dream is for all of you white people to fill up your boats and leave.*

The new home in the Dakota Territory was within the stockades at Fort Thompson, and their treatment there was atrocious. There was little food, no blankets, poor soil, no willows to make lodges, and no game to hunt. Everything would have to come from the government. The message was clear: the red man was to be pushed off the continent of North America.

The harshness of the windswept Dakota stockades was too much for William's mother. One night she went to sleep and never awoke. William couldn't even grieve his mother's passing since there was no place to go to fast and pray. They couldn't hold the traditional four-day wake since they had no extra food for a feast. All they could do was talk about how it used to be—before the white man, when they lived in peace and no one owned the land.

"This is not our homeland," the old ones kept saying. Many wished they could return to their old home and ways. "That's where I want to die," they would say. In the morning, the soldiers would come around with a wagon and load the dead, taking them out to a common grave. The Ho-Chunks were not allowed to even bury their own "the Indian way."

William was not alone in mourning; many Ho-Chunks lost members of their families in the stockade. But the chief kept asking the members of the tribe to be patient. Things would get better!

It will only get better when we are in the spirit world, thought William. Inside, he was ready for war—sick of losing loved ones, suffering at the hands of the white soldiers, and hearing promises that were never meant to be kept.

When General Alfred Sully's cavalry of 1,200 men arrived in Fort Thomson, the general passed the word that he wanted to speak with Chief Little Priest. He had held council with the chief back in Minnesota and was sympathetic to the plight of the Winnebagos. "A few years ago, we signed a treaty and were given the Blue Earth reservation as our permanent home," one of the Winnebago chiefs stated at the beginning of the meeting. "That *permanent* home only lasted twelve years, and now we are here on the Crow Creek Reservation, where the land is too hard and too poor to grow crops. There is very little rain, no game to hunt, and if we go west to hunt buffalo, we will be killed by the Lakota. Our people are starving. We have no rations, no blankets and no medicine."

"I am sorry that the Winnebagos are starving and have no rations," the general said, rising from his chair. "I will send word to my superiors in Washington for more food and medicine. Your people shouldn't have to starve here!"

"General, can you help us move to the northern end of the Omaha Reservation in Nebraska?" Chief Little Priest asked, standing up. "We have been there, and it is good for my people. There is plenty of water, game, timber, and good soil for corn and squash; and our brothers, the Omahas, already said that they would sell us part of their reservation."

General Sully wondered how the chief could have made a deal with the Omahas, when he and his tribe members were always under watch of the guards. Nonetheless, he sent word for more rations and to purchase part of the Omaha Reservation for the Winnebagos. "This," he told his superiors, "would be both a humane and an economical thing to do."

Over the next year, six hundred Ho-Chunks left to travel along the Missouri River to the Omaha Reservation in Nebraska where there were lots of trees, rolling hills, good grasslands, plenty of game, good fishing, rich soil for planting, and—they hoped—far enough away from the Sioux Indians! Gradually, the rest of the Winnebago Nation joined them.

Chapter 4

Company A Omaha Scouts

William Cloud blinked in disbelief. "You want us to *join* the white man's army?"

"It is the only solution," Chief Little Priest told him. "We don't want to be moved anymore, do we?"

William sighed. "No, we don't."

"Volunteering the services of Ho-Chunk warriors as scouts for a war against the Lakota Sioux is our chance to make peace with the white man's army and stay put," Chief Little Priest told him. "My plan is to take about seventy-five warriors to join the Nebraska Cavalry Regiment."

"Including me?" William asked.

"Including you. You are about to turn thirty-one," the chief told him with a smile. "That means you are young enough to have the strength, agility, and stealth to fight, but old enough to have the wisdom and common sense that come with age. You are very much needed, William."

The plan was not immediately popular. Some of the Indians thought joining the U.S. Army was giving in to the white man, that the Ho-Chunks would be labeled traitors. Most of the elders understood, however, that it was the right thing to do, and it would also give the Ho-Chunks a chance to get back at the Sioux.

With mixed emotions, William made his mark on the paper.

Other Ho-Chunk warriors had joined in the great battle of the North and South. Some had joined the Northern army, and some joined the Confederacy. Most of those warriors were the young ones. They did not remember the raiding parties from the Sioux. They didn't remember the treatment by the bluecoats, even though some of their own brothers and sisters were left on the trail and killed by the rear guards, which chose to kill them rather than pick them up.

William's wife and child would live with her Day-ga Herman while William was in the army. Their new home would be in northeast Nebraska along the Missouri River. A leader and a medicine man, William was in good standing within the tribe, sought out by others for his advice and wisdom. Inside, however, he was still the hard-charging, scalp-hunting warrior that he always wanted to be—ready to charge into the enemy and let the bullets and arrows fly. It was time for war.

The seventy-five new scouts were taken to Fort Omaha, given a quick medical check up, and issued army regulation hats, shirts, boots, and trousers. Chief Little Priest was given the rank of sergeant; the rest of the scouts were privates, and the group was known as the Company A Omaha Scouts.

A bluecoat soldier, William thought, *look at me now. They were what I despised most, and now I am one of them.* It was hard to get used to being in the white man's army, let alone being called a private. At least, William reasoned, they gave you a horse with a saddle and bridle and a repeating rifle. He and the other recruits spent days on the rifle field learning how to shoot this new weapon. After a quick lesson in army behavior and a quick orientation on military rules and chain of command, William and the other new scouts rode north to catch up with the main cavalry. In William's mind, wearing the blue uniform made them an easier target for the enemy. Wearing a cavalry man's hat would take some getting used to.

Little Priest asked William Cloud if he would like to lead and be the tracker for their group. William thought it was an honor to take on such a risky position, so he agreed without hesitation. It was settled that William Cloud would lead the column in the search for their adversaries, the Sioux.

It took a couple of weeks for them to catch up to the cavalry. William was the first to pick up the army's trail. At the crest of a small hill, he could see the dust, and he could actually hear the movement of the army. He motioned for Chief Little Priest to join him. The chief motioned for his scouts to move in a single file as they approached the army column, and soon they made contact with the tail end of the column. Little Priest identified himself, and they told him where to report.

Later that evening, the commanding officer told Chief Little Priest that his scouts would ride in front of the column. "This is where we do our best work!" Little Priest told the commanding officer.

The command officer had a smile on his face when he left the chief. Chief Little Priest knew that was because every soldier's eyes would be watching them, and if it looked as though they might switch sides, the soldiers were instructed to shoot the scouts.

The next morning, the commanding officer instructed Chief Little Priest to send out his scouts; he showed them the direction that they would be moving. William was in the saddle and was waiting for his instructions from the chief. The chief showed William where he wanted him to look, and William rode out into the new day. The grass still had dew on it, and this would help him look for signs of movement. Soon William disappeared from sight. He rode straight out for about a quarter of a mile; then he turned to his left and rode in front of the camp.

Halfway across the front of the column, William picked up a new trail. He saw where the grass was worn down by many horses, so he followed the trail for a short while until he came upon some horse dung. He got off his horse and checked the dung. It was only a few hours old. They were close. William rode back to tell the chief, who told the commanding officer, who made a note in his log. "Omaha scouts have found a new trail, made by many horses. We have entered into the Heart River area of North Dakota Territory; soon we may engage the Teton Lakota Sioux."

The Ho-Chunk warriors rode out in front and on the flanks of the column, since they were better at picking up the trail and looking for signs of an ambush. Private Cloud, one of the trackers, could be found every day in the front, sometimes a half mile from the column. With his senses working at a 100 percent, there was not a bird or a movement in the grass by a small animal that William didn't catch. This wasn't quite what he had in mind when he wanted to be a warrior, but at least he was fighting against his old enemy, the Sioux. Alone in front of the column in the danger zone, the kill zone, the death zone, William Cloud did his best work. Not all scouts would ride up front, but then, not all warriors were like William.

Some days it was hard to concentrate on his job because it got boring—long rides looking and finding nothing, riding ahead, and reporting back to the general, "Nothing to report," then heading back out to the front. At night the scouts camped together in their own little circle. They talked in their own language, and sometimes they would laugh at one or two of the soldiers. It always ended the same way because Chief Little Priest didn't like his braves talking about the soldiers. They had to take turns on watch just like the soldiers did; they ate the same food. It would take some time before the soldiers really trusted them, because some still thought that when the Sioux attacked, the Winnebagos would turn on them and join the Sioux.

As the column moved north, William saw more signs of the Sioux; he could tell how many were in their camp, how many horses, even how many dogs were with them. The signs were getting fresher every day; soon they would be within gun sight of the Sioux.

Finally, one night, William told Chief Little Priest that they would make contact with the Teton Lakota Sioux the next day. The chief passed on the word to the general, and plans were made for the attack. A handful of the scouts would sneak ahead and check out the Sioux camp, check on the number of warriors, count their weapons and the number of horses they had, and see if they had any hostages. If they could get close enough to kidnap a guard, they were told to do it; if not, they were not to spring the attack. The column would ride as close as possible to the camp, and then the scouts would ride in front of the troops on the attack; in fact, the scouts would lead the attack.

William could not sleep. There were too many things going on in his head. Tomorrow he would lead the attack on the Sioux. This was not something that Indians talked about; you didn't brag about what you would do—you just did your job. William wondered whether he would lose his courage and do nothing. He put those thoughts out of his mind. He was a Ho-Chunk warrior, and he had a job to do. He would lead the charge; he would kill the enemy. Just the thought of it caused goose bumps to form on the back of his neck and arms. Maybe tomorrow would be a good day to die. When you choose to be a warrior, you choose to die. That was why not all of his friends became warriors—some became farmers, others did artwork, and some became drunks.

The next day, as William led the column out, he could feel the blood rushing though his veins, his heart pounding in this chest, his hand steady on his Winchester. The tall prairie grass and rolling hills could hide a small war party. Sometimes the rolling hills would drop off, and the flanks would disappear from sight. This made the soldiers nervous, but they always gave a sigh of relief when the flank reappeared. As William pushed forward, he caught a whiff of smoke, very faint, but still it was the odor of smoke. Scanning the horizon William looked hard into the distance but could not see any telltale sign of smoke. William turned his mount around and rode back to the lead element; he told the other scouts, and they passed the word. It could be a trap, maybe a small hunting party or a scouting party. As William rode out to the point, he looked at the flanks. Both sides were looking hard into the horizon. He started to climb a small rolling hill. Two-thirds of the way up, he spurred his mount hard and galloped over the hill, hoping to surprise or spring an ambush and catch them off guard. This movement startled the rest of the company; some didn't know if he would be back or get killed.

As William charged up the hill, he rode low on the right side of his mount, making a smaller target, his eyes searching the grass and the horizon, his ears tuned to the wind, listening for any signs. Why was that flock of doves startled in the distance? Why was the grass bent down like that? At the top of the hill, William could see for miles; the hill rolled down into a long wide valley. He could see the grass was bent down; he could smell the enemy horses. This was a good site for an ambush.

William rode back over the hill and passed word about the valley. All of the scouts agreed it would be better to turn to the left and ride around the rim of the valley, but off on the side of the hill. Another thirty feet and William would have ridden over the Sioux war party, which would have closed the gate on the troops—there would have been no way out.

As William led the troops around the rim of the valley, he could see movement in the grass. Word was passed, and the column was put on line for an attack. The Company A scouts formed a line in front of the cavalry, at a fast trot and then to a full gallop.

This is what Private Cloud had waited for, for so many years. His Winchester ready, he rode low in the saddle, eyes wide open, adrenalin racing in his body at a full charge: the battle was on. It was time to see the enemy and kill him, take as many of them as he could before he went down.

The fierce Dakota warriors, always ready for a fight, did not let the war come to them; they mounted and attacked the onrushing soldiers with vigor, speed, and bloodcurdling war whoops. Private Cloud and the rest of Company A returned the war whoops. Soon the first shot was fired, and the battle was on. William took aim on his first target, a Sioux warrior bearing down on him. He squeezed the trigger, and the lead projectile zipped through the grooved barrel at high velocity, finding its target. The young Sioux warrior was snapped backward off his mount, as if he had been hit by a tree branch that was pulled back and released.

Bullets were flying, dust rising, and men falling and dying, as cannon shots fell in and around the brother Indians. Soon the two warring tribes clashed, and war clubs and hatchets were flying in the air. Private Cloud holstered his Winchester, which was out of bullets, and pulled his hatchet from his cartridge belt. An enemy warrior tried to pull him off his horse, with one swift swing of the hatchet, the Sioux warrior's head split open like a ripe melon.

With many dead and the battle going badly for them, the Lakota warriors broke off the attack. William quickly reloaded his Winchester and continued to shoot and then reloaded for the second time and waited, certain they would attack again. The soldiers set up a 360-degree perimeter and waited for a new attack, but it never happened. The Lakota had suffered a major defeat, caught off guard by the surprise movement of the cavalry. Rather than take more casualties, the Sioux broke it off, they would return to do battle another day.

That evening while the white soldiers sat around and talked of the next day, the Ho-Chunk scouts were telling their own war stories, reliving the battle, reliving the moment that they had each been transformed from a scout to a real Ho-Chunk warrior.

They savored the look on the enemy's face when he was hit with a rifle shot, the hand-to-hand combat, the feel of victory, and the pride in knowing that they had done it and had lived to talk about it. They talked about the songs, they would sing about this day and how it would sound on the large drum in the Big Bear Hollow. All of the Winnebago people would know how the army led by Chief Little Priest and seventy-five brave warriors defeated the Teton Lakota Sioux at the battle of Heart River in North Dakota Territory.

When it was William's time to tell his story, he couldn't wait; first he started out by telling them that it was he who had told the army to go around the rim of the valley and not through it. He knew that something would be waiting for them if they had gone into the valley. He had sensed an ambush.

William didn't tell them how hard his heart had been beating. He didn't tell them of the sweat breaking out on his forehead or of how his hair was standing up on the back of his neck. But he told them of how he could see his enemy in the grass (even though he hadn't seen them), waiting for them, how he had been out in the front where only the warriors were. William told them of how with one good shot from this Winchester, the Lakota warrior had gone down.

None of the Ho-Chunks were killed, but four of them had been wounded, and all of them told their stories of victory. The four lucky ones would have the scars to show the rest of the tribe when they got home. It was a good day for the army and the Ho-Chunk scouts. It was a victory that could have been a disaster had it not been for one scout named Private Cloud.

William felt too good to go to sleep. He thought of how easy it had been for him to be in a battle and how at last he had lived up to the name he chose, of Hatchett.

The next day, the commanding officer of the cavalry told Chief Little Priest that his scouts had done a magnificent job of scouting and definitely showed the warrior spirit in battle. The cavalry formed up and rode out; the scouts were put on a line in front of the army. Their job today was to look for any survivors, dead bodies, weapons, and any other things of war.

As the scouts swept though the battlefield, many bodies of the Sioux were found—some with many bullet holes in them and others with cuts and wounds on them. They found bloody trails and drag marks were they had dragged off their wounded.

William found his first kill. While the other scouts were busy looking for other dead Sioux, William quickly dismounted and pulled his knife out. With a quick slice around the crown of his prey's head and a quick jerk, the scalp came up off the top of the young warrior's head. It was a custom back then to give a war whoop, when they lifted a scalp; but because of all the young soldiers around who wouldn't understand, William gave a sharp whistle, and only the scouts knew what that meant. They came over to see what William had found.

With a large smile on his face, William held up his trophy. The scouts held their rifles in the air. Instead of being a big celebration, it was kept to a small victory. This was William's first Sioux scalp. He quickly stuffed the scalp into his saddlebag. Once William did this, other members of the scout company did the same. It was a good day for the Winnebago scouts of Company A.

William rode a bit taller in the saddle as the other scouts said that they would go into battle with William Cloud at their side any day. It felt good to know that his fellow Indians trusted him in that way! Some said that he had power; others said that he had good medicine. After the search was completed, the bodies were thrown into a large pit and buried. The Company A Omaha Scouts gathered around the site and gave a silent prayer for their brother Indians. True, this was no way to treat a warrior, but this was war!

"Move out," came the order.

The Sioux had moved out. The trails headed in all directions. They would scatter for now, but later they would gather and become a formidable force again. If this was Indian against Indian, William thought, they would be moving a lot faster and keeping the pressure on the Sioux war party; but this was the U.S. Army, and they did things differently. They would stop and walk the horses, to let the cannons catch up, and give them a rest too. They would stop and look through the field glasses, ask questions, and talk among themselves. It was a different way to fight a war.

The scouts followed the trail west until they came to the headwater of the Heart River where the trail was more definite, and William could see more Indian ponies had joined the war party, but the tracks turned right, heading north into the Killdeer Mountains.

General Sully informed the Winnebago Scouts that the cavalry would winter it out in Fort Pierre and that if they wished to move back to their families at Fort Thompson, they could leave.

Chapter 5

A New Home

Chief Little Priest and his scouts did not like what they found when they returned to Fort Thompson. The Winnebago people were still starving and dying. Women were picking undigested corn from horse and cattle manure to feed their families, and building material was scarce, so the wigwams were poorly made. Some of the younger Indian women were selling themselves for money, food, clothing, and things that would help them survive. The war chief contacted the Indian agent who promised he would get more rations and medical supplies for the Indians.

Some six hundred Winnebagos had left Fort Thompson for Northeast Nebraska, including William Cloud's wife and family. He and many of the Company A scouts decided to join them. It was a difficult journey. They moved down the ice-filled Missouri River by dugout canoe, but it was a cold and miserable trip. They had to pass Fort Randall at night so the soldiers wouldn't fire on them. They made their way to the mouth of the Niobrara River, but because it was frozen solid, they had to travel the rest of the way—another hundred miles—on foot.

The second day on foot, a blizzard caught up with them, and it was all they could do to keep pushing through the deep snow. By luck, they found a small cave. The men gathered firewood and made a makeshift door over the entrance. Two of the warriors went out to hunt and shot two rabbits. With the rations that they had brought with them, they had a good meal. This cave served as their home for two days as the blizzard raged outside. The Indians were warm inside the old cave, but after a while, the inside of the cave got muddy because the walls were defrosting from the fire.

The knee-deep snow left in the blizzard's wake made walking very hard, so they put the strongest man in the lead to make a trail for the rest to follow. Occasionally, they would change lead men to give that hardest worker a rest. After a heavy snow, game was always plentiful because the animals were out trying to find something to eat too. This was good for the Indians. A deer was shot and cleaned, and stomachs were filled with venison. Later that day, they found a downed tree in a deep narrow ravine. It wasn't much, but once a fire was built beneath, it had some warmth to it and protected them from the wind.

The tree had dropped into a narrow ravine where two walls came together, and the trunk and branches served as a roof. The women cleared the snow out and used the new deer hide for a door; it was crowded, but it was warm. The next morning, everyone was up early, and soon they were on their way. With the fresh snow on the ground, game tracks were plentiful. The warriors kept their eyes open, and by midday, they had captured enough game for a good feast.

By late afternoon, they saw smoke and knew that they were close. As they entered the Ho-Chunk village, family members came out to greet them and invite them into their lodges. William found his family. Their lodge was in bad shape, but it was still warmer than the outside. They told him that there was plenty of game in the woods and that those who lived on the river liked to trade their fish for fresh deer meat. There was plenty of small game for trapping. The Winnebagos had taken over an old Omaha village that had been ransacked by a Sioux war party, which was why all of the lodges needed repair. The Omahas had left because that part of the reservation had been too dangerous to live on. Now the Winnebagos would be living amid the threat of Sioux war parties.

Even with plenty of game and fish in the river, the first group of Winnebagos living in northeast Nebraska still needed government rations to survive. They had very few cast-iron pots and pans, their blankets were old and thin, the buffalo robes were worn and splitting. Most of their axes and other hand tools were very old, often with improvised wooden handles that didn't fit. They had neither horses nor any other livestock, and the government would not let them have firearms for either their own protection or game hunting.

In the early spring of 1864, the Indian agent Robert Furnas, from the Omaha

Agency, sent word that he would need to meet with the Omaha Scouts of Company A in the Big Bear Hollow. Robert Furnas first thanked the men for the work they did for the U.S. Army and went on to tell them that the army wanted them to return and scout for them that June. The army would start a major operation against the Sioux. Hearing this, Chief Little Priest stood up. "We need weapons and horses for us and for the men that stay here and protect our people," he said. "And those who stay here will need some training."

"This will be arranged for you and your men," said Agent Furnas.

In the following weeks, men of the Winnebago tribe were sent down to Fort Omaha for training and were issued rifles and ammunition and the army blue coat and uniform. Those who stayed behind were also given blue coats, because it was felt that if the Sioux war parties saw the blue coats in the Winnebago villages, they might leave them alone. Unfortunately, it had the opposite effect; the war parties considered Winnebagos who worked for the army to be traitors, and Sioux war parties began attacking the new Winnebago reservation. One encounter was against some Winnebago farmers who were in the fields planting corn, and the war party killed three of them, leaving the fourth to live to tell about it.

In another battle, east of (present day) Homer, Nebraska, the warring Sioux weren't as lucky. They sustained many deaths and many wounded before they could break off the engagement and scatter west following the bluff. Marauding bands of Sioux warriors continued to pay such visits to the new Winnebago reservation.

On June 10, 1864, fifty Winnebago scouts rode up from the Big Bear Hollow under the leadership of Chief Little Priest and made their way to Sioux City, Iowa, twenty miles away. There they met with Captain Christian Stufft and his army of fresh soldiers, ready to do battle with the Sioux Indians. They loaded on to steamers, along with the supplies they'd need, and headed up the Missouri River. Since it would take three days for the army to unload and prepare for the upcoming campaign, the Winnebago scouts had time to look for the Winnebagos at Fort Thomson who had decided to stay in the area because they were tired of moving and just wanted to be left alone.

Chief Little Priest urged the remaining Winnebago Indians at Fort Thompson to go to the new reservation, insisting this would really be their "permanent home."

His words fell on deaf ears.

When the huge column of men and material finally moved out of the fort, they did so at a snail's pace, with large clouds of dust rising from the many wagons and horses. William Cloud was again out in front of the column, looking for enemy tracks and hoping that the men left to guard his family back in Nebraska would be strong enough to do the job.

That summer, the scouts and the U.S. Army had many run-ins with the Sioux, as they made their way to the Heart River and the area north of there, in North Dakota. Private Cloud was promoted to the rank of corporal, but even with the new rank, William still liked to lead the column. It was just as well, because the rest of the army liked to see William lead. It had been over a year since the scouts joined the cavalry. They had ridden many miles and fought many battles large and small, and the white man's army not only trusted them but was glad the Company A Omaha Scouts were on their side. They were fierce in battle, able to read the wind, and skilled hunters who had kept the army in fresh supplies of meat.

By early August, when the column made its way into the Killdeer Mountains of the North Dakota Territory, the trail was fresh and smoke was detected in the wind. It was as if the Sioux were leaving a calling card or an invitation to a battle—the signs were all over.

On August 10, 1864, pushing north into the open plains, the prairie grass was almost saddle high. To William's left, a young Sioux warrior stood up to have a better look, but his eagerness and inexperience cost him his life as he was shot by one of the scouts.

The element of surprise was no longer on the side of the Sioux. Within seconds, the scouts formed an attack line and charged into the Miniconjou Lakota Sioux. The lead element was met with rifle fire and arrows, some of which found their targets as some scouts went down. Soon the cavalry was fighting alongside of the Ho-Chunk scouts. Hand to hand, war club to war club, the battle raged on, with hundreds of rifles firing and arrows flying in an area about the size of a large corral. But the Miniconjou Lakota Sioux were no match for the firepower of the U.S. Army; even as the Sioux pulled back, they were chased with exploding cannonballs until they managed to scamper out of range. This was a hard-won battle for the cavalry: ten troopers and two scouts died, and many were wounded.

William Cloud could see many of the enemy spirits leaving the earth for the spirit world even before the battle began. He wondered whether the other Indians could see the spirits too. How was it that he could see the enemy waiting or feel the danger that he would be riding into?

William contemplated the spirits that he saw coming up from the battlefield before the battle. He didn't say anything to the other scouts about this; they might say that he was just making it up. That night William turned to another scout who came from a strong longhouse clan. His name was Joe Who Respects Nothing. "Do you think it's possible to see the spirits of the living before they die?" he asked.

"I have heard that some of our very powerful medicine men could see into the future," Joe replied. "It's not good medicine to talk about someone's death before they die. Why do you ask?"

"Today before the battle, I saw the spirits coming up from the battlefield," William told him. "I saw many of the Sioux warriors, the white soldiers, and two of our scouts. They didn't look at me, nor did they look around. They just passed on into the heavens."

"This could be a blessing or a curse for you, William Cloud. I won't tell anyone of your power because this could cause many of them to ask about their futures, which would not be a good thing."

William thanked Joe for his words of wisdom and for his promise to be still about the matter. It was accepted to talk about your own death, but not about someone else's death in the Winnebago tradition.

On August 15, 1864, Chief Little Priest and his scouts came upon a band of Northern Cheyenne, and a battle ensued. William did not see his spirit fall. At a fast gallop, he rode into the hostile encounter, and something hit and spun him right out of his saddle. Dazed and wounded, William tried to find his horse and rifle, but he was on the ground with only his hatchet. A rider came charging at him, swinging a war ax. William ducked. As he turned, a Cheyenne warrior was coming at him on foot, armed with a war ax. They squared off, and the death battle began, moving sideways, backward, dodging the swings.

They locked weapons, and the Cheyenne was thrown to the ground. He rolled and tried to kick William, but William was too fast. The warrior threw dust into William's face, but that only made William mad. The Cheyenne warrior rolled again and tried to get up, but this time, he had his back to the scout. William threw his hatchet, and it stuck in the back of the young Cheyenne. The young warrior was trying to reach around and pull the hatchet out of his back, but the hatchet was buried too far into his back. Blood gushed out of the wound every time his heart beat, and the young warrior was too weak to sing his death song. He collapsed on the ground.

William hurried over to retrieve his weapon, quickly wiped it off, and holstered it; and then he looked for his rifle, which lay quite a few feet from where he stood.

By this time, the bands of Cheyenne were either dead or running for their lives. His men came to help William. He was bleeding, so the army medic put a bandage on his wound, and then the teasing began:

"Now you have something to show the people back home—Chief William and his battle scar. 'Just look at my shoulder; touch it if you like.'"

It went on and on. But in reality, William was in pain, but he couldn't show it.

"How will your warrior song go?" asked one of the scouts.

"Maybe something like 'I took care of the Cheyenne at the Little Missouri River battle,'" sang another.

Still the teasing went on. All William could do was to give them a little smile.

The next morning, the detachment of the wounded left the column and made their way back to the camp, where the company surgeon cleaned out the wound and put William on light duty for a few weeks. Although it was embarrassing to be on light duty, it felt good to get a few days off. The wounded scouts had a tent with cots, but all of the other scouts slept outside on the prairie, because they liked to feel Mother Earth beneath them.

One night William was lying on the ground, looking up into the vast heaven, and wondering about this power that he had and why he could see into the future. Why didn't the other Indians have it? He finally fell asleep, but what he saw in his dream he would never tell anyone.

The men wore uniforms, but they were not blue like his, and their weapons were very different. All of the men spoke in English. Somewhere he saw an American flag, so he knew that they were American troops, but the flag had more stars on it. The young man in his dream was his own great-great-grandson. He was fighting a losing battle with more and more of the enemy coming at him. Soldiers were charging and shooting at him and his men, but the young warriors stayed their ground. His great-great-grandson and his men were in a vicious battle against overwhelming odds. The enemy had slits for eyes. They were small in build. There were hundreds of them, and they just keep charging up the hill, shooting and throwing some kind of exploding device. Many dead enemy bodies lay around his great-great-grandson's position. William had no idea how long the battle had been going on. He looked to see if any spirits were rising from the battlefield, but he saw nothing.

Instead, William saw blinding flashes of hundreds of explosions going off and hundreds of wounded and dead. His grandson and his men were cut off from the main body; the enemy had cut them off and was making a circle around the small group of warriors.

A group of enemy soldiers had made their way behind his great-great-grandson's position; they were sneaking up from behind them. One of the enemy soldiers was taking aim at the back of his great-great-grandson's head. William watched in horror as the enemy soldier began to squeeze the trigger.

"STOP, STOP, STOP!" William screamed.

His grandson could not see the enemy coming up behind him. William had to do something. He hollered, he screamed, "TURN AROUND, TURN AROUND, LOOK BEHIND YOU!"

He heard a bang.

William woke up in a chilling sweat. This dream seemed so real, so very real, but where was it? Part of him wanted to go back to the dream, but the other part of him didn't want to know how it would turn out. Where was that place? Why did the enemy look so different? And how did he recognize who the young man was? In this dream, the battle wasn't against other Indians or even against the whites, but against some people that William had never seen before.

His blanket was wet with sweat. Trembling and shaken, William sat up. He hoped that no one saw him or heard him yelling and screaming in his dream. He would fast and pray the next two days and hope that this would never happen. The next day, other scouts wondered why William wanted to have a sweat and fast for two days—he didn't seem like himself. He had a look of loneliness, or maybe it was a worried look about him, and he had a far-off distant look in his eyes. After the sweat and fast, William put this matter in the hands of Mah-oonah. This was all he could do!

The scouts had received word that the Sioux were raiding their villages back in Nebraska. More Winnebago braves had joined with allies from the Omaha tribe to defend their homes from the Miniconjou and Ogalala Sioux. In late December of 1864, Chief Little Priest led his scouts back to Nebraska and, in January of 1865, led the charge against the Ogalala and Miniconjou Lakota. The battle took place near what is now the town of Winnebago, Nebraska. Most of the year, the scouts had running battles with the Sioux in and around the Winnebago Indian reservation in Nebraska. Most of the encounters were with small war parties. This was the Sioux way of getting back at the Winnebagos—to harass and kill the ones back home. This would keep the Ho-Chunks out of the Dakotas.

In February 1865, the Winnebagos held a name-changing ceremony in one of the villages in the Big Bear Hollow. This kind of ceremony hadn't been held in many years, because the tribe had been moved so many times. Many of the elders wanted to get back into the old ways—feasting, name changing, and listening to stories.

It was in this ceremony that William Cloud would officially change his name to William Hatchett.

In the celebration that followed the naming, William and others were asked to tell of the battles. William was last to talk about being a scout. He told the story of the valley and his first kill; he also told how he got wounded and described other battles. He told the people how he could see into the future, but he never told them how far he could see into the future.

"When you choose to be warrior, you choose to die," said William Hatchett. "And many of our warriors have died for our place on this earth. It is here in Nebraska that the government has decided to let us live. We have earned that right to be here. We have paid the price for this land that we now call home. I hope that we can live in peace and not be moved ever again."

A few months later, the commissioner of Indian Affairs, William P. Dole, authorized agent Saint Andre Durand Balcombe to move all Winnebago belongings to Nebraska. The Ho-Chunk Nation lost 610 people at Crow Creek due to starvation and the cold. No one would know the actual loss of life due to heartbreak and loneliness or the numbers of those who had tried to walk back to their ancestral burial ground in Wisconsin.

As the weather warmed up, the rest of the Ho-Chunk Nation left the Fort Thompson area, glad to get out of that hell. When they reached Nebraska, the spring rains had begun, but they didn't mind. It felt good to be in the woods again and have fertile ground under their feet. The Omahas told them that in the month of May, the mushrooms came out, and then they would have some good eating.

On May 1, 1865, Little Priest and his scouts battled bands of Oglala and Miniconjou at Honey Creek on the Missouri River. Later that same month, on the fifteenth, they managed to annihilate a complete Sioux war party down by George Snake's old residence. The Omaha scouts and warriors from the Omaha tribe continued fighting the marauding Sioux war parties that came into the reservation. It was easy for the Sioux war parties to hide in the thick timbers, the large wooded hills made it very easy to move about without being seen. By now many more Winnebagos were moving into the Big Bear Hollow and other parts of the new reservation. This made it harder for the home warriors to keep watch over all of them.

Small battles would occur all year long on both the Omaha and Winnebago reservations. More and more young men joined the warriors to protect their homes from the Sioux, and still more young warriors joined Chief Little Priest and the Company A scouts.

In the spring of 1866, the New Company A of Fort Omaha left their homes in Northeast Nebraska and made their way to the Tongue River in Montana, where they encountered Red Cloud's band of Ogalala Lakota with Northern Cheyenne and Northern Arapahos. This battle would be known as the Battle of the Tongue River. Again, the Company A scouts distinguished themselves in battles with their brother Indians.

The Sioux war chief was wounded in the leg, while others were not so lucky. Although the Company A scouts had been with the army since 1863, there was never a shortage of new scouts coming from Nebraska.

William looked at the new scouts and wondered whether he had looked that young and ready for war back in 1863. When would it end? The Sioux never seemed to quit. Always in raiding parties, they attacked Omaha and Winnebago villages and some white settlers. Even with the big War Between the States over, the Sioux kept the war clubs swinging.

In August 1866, Chief Little Priest was badly wounded when a band of Ogalala Sioux caught him and three others on the Powder River. Although shot four times, the war chief managed to kill nine Lakota warriors and their war chief. The Lakota remember the day also; they have a song honoring the Winnebago war chief. The song claims that he changed into a "grizzly bear" and stood his ground. Chief Little Priest was carried back to the fort with his trophies: the other war chief's horse, his rifle, shield, and his bearskin—all big medicine.

It didn't look good. Some of his wounds were infected, and he was still losing blood. He died a month later. The war chief, Little Priest, was buried in a small mound in the Winnebago area. In honor of his dead brother, the new chief, Gray Wolf, held council in the Big Bear Hollow council house and proposed a celebration in honor of his brother's death and in honor of all veterans of Company A Omaha Scouts, Nebraska Volunteers.

This celebration took place at the Flag Pole Hill, which was on William Hatchett's land. William recalled many times when he and the war chief would talk about the old days, the battles, the army, and what would happen to the tribe. Would they be left in peace, or would the government try to move them? It was a sad time, but also a good time. The drums beat out the new war songs of the war chief and the rest of Company A. William's uncle had made a song for William Hatchett; it told of how he saw the war party in the grass and of how he could see the spirits rising from a battlefield before it became a battlefield. It was a warrior's song, because every warrior has his own song!

The celebration lasted several days, and stories were told and retold. Different members of the Omaha scouts talked about the big battles with the Sioux Nation on the great plains of the Dakotas and battles with the Ogalala Sioux on the Winnebago reservation.

On the last day of the celebration and after the last song, the flag was lowered, and it was agreed to meet every year on that date at the flagpole and honor the war chief, Little Priest, and members of Company A. (This powwow would become the oldest continuous powwow in North America.)

The death of the war chief, Little Priest, did not stop the Ho-Chunks from scouting for the U.S. Army; in fact, after his passing, there were still Winnebago Scouts in the Wyoming Territory helping the army. After his death, however, William Hatchett and some of the original scouts stayed home and provided security for the new reservation. They would have run-ins with the die-hard Sioux for many months.

The Winnebagos had finally made their last move. In the past thirty-four years, they had been moved five times, and each move was with bitter tears, heartbreak, and loss of the old and weak who could not make the move and those who fell behind. Being woodland Indians, they adapted to their new environment very easily; and once the fear of the Sioux war parties was gone, life in Nebraska was finally pleasant. The census of 1869 found 1,343 Indians living on the Winnebago reservation: 408 men, 448 women, and 487 children. Most if not all lived in fourteen villages ranging from the Omaha Reservation border to three miles north of what is now Honey Creek Road.

Not all of the Winnebagos liked to live in the villages; some of them liked to live in private. William Hatchett's family lived by what would become known later as the Hair Pin Turn about two miles above Big Bear Hollow. The Hatchett family had a lodge down by the river where they stayed during the summer months. It was close to his brother.

Talk of a railroad coming into the reservation was on a lot of lips. This would mean more white people, more of their way of life. William stayed at Hair Pin Turn and raised his family by the old Indian ways. His lodge was open to anyone, for guidance or for talk of the old days or talk of what would happen to the tribe. William knew that the old ways were fading fast and that soon his own children would have to learn the white man's way. Already the white man's schools were being built on the reservation, and more and more of the young people were learning the white man's language.

William often retreated into the timber and fasted. There he would remember the vision that he'd had about the young warrior in a different war in a foreign country … his own kin. But he didn't want to know how it ended; he hoped that maybe someday, somehow he could help this lone warrior and his men. William was a member of the medicine lodge, but he never told the other members of his vision. It's true he could see into the future, and what he saw, sadly, was the Ho-Chunks living in two different states, Nebraska and Wisconsin—a divided nation.

William's son, Louis, was raised in the old traditional way. By the time Louis was six, he could run a fish line, clean fish, skin out small game, know what berries were good to eat, and survive on his own in the timber. Louis didn't attend any white man's school; this was not the traditional way. When spring was in the air, it was time to move to their summer lodge down by the river. It would need some repair, but it always did, and William felt this was a good time to be free. He built a longhouse in the woods not too far from his lodge, and he and Louis loved to go mushroom hunting. He liked the way his wife cooked the mushrooms. She would dip them in egg batter and then roll them in flour, and then she would drop them into hot bacon grease.

You could smell them cooking all over the river bottoms. Sometimes she would add a few potatoes and maybe some wild onions. Later on in the summer, they would all go out and pick raspberries, gooseberries and sweet strawberries.

This was Louis Hatchett's favorite time of the year because he didn't have to chop as much wood, and the days were getting longer and the nights warmer. He liked his mother's stories about the Neutral Ground and moving from one place to another. He liked the ones about his father the most, about how he became a Ho-Chunk warrior—to see the enemy and then to kill him. Louis wondered if he would ever become a warrior. Louis was told that Nebraska was his home forever. There would be no more moving from place to place, at the point of a bayonet. His father and the rest of the Omaha scouts had made sure of that.

However, some of the Ho-Chunks were still hoping to recapture the past, swimming across the Missouri River and walking at night across Iowa. They had to stay out of sight of the white people because they would call out the sheriff who would arrest them and send them back to Nebraska or shoot them on the spot. If they made it across the state, they still had to deal with the Mississippi River. In the summer, they could find a shallow part on the Mississippi and cross it at night and make the final leg of their journey to their old villages. Most of those villages were gone, but some of the locals who knew them would take them in. They could stay in Wisconsin if they were landowners, and with the help of some good white folks, this was arranged. Ho-Chunk people who had land sent word back to the Winnebagos for their relatives to come and live with them, back in their own country.

And this is how the tribe split into two nations.

For those who managed to make it back to Wisconsin, there were still problems. They found work, often laboring for the local farmers, saving as much of their earnings as they could to try to buy land—the very same land that had been theirs years ago. William had a chance to go back to Wisconsin, but he thought it was better to stay on his own land and try to make a living. Besides, they had been promised by General Sully. It was their right to be here!

All was not perfect on the reservation, however. William's eyes took in the group of men huddled under a tree, passing around a bottle. "All my life they've been telling my people to become more like the white man," he said aloud. "They put us here on the reservation and took away our way of life to make us live more like the white man, and now I'm afraid all too many of our people are doing just that—drinking the white man's whiskey and getting put in jail like some white men."

He turned to the warriors standing around him. "Is this why we fought our brother Indians? To become useless and drink the white man's whiskey?" Frowning, the warriors looked from William to the men huddled under the tree.

This problem would plague the tribe for years. There was a law against the bootleggers coming into the reservation, but no one enforced it.

Chapter 6

Educating the Ho-Chunk Child

"What do they teach at the white man's school that I don't already know?" Louis asked. He was ten years old, and as far as he was concerned, spring was a time to enjoy life. There was good hunting and good fishing, and there was the planting to do. He was very disappointed when his parents told him that maybe this year; he would have to go to the white man's school. "They will teach you to read and write," his mother told him. "This is an important thing for Indians to know, important for your future."

"Where do I have to go?" Louis grumbled.

"It's a place they call the Mission Day School," his mother explained. "It's in a big building."

Louis didn't like this white man's school already, and he hadn't even seen it yet. How could they think of sending their own child away every day?

It was a decision that had not been reached easily. The missionaries who taught in Indian schools had no comprehension of the complexity and sophistication of the traditional native educational, social, and cultural systems. Their religious zeal to spread Christianity among the Indians and their condescending attitudes prohibited the missionaries from understanding why their goals were stymied and why Indian students clung to their cultural and spiritual values with such tenacity. Most missionaries harbored deep prejudices against Indians, and most

Indians, including Louis's parents, deeply resented the missionaries and their activities.

William, however, was having second thoughts. "Times are changing for the Ho-Chunks," he explained to his son. "We will have to learn how to live like them, to speak like them. Already we farm like them. We eat their food and use their blankets. Son, don't look at this as punishment; it's just the way it is. Besides, the school is on the reservation a few miles from here; it's not like it's in the Dakotas. I know what it's like to be away from your family. When I was a scout, I would miss my home and my wife, but I knew that what we were doing was for the good of the tribe. We all agreed to help the army so we wouldn't be pushed around. We must learn the white man's ways, or we will disappear like the buffalo. We must set the example now so our children's children will know—even seven generations of Ho-Chunks will know—that we must live with the white man and learn his ways."

Hearing this from his father, Louis knew that he had to do it, but he still wondered why his family couldn't just stay down at the river all year. No one would miss them because sometimes, they didn't pick up their rations. There was enough deer and game to last the year around. Plus they had new traps, and they worked very well.

One day a lot of men came to meet at their lodge. Louis knew most of them because they had been over to his lodge before, and they were medicine men of power. The medicine lodge had been set up, far from the wigwam. The night of the meeting, Louis made his way over to the lodge to hear the men talking and singing the songs of the medicine lodge. Louis listened and learned the songs. He could understand most of what was going on, but he still had trouble with some of it.

In the morning, when the meeting was over, William took a nap. Later that afternoon, Louis was singing one of the songs, when his father heard him. "Louis! Come over here! Where did you learn that song?"

"I was outside of the medicine lodge, and I heard it."

"Do you understand what the songs are about?"

"Some of them."

"How long did you stand outside of the medicine lodge?"

"I listened to a lot of the meeting."

"So what do you think about our medicine lodge?"

"I would like to learn more about your medicine; they say that in battle, you had strong medicine."

"But even with good medicine, I was wounded."

"But the songs tell of your bravery and how the others always wanted you in battle with them."

"The songs tell the truth, but there is one thing that I never told anyone," William said softly. "I can see into the future." He told Louis about the dream he had had after he was wounded, the dream about the young warrior who was his great-great-grandson—Louis's great-grandson—in a battle in a foreign land against an enemy with slits for eyes.

Louis didn't know what to say or think. He had heard stories of how his father had looked into the future and how he could see spirits on a battlefield even before the battle happened, but this was a lot to take in. How had his father known that the warrior was his kin? Did he look like his father? Was this young man that wasn't even born yet a medicine man too? How could all this be?

Louis wondered about this for the rest of the day. At night he tried to dream about a battle in the future, but it wasn't there. The next day, Louis was still puzzled, but his father told him not to dwell on the dream because it wasn't about him or even in his lifetime. If this was part of the medicine lodge, it was scary and exciting, yet it kindled a feeling of belonging at the same time. Louis wanted to learn more about the lodge, but once you're in, you can't leave—you're a member for life. Knowing this, Louis accepted the challenge; he wanted to be like his father: respected, liked, and maybe feared by some.

Their summer lodge was not far from the river. His father had a canoe, so they fished a lot. There was always something for Louis to do; if it wasn't cleaning fish, it was getting firewood or maybe skinning out a mountain lion that they had trapped in the night. Some days his mother would have him working in the fields. He thought, *this is women's work.* But he did it anyway.

Much had changed since Little Priest sent two of his braves over the side of the steamboat to find the Omaha village, and their chiefs and make a deal with them to buy the northern portion of their reservation. After the warriors of Company A returned home, many villages had been built in the Big Bear Hollow area of the river—fourteen in all.

Some of the villages were actually dug into the side of a large cliff that loomed several hundred feet up. These lodges were easy to heat in the winter and were very comfortable in the summer months. The main living space was in the cliff, and the entrance was used for storage or a spare bedroom. The entrance was covered with canvas if they could afford it, but most were covered with bark. This was one of the old traditional lodges of the Ho-Chunks.

Louis had relatives and friends in each village, and sometimes his father would let him go visit them for a few days. Most of the villages were close, but two or three were on the west end of the reservation. Louis had all of his work done, so he asked his father if he could go and visit his Day-ga for a week or two.

"Take the war pony if you like," said William.

The army had let his father keep his horse in return for some of his pay. The pony had a battle wound and moved with a slight limp, but he was still strong. He was getting old, so Louis had to ride him slowly, but he loved thinking that this horse had taken his father, the great William Hatchett—medicine man, Indian tracker, the man who could look into the future—into battle. Louis wondered what kind of stories this animal could tell if he could talk. As Louis approached the Big Bear village, he could smell smoke and the cooking of the milkweed soup. What a delight. He'd made it just in time for supper. "A-ho, Day-ga, is it time to eat?"

"Come in, nephew. The soup is done, and the fry bread is coming out of the grease."

Milkweed soup made with salt pork and some fry bread. What more could a boy want from life? Maybe a good war story from his Day-ga or a funny story. It was a good meal: soup, bread, and fresh berries. "My father sent over some dried fish and some tanned hides," said Louis.

This pleased his uncle. His woman would make clothes for the winter and use the lighter skins for his dancing regalia, now that they had an annual powwow coming up. Louis liked his Day-ga very much. He was the one who wrote and sang the Hatchett warrior song, and Louis hoped that maybe someday he might make a warrior song for him.

"Tomorrow you can help me and some of the boys cut down a cottonwood tree," his uncle told him. "We'll make a canoe with part of it and make a drum out of the largest part of the trunk."

Louis liked this kind of work. He wanted to show his Day-ga that he was a hard worker, and he was anxious to learn about drum making.

Louis was up early the next morning, and he couldn't wait to get started on the cottonwood tree. The rest of the boys showed up right after breakfast, and soon they all walked into the woods. Two of the men were carrying the longest cross saw that Louis had ever seen. It had two long wooden handles and huge saw teeth. The saw was almost two men long, and it bounced up and down as they made their way into the timbers; soon they found the tree they all liked.

"That's the one," Day-ga said. "We will all take turns on the saw."

One of Louis's jobs was to bring the water bags and food. He wondered why they needed so much water, but he would soon find out. The first cut was made, and then they cut out the notch; and then the sawing started, first one team and then another and then another. This went on for quite a long time. Everyone was up on their feet as the last few pulls of the saw were being made into the tree. Soon the large cottonwood leaned into the direction of the notch. With a large crash that shook the ground, the tree was lying on the forest floor. They all went to work cutting off the branches and making room around the tree to cut and move it.

"The bottom part of the tree will be cut into a drum circle," Day-ga told them. "And the middle will be the canoe."

Back and forth, they sawed as the teams took their turns cutting the monster. Finally, by midday, the drum circle lay on the ground, and they had measured off the length for the canoe. The smaller branches would be used for making drying racks for fish and other game. Some of it would be used as fuel for the lodges, and most of the leaves would be used for new bedding. It would take the lumberjacks two days to get all of the cottonwood back to the lodge so they could start to work on it.

Axes, sharp tools used for cutting, chisels, hammers, and fire—all would be used on this project. Louis was tired from the dragging, lifting, and rolling the big logs; but it was exciting to learn a new trade. The next day, Louis would start on the drum. Louis's job was to trim off all of the bark around the circle. He had to be careful to not cut into the meat of the drum. "One good thing about cottonwood trees is that they have a lot of water in them, and they clean up real good," said Day-ga.

It took two deer hides to make one drum. They put the skins into a large tub filled with water and left them in there until it was time to stretch them over the drum. Louis was given a small ax and a chisel and was told to keep the fire going. Day-ga started on the drum circle with an ax. He made several chops into the middle, working his way to the outside but leaving enough room around the edge. Then Louis would clean it out, and they would start over again.

After several repetitions, they set a small fire into the circle, paying close attention to the edge of the drum. This took most of the day. Progress was good, and they finally turned the drum over and started all over again on the other side. This time, they had to be more careful because the edge was getting smaller, and they had to work with more care. Soon they had a very small fire going in the drum itself. This time, they had a jar of water and used it when the fire got too close to the edge. Louis could see the drum taking shape, and he learned how to use the chisel.

"You make small chips," his Day-ga told him. "If you take too much, you might break the drum. Then it's only good for firewood."

Louis sure didn't want to do that. Instead of using fire this time, they used small hits from the chisel and then smoothed out the wood with small hand stones. Louis was getting sore hands from all of the chipping and scraping, but he was proud of the drum. It looked like a real drum! After days of continuous work, the circle was ready to be painted by his Day-ga. The base coat of blue was put on first and then came the artwork. The hatchet and the war pony were part of the story. This drum would be known as the Hatchett drum.

Finally, on the sixth day, they were ready for the skins. The first one was laid over the top and trimmed; holes were cut for the deer hide straps. Next the drum was turned over very carefully, and the bottom skin was placed on it. The skin was trimmed, and holes were made. Next it was time to lace it up. Very carefully, they pulled the deer hide while keeping the skins even. After the initial lacing, they would adjust the skins and put more tension on the deer hide straps. Once that was done, the Hatchett drum was complete and just had to dry in the sun for several days.

The Hatchett drum was big enough that eight singers could sit around it and still have enough room. Louis was told that he had to make his own drumstick. His Day-ga showed him how that was done. His Day-ga had taken a small branch from the cottonwood and cleaned it up and smoothed it down. Then he told Louis to take some of the hide that they had cut off for the drum and wrap it around one end, making sure that it stayed even. Day-ga cut a larger piece and showed Louis how to wrap it around the end and sew it together. Louis had to do the sewing of the hide. This was hard; it hurt his fingers to push the needle through the hide. His mother had always made it look so easy when she was working on hides. He got the job done. This would have to lie out in the sun also.

Louis was told that he could put his own design on his drumstick—maybe a hawk feather, maybe some beadwork, something that told the people that this was his property and his markings. He couldn't wait for the drum to dry; he wanted to be one of the first to use it, and he knew his father's war song by heart. His Day-ga told him that they would have to be careful the first few times because the wood was still drying inside.

They let the drum set for a week. Then one afternoon, they smudged (a bundle of sage would be lit and the smoke would be pass over the drum. Smudging was done so the drum would have many good songs and only good spirits in its lifetime) and placed tobacco on the circle of life (the middle of the drum). Day-ga said a prayer for the drum, and Louis and the rest of the boys sat down with the new Hatchett drum.

Day-ga let Louis make the first hit on the drum. This was a proud moment for Louis. He had helped make this, and now he was the first to use it. The first hit and the drum came to life. The sound carried all through the Big Bear Hollow. Louis could feel the beat vibrate through his body. The rest of the boys joined in, and the William Hatchett war song came to life in the Big Bear Hollow.

Other members of the village came over to see what was going on. As the song progressed, one of the village members pointed up into the sky. An eagle was flying over the village and looked down on the singer and the Hatchett drum. It was said that the Hatchett drum was blessed by the eagle and that nothing could ever stop the words and songs that the drum made; it was the heartbeat of a warrior.

On and on the singing went, and someone brought water over for the singers. Everyone agreed that the new Hatchett drum carried a real human heartbeat. People who were standing twenty feet away could feel the beat go though their bodies. Women joined the singers, standing behind them and singing with them, and some did a two-step around the drum. Louis was very proud to sit with real warriors and sing their songs.

"It's good to hear a good drum and good singing," said one elder. "This is how it used to be when we lived in Wisconsin many years ago. Someone would make a new drum, and we would all gather around to hear it."

After several hours of singing, Day-ga said that was enough. "We will have more time to practice later, but I don't think we will need a lot of practice for the powwow. We already sound good enough-ah."

Louis had been so involved with the work on the drum that he hadn't noticed the new dugout canoe that was gliding across the river. This had also been created from the cottonwood tree that they had taken down just a few weeks earlier. It too had its owner's markings on it. Louis wondered why anyone would need to go to the white man's school when there was all of this to learn right here. He knew that the white man didn't teach young Indians this in his school.

It had been three weeks since Louis left his father's lodge, and he was anxious to get home and tell his family about everything that he had done. He rushed into where his parents were sitting with a smile on his face, and they both looked up.

"What did you get into now?" his father asked.

"We made the Hatchett drum," he told him. "And it has your story on it; even the war pony is painted on the side of the drum!"

Louis told him about the cottonwood tree and how it gave up its life so they could make the drum and a canoe for fishing. Even the leaves and lesser parts of the tree were used. "When I hit the drum the very first time, it came to life," he told his father. "I could feel its heart beating. Every time I hit it, it spoke to me."

"I thought I heard a drum the other day," said William. "It was far away, but I could hear it very well. It seems like they drummed all afternoon."

"We did. You could hear us all the way over here?"

"When you have a good drum, it will send the message out for everyone to hear."

Louis showed him his drumstick and described the new canoe that could glide over the water with very little paddling.

"Tomorrow we will go to the agency to get our rations, and we will stop by our lodge up by the hairpin turn," William said. "Maybe we will stay the night on the way back to the river."

The next morning, they put everything away and got the team ready for the trip to the agency. It would be a long ride for all of them, since the roads were very rough. The war pony was left at Day-ga's lodge, since the ride to the agency would be too much for the old horse. He didn't mind being left, and he liked to be around people, especially when they had fry bread.

Louis walked while they rode through the flat river bottoms and caught a ride on the wagon when they started to go up Big Bear Hollow. It was a long hill with a slight turn to the left on the upper part.

The team worked hard to pull the wagon up the big hollow hill, and when they finally made it to the top, William pulled the team off the road to give them a short break to catch their wind. As they waited for the horses to get their rest, William told Louis how he had participated in a battle with the Sioux just over the hill from where they were standing. "It was in the afternoon, and we were getting ready to move out when one of our scouts saw a Sioux war party. They were moving along the top of the hill, so we hid the best we could and waited. When they got within rifle shot, we set up on a straight line and let them ride into the ambush. It didn't take long once the shooting started. One or two may have gotten away, but the rest of them were dead. It doesn't seem like that long ago, but it's been a while since we moved the Sioux war parties off the reservation. I hear that the Sioux are still fighting with the army out in Montana and western South Dakota."

After a few more turns in the road, they were at the hairpin turn. Then they went by their winter home and on their way to the agency. The team and wagon rumbled along the dusty road, passed through the four corners, and kept going west. They topped the next hill and gazed out into the valley below them. In the distance, they could see the last turn to the left, which would take them to the agency. It was afternoon when they got there. William went into the agency office to see if he had any mail and to get any new information on the day school and the new homes that were supposed to be built for the tribal members.

They drove around the office to a yellow building to pick up their rations—flour, beans, meat, salt pork, baking powder, lard, salt, a few used army blankets, and other things. Other Indians were picking up their rations too. William stopped and talked to a few of them. Louis met a few of his friends, all of whom were eagerly anticipating the powwow.

Louis thought they would head back to their winter lodge, but instead of heading home, William went south to where they were building the new schoolhouse. Louis looked out at the people working on the building and putting up fences for livestock and chickens. Louis had never seen a building with so many windows. He wondered why they built such a building and what the purpose was for having all those windows.

William left the wagon and went inside. When he came out, he got back into the wagon and headed for home. "The school will open this fall," he told them. "And you will be going there, Louis."

"What do you mean I will be going there?"

"I mean that you will go there every day."

"Every day?"

"Every day that you can make it."

"How long will I have to go to this school?"

"A while until you can speak the white man's language."

"How will I get there?"

"You can ride the war pony."

"Don't the Y-Sapes run the school?"

The question caught William off guard. He had never thought about the Y-Sapes running the school. He didn't answer for a long time; he had to think about what to say, because he had always said such bad things about the Y-Sapes. "Yes, the Y-Sapes run the school, but this one is different; it's called a day school." That was a weak answer, true, but William let it go at that.

Louis wondered what they would teach that took so long to learn.

The July afternoon sun was very hot. William turned the team into the long drive to their winter lodge. He held the team back as they went down into a meadow and then let them have the reins as they pulled up the small hill that took them to the lodge. They would leave some of the supplies in the lodge. William and Louis took the team down to the creek to get water for the lodge and let the horses have a good long drink.

The next day, the whole family went into the meadow to pick milkweeds for supper. Louis liked salt pork and milkweed soup, and the fry bread he always used to soak up the soup. On the way back to the lodge, as they stopped by the flagpole, William and Louis realized they would have to come back the next month and knock down the weeds and clean it up before the powwow.

"How many warriors and dancers do you think will come to the dance this year?" Louis asked his father.

"I think we will have plenty of Ho-Chunk warriors here next month. This is a good time to get together and see old friends and family, maybe do a little trading of goods. We will put up many tents and lodges here."

The next morning, everyone was up and ready to go back to the river. They closed up the winter lodge and headed east, passing other members of the tribe going to the agency. Some stopped and talked for a while, as others just went about their way and kept going. When they got to the bottom of Big Bear Hill, Louis spied a snapping turtle trying to cross the road. He jumped off the wagon and went over to catch it.

"Grab it in the middle where it can't hook you with its hind legs," William shouted.

Once Louis had the monster, William held out a gunnysack, and Louis dropped the turtle into it. "Good eye, son! We'll have turtle soup tonight, and your Day-ga can have the shell for his dance regalia." William looked around. "The woods are full of game, and the forest floor can grow anything. The wild onions are ready, and in a few months, the squash will be ready to pick. Later this fall, we'll gather walnuts for the winter months."

It was lunchtime when they got to Day-ga's lodge, and his wife had prepared deer meat and *Wa-da-shoh-ttohch* (hominy soup) with lots of fry bread.

"Soon we will dry corn and put it up for the winter," Day-ga said. "How about you, William?"

"We will leave before the powwow and stay in the winter lodge."

"The government said that they will start to build next year, so we can have a more permanent home. Maybe this will be good, I don't know."

"They talk about the railroad coming through the reservation and maybe having some kind of village by the railroad tracks somewhere." He looked at his brother and grinned. "I heard the Hatchett drum the other day."

Day-ga grinned back at him. "Yeah, it sounded pretty damn good, huh?"

Louis liked it when they talked about his drum.

"It is nice and big, with room for lots of singers," said Day-ga as he took it out and showed him.

Day-ga sat it up; and William, Day-ga, and Louis sat down at the drum and started to sing. The wives stood behind them and joined in. In the Winnebago tradition, only the men can sit at the drum and sing, but it always sounded better when the women joined and hit the high notes. Again, people came out of their lodges to see who was singing. More of the old warriors joined William, Day-ga, and Louis. One of the songs was an honor song to Chief Little Priest. The men removed their hats, and everyone who had been sitting stood while the honor song was sung. The Hatchett drum carried the beat throughout the Big Bear Hollow.

William agreed that the drum had a real heartbeat. "We will use this drum for the opening song at the powwow this year. This drum will tell the stories of Company A Omaha Scouts. It will let the people know how it was out in Sioux country. This drum will pass down the stories and pass on the tradition. Years from now, when this drum is very old, it will hold the stories and will be the next storyteller," he predicted.

William and his family headed home in late afternoon. It was a great day in the timbers, with so much to see and do, but little time to get it done. Louis knew that he would have to get firewood for the lodge just as soon as he got home. Next the turtle would have to be prepared for supper. Louis would have to get the turtle's head out of its shell. He would do this by putting a stick in front of the turtle. It would bite on the stick and pull its head out of the shell. Once the head was out, Louis would place a piece of rawhide around its neck and pull the head all the way out. With a quick chop from the ax, he'd have a headless turtle. Next it would go into a pot of boiling water. Soon it would be ready to split open and get the meat out. Louis was certain that the white man's school didn't teach that!

A few days later, the Thunderbird Clan held its summer feast, an event that took almost two weeks and kept William and his family very busy. Louis enjoyed the feast, especially seeing so many of his relatives and friends. In fact, this was just one of many feasts that month and the next. The Bear Clan held their summer feast over by the bluffs. That was an exciting time for Louis because he and his relatives would try to climb the face of the bluff and try to get to the top so that they could survey the valley and the Missouri River. The whole valley floor was full of large cottonwood trees. Some said that you could get lost in there because the trees were so thick. They could see far into the state of Iowa. It was very flat, but in the far distance, they could see hills and sometimes a steamboat on the river. This brought back many unpleasant memories for the older Indians. From this high point, they could see the smoke coming from the different villages that were along the river. Many years later, this high spot would be called Engineer Point, and the CCC (Civilian Conservation Corps) boys would construct a fire tower with a small house for the watchman or ranger.

A month later, the William Hatchett family was packing its belongings, and heading for the winter quarters by the hairpin turn for the powwow celebration at the old flagpole. By the time the Hatchett family arrived home, some early arrivals were already setting up their camps, and more would be coming every day. By the end of the week, several more members of the tribe had arrived. Louis could only think of how it must have been years ago to see the whole nation on the move and setting up every night on the prairie. The tribe would follow the herds of buffalo and kill enough to dry and pull jerky and tan out the hides before they would move on.

Every afternoon and evening, the drum groups got together and practiced. Different clans had their own drums, as did different families. It was an exciting time. The following Monday, the ceremony started. One of the elder scouts blessed the sacred circle and made an offering to the spirits.

The American flag was raised, and the men of Company A Omaha Scouts led the grand entry into the great circle. That started the powwow. Then there would be a lot of storytelling, a lot of laughter, good food, and singing well into the night. "Next year, in the month of the mushroom," one member predicted, "a lot of babies will be born!"

They all laughed as someone else said, "Yes, and those will be powwow babies!"

Day-ga entered the sacred circle in full regalia with the new turtle shell shield, went over to the new Hatchett drum, and took his place as the head singer.

The next song was an honor song for William Hatchett. As William entered the great circle, members of his family followed behind him. William led the Hatchett clan around the drum. Louis waved as they passed by, and then he joined in. What an honor to be there in the sacred circle with the great warriors that rode with their fearless Chief Little Priest. Louis could almost see himself as one of them. He knew all the war stories. He knew when they got shot. He knew the ones who were killed, and it was as if this honor song was for him. That evening Louis went over to his Day-ga's tent. There was an old man there, and he was telling a ghost story.

He started out by saying, "This happened to my nephew when he was a young man. One time my nephew was getting ready to go to a white man's celebration. I think it was a Fourth of July party or something like that, something that the white man celebrates. There was much to eat and drink, and a lot of pretty white women. Some of the white men were getting drunk and acting stupid. They sang songs and did all kinds of things. Mostly my nephew just stood around and watched them. Sometimes one of the white ladies would come over to him and talk, but my nephew didn't speak very good English. A few of the white men came over and told my nephew to have some drink. He did, and he didn't know that it was whiskey.

"This went on for quite a long time. He drank more and was acting stupid just like the white men. There were a few other Ho-Chunks there. Some had the drinks, but a few of them didn't drink any whiskey. After a while, it was time to go home, so the Indian boys loaded up into their wagon and headed back to their lodge. Some of the drunken ones were singing a song in English. When they didn't know a word, they would sing it in Ho-Chunk and then laugh about it.

"Moving through the woods, they crossed over a small bridge. One of the boys just happened to look down into the water, and he saw a ghost following them. He pointed and said 'Ghost!'

"Everybody stopped and looked. Sure enough, there it was just floating along by the wagon. Everybody was scared, and the driver hit the team and had them at a full gallop. Soon they were at their lodge. They all jumped out and went into the lodge, and they built a big fire. They grabbed weapons and went outside to put the horses away. They didn't see anything, and they didn't say anything to anybody. They didn't want people to make fun of them for being drunk."

Did they really see anything, or were they just drunk? Louis wondered.

On the last day of the ceremony, they had a great feast. The warriors were first, and then the elders next and then the rest of the members of the tribe. Louis worried they might not have enough food for him because he was in the back of the line, but they did.

"There is sadness at this powwow," said William. "Over four hundred of our relatives and friends have moved back to Wisconsin. I don't know if they are dead or safe in Wisconsin. I don't know if anyone helped them along the way. I only hope that they are safe and well. They don't have a reservation there like we do here, and I don't know how the white man will let them live. We as Ho-Chunks signed our land away in Wisconsin many years ago."

As the afternoon started to turn to evening, they sang Chief Little Priest's war song as their last song. One week of celebration, and it was over. It had been a good powwow. It seemed as though they had no sooner come than they were gone, back to their villages in the timber and to the west end of the reservation.

William lowered the flag for the last time and put it away for another year. It was quiet on the Hatchett allotment. Gone were the singing, feasting, laughing, and the stories.

Chapter 7

Mission School

Missionaries were encouraged by the U.S. government to move onto the Indian reservations, to establish schools and churches, and to teach the youth the American way of life. By doing this, it was hoped that it would drive a wedge between the educated youth and the old Indian ways, but the program failed miserably. What little the students learned in school was forgotten as soon as they walked into their lodges. The family and the Indian ways of life were too ingrained into the youth, and going to a day school meant nothing or very little to the children.

Louis Hatchett was ten years old when his father, William, enrolled him in the Mission Day School that was built close to the agency grounds. He attended the school for three years off and on and learned the basics of education, enough to help him and his family. This chapter offers a capsule version of the experience that many Ho-Chunk children went through. No one will ever know the full story of the tough times the young Indian children endured at the hands of so-called religious saviors.

Louis was told to put on his best clothes and shoes. He knew what was going on, and he didn't like it. His parents climbed into the wagon, and William told Louis to ride the war pony, since the horse needed the exercise. The Hatchett clan made its way down the pasture and up the hill to the rough wagon road. They turned left and headed to the agency.

Now Louis understood what his father must have felt like when they were loaded onto the steamboats and sent down the Mississippi River to South Dakota Territory. No one said a word on the trip. They passed the agency and headed toward the mission school. William stopped the wagon in front of a big building and went inside. After a while, he came out and told Louis to tie the war pony to a tree on a long lead and go into the building. Slowly Louis did as he was told and headed off to the open door. He looked over his shoulder and made a small wave.

Once inside, he met a Y-Sape and other white people. There were several Indian boys and a few girls inside waiting. Most of them were little, but a few were older than he, and all had fear on their faces. There was also a young Winnebago boy who translated for the Y-Sapes. He told the children to go into the classroom and sit down. "Do it, or they will do it for you," said the young interpreter.

Soon a bell rang, and a teacher stood in front of the class. He spoke in English, and the interpreter spoke in Winnebago.

The teacher told the new students that they were there to help the Indians and that in time the students would be thankful for the help that they received. He went on to tell them about the rules of the school and how important it was to come to school every day and learn. They would learn how to read and write, add and subtract, and, most of all, how to become good Christians.

Then the teacher wrote his name on the chalkboard. By Christmas, he told them, they would all know how to read and write his name.

It was a boring day for Louis. He didn't understand most of what was said, and furthermore, he didn't care about it. At noon they took a break and served the students some soup and biscuits. Then they told them to go outside and play. Louis didn't know what the word "play" meant, but he went outside and watered the war pony. Soon a bell rang, and the students were told to take their seats in the classroom again.

Again, the teacher talked, and the young student interpreted. On and on it went, until finally, they were told to go home and to make sure that they came back tomorrow. On the ride home, Louis pushed the old war pony on and thought about the day. He still couldn't make heads or tails of it, and he told his parents just that when he got home.

"Maybe it will get better tomorrow," said his mother.

"All I know is that they have a lot of rules, and they say that you can get a beating if you don't follow them," said Louis.

"That's sounds like a tough way to teach a person," William admitted.

Louis attended school most of the fall. One day before classes started, the teacher asked the boys if any of them would like to go and cut wood for the school. Louis's hand was up in a flash, and so were others'. In fact, so many of the boys volunteered that they were divided into two groups. This was Louis's lucky day. Any day was a good day if you didn't have to be in school, at all. His work party left the school building in a large lumber wagon with sack lunches. The work was hard, but it made the day go by fast. After they headed back to the school with their load of wood and unloaded the wagon, they were told to go home. Louis pushed the old war pony a little faster on his ride home; he couldn't wait to tell of his day in the woods.

For the next few weeks, the boys made trips into the timber to cut firewood. By now the days were getting shorter and colder. By Christmas, Louis could pronounce his teacher's name, but he could not write it, and that's where most of the students were with their English. Louis didn't go to school on bitter-cold days, nor did his father let him go in the deep snow. He said it would be too hard on the old war pony.

In the spring, Louis and the other students got together before they arrived at the mission school and didn't go to class. There was no way of telling their parents of their absence. It was common for Indian kids not to go to school.

After the first year at school, Louis was glad to leave the classroom and the boring teacher. He couldn't wait to get home and be an Indian again. The old war pony didn't make it through the winter, so on the last day of school, Day-ga and his father picked Louis up from the day school.

The Hatchett family had made plans to leave for their summer lodge on the Missouri River that day. The supplies, blankets, and food were packed and ready to go. The winter lodge was closed up for the season. (This was accomplished by propping a stick against the door.)

"Well, I learned some new white man words at your school today," Day-ga said. "I don't know how to use them. Maybe I don't need to know how to use them."

I feel the same way, Louis thought to himself.

The ride down to the summer lodge was very enjoyable for Louis. It felt good to be out in the timber. When the road got too rough, Louis would get off the wagon and walk. One spot in the road was very rough and even Day-ga got off the wagon and walked with Louis.

"How is the Hatchett drum?" Louis asked his uncle.

"It is fine. We used it last month. One of the older warriors died, and the family asked if we would sing his song on the Hatchett drum. It still sounds good. The spirit is still there."

William pulled the wagon up to Day-ga's lodge and off-loaded his rations and supplies. "I will see you soon, Louis," Day-ga said.

Louis looked up at the cottonwood trees. He had forgotten how large and green they were this time of the year. He could hear the wind moving through their leaves far above his head. He looked over at their summer lodge, and as usual, it would need some repair, but that was an ongoing thing.

Louis helped put the supplies away and unhitch the team. Then he walked over to the river and sat down. It was so peaceful there on the banks of the Missouri. It was time to get recharged, to be an Indian again—to go shirtless, to let the hair grow, to feel Mother Earth between his toes. This was a good time of the year. The hard winter was behind them, and growing season had begun. The Y-Sapes couldn't get him here.

There were mushrooms to pick and cook and work to do on the lodge, like cutting new poles for the tent. Louis and his father put some fishing lines in the water right away. They would have catfish for supper tonight and maybe some fried mushrooms if they looked hard enough. Louis and his sister looked for mushrooms while his father fished the river; all three had good luck. "Now this is what I call a real meal," said Louis, looking around at the fried mushrooms, fried catfish, boiled nettles, and green gooseberries.

After supper, William wanted to talk more about the mission school.

"At first it was very hard," Louis told him. "They have a lot of rules. You can't talk in the lunchroom or the schoolroom, and you get a beating if you talk Ho-chunk."

"What do you mean 'you get a beating if you talk Ho-Chunk'?"

"The Y-Sapes don't want anyone to talk the Ho-Chunk language," Louis told his father. "If you do and get caught, they send you to see the head Y-Sape, and he beats you with a club or his fist." Louis could see the anger in his father's face.

"The Black Robe would hit you with his fist or a piece of wood?"

Louis nodded. "A lot of the students talked in Ho-Chunk about the Y-Sapes and made fun of them. That was the reason they didn't want anyone talking in Indian." Louis shrugged. "They say if you are to learn the English language, then you have to speak it every day."

"How many times did they beat you?"

"Never, I am a fast learner."

William liked that answer. "Well then, you have learned something from me. It's better to keep your mouth shut and learn."

That evening as Louis lay on his bed, he could smell the earth and the forest. He listened to the call of a whip-poor-will and the slap of a beaver tail on the water. It almost sounded as if the frogs were glad to have him back. These were the sounds that he missed, the odor of Mother Earth, the gentle breeze blowing into the lodge. Every now and then, he could hear a pack of coyotes howling. He knew where their den was; it was over by the bluff. He had seen their den dug into the side of the hill. He could hear the young ones trying out their new howls.

He awoke to the smell of the campfire and bacon. The sun was high in the eastern sky, even though it was still early in the morning. "Mother, do you need any more firewood?"

"I can always use a good stick to burn."

It was good to see a friendly face in the morning and not the pinched faces of the old white women from the mission school. When Louis got down to the river, his father was pulling in a fish trap that he had set the night before.

"It's a good day, Louis. I have already caught eight fish this morning, and we will get them ready to dry and cook later."

The next day, the family traveled over to the Big Bear village for a Ho-Chunk feast. The preparation took five days. William, Day-ga,

Louis, and other hunters went out and killed three deer for the feast, field-dressed them, and brought the kill back into the village so the women could cut and cook the deer. They made soup and fried venison, and later, they tanned the hides for winter. A clan feast was always fun for Louis because many of his friends came, some of whom had gone to the mission school with him. This time, he would try to "talk white man talk" to them, if he could remember enough words to impress them.

Soon another hunting party was organized.

"It's a good day to shoot deer," Day-ga told William.

"Yes, I know, I brought three bullets with me."

"Listen to this old warrior; he only needs three bullets for three deer."

"I might even shoot one from my hip, just like the old days," William told him.

"Well, if you can shoot one from the hip, maybe I will kill one by looking through a mirror with my gun on my shoulder," said Joe Little Soldier.

Everyone burst out in loud laughter.

The mighty hunting party left the village and headed in different directions. It didn't take long for any of the group to fill its quota. Deer was very plentiful on the river bottoms of the reservation; soon there was much laughter and teasing in the village again. "I jumped on the back of this big buck and wrestled him down to the ground," Joe Little Soldier said. "I didn't even have to shoot him!"

"Yeah, he probably was old and sick and just fell down," Day-ga said.

William said that his deer was running away from him, so he whistled real loud. The deer stopped and looked around, and that's when he put a bullet into his head. It was a good kill.

Day-ga told the group that he went into the timbers and sat down, and soon a large buck came up to him and said, "I am here to offer myself to the feast of the clan."

This caught everyone's attention; it became very quiet, and every ear was tuned into the story. Day-ga went on to tell them that he asked the buck, "Who told you of this feast?" The buck replied, "I was told by the wind to go and find Day-ga and that he would take me to the feast."

Day-ga said he told the buck, "How can I kill a friend? We have just become friends, and now you want me to kill you?"

"It is so," the buck said upon hearing this. "You must do your duty!"

Again, Day-ga said, "How can I kill you? You are special."

The buck reared back and charged Day-ga. Within a split second, he lay dead on the ground.

The young boys just sat there with their mouths wide open.

Day-ga winked to the other hunters but never said another word about his kill.

Soon the womenfolk took over on the kills, and they told the men to go and have a cup of coffee. Louis liked to be around the men of the village, and he even drank coffee with them. Other young boys also stayed with the hunting party.

When the coffee was gone, the men went to work on the longhouse. It needed to be cleaned out with new poles put in. Wood for the fire pits needed to be gathered and placed outside of the lodge. Louis said that he would gather the wood. He told everyone about the name that someone had given his wood-cutting crew. "They called us the Wood Ticks."

"The Wood Ticks, what a name," said Day-ga.

"Only Ho-Chunks would think up a name like that, but it's a good name," said William.

By the next day, the feast was ready. The food was cooked, the soups came off the fire, and the fry bread was fresh and ready to be served. An elder gave the blessing, and the feast began.

After the meal, different members of the clan stood up and told stories. Some told of their families. Others told of how the young ones had gone off to the mission school to learn the white man's ways, his language, and his way of life, his beliefs, and his manner of worshipping his god.

William stood up. "We are glad to be here," he said, "glad we don't have to move anymore. I and others of the tribe made it so. We fought hard battles with the Sioux. We lost many men, and now we send our children off to the white man's mission school to learn how to live like him. Now I hear that they call my son's work crew the Wood Ticks, but unlike the wood tick that gets full and falls off, our young children will get full of the white man's knowledge. They will not fall off; they will go on forever."

Day-ga stood up next. "I don't like to send our children off to the white man's mission school," he told the gathering. "But if this is what it takes to live a better life, then yes, it is so. We no longer have the right to hunt the buffalo or to even leave this reservation. I don't believe in the white man's drink. The whiskey is a bad thing. It has made many fools out of our young warriors. They no longer walk with pride. They no longer hold their heads up and take their place as young men in the warrior society, men that would put death before dishonor. I know that it is a change for our people, and we will never live the old ways. We are here, and we must make the best of it for now and forevermore."

It was late in the afternoon when the Hatchett family headed for their lodge.

"It was a good feast, and I had a lot of laughs and heard some good stories. I just hope that this will continue in our clan," said William.

"Was the story about the buck true?" Louis asked.

"That's one story that you will have to ask your Day-ga about someday."

William saw the need to teach the young people more about the various healing plants before they were brainwashed by the Y-Sapes at the mission school. He wanted to hold a meeting before Louis returns to school. He wanted to make sure that Louis had good medicine around him and with his spirit so that the Y-Sapes could not break him of his beliefs. He called a meeting in the longhouse located by his river lodge. William's old friends and veteran scouts came for this meeting, and William was very happy to see so many: John Rise Up, Walking Over Earth, Young Prophet, Walking Soldier were just a few of the old Company A Omaha Scouts to arrive. No longer did Louis lie on the outside of the lodge and listen. This time, he was inside with the rest of them. He knew how the meetings went, and he knew the songs because he was now a member of the medicine lodge, the longhouse.

Louis asked for protection from the Y-Sapes at the mission school. All agreed that young Hatchett would need help and protection. The meeting took several days, but when it was over, Louis felt strong and was ready for the Y-Sapes, but he was warned not to overdo it.

The Hatchett men went fishing late in July. They needed to have some dried fish on hand and some fresh fish for trading. Grain for the team was getting low; they would need to take a trip to the west end of the reservation, where they grew corn and other grains. The farmers were too busy to come down to the Missouri River and fish, but they did like to eat fish. By midday, the men had enough fish to do a lot of trading, so they loaded up and headed west. It would be late by the time they got home. It was a long day of fishing and trading and picking up on the latest news.

By midsummer, Louis was thinking about the mission school and that he only had a few more weeks until he would have to go back to it. He didn't like the thought. He didn't like the way the Y-Sapes talked about the Ho-Chunks' way of religion. He didn't like all the rules, and most of all, he didn't want to be there. But this year, he had protection; he would use it with common sense.

The first week of August, the Hatchett family moved back to the hairpin turn lodge to prepare for that year's powwow. One day a man from the agency came out to talk with William, and they went in the backyard and remained there a long time. Then they went out into the meadow and walked around; finally, the agency man left.

William told his family that the agency man wanted William to farm the land and that if he did, the government would build them a new house. He told the agency man that farming was women's work and that he didn't like it. The agency man said that this was a good way to make money, by planting corn and selling it in the fall. William told him that he would have to think about it.

Soon the early campers came to the Hatchett allotment for the annual powwow. Within a few days, there were many teepees, and at night you could hear the drumming and singing. The next day, Day-ga set the Hatchett drum out in the sun to stretch the head of the drum. "This is what gives it the best sound when the drum is very tight," he told Louis.

"Will we sing tonight, Day-ga?"

"You just come around about sunset."

The sun worked wonders on the Hatchett drum. From the first hit, it came to life, and everyone could feel its vibrations. It was the host drum of the annual powwow. Many drummers would sit around the drum; women dancers would stand behind the men and sing. The Hatchett drum could be heard many miles away. The old flagpole sat on a higher elevation than Big Bear Hollow, and the rolling hills were treeless. This helped carry the sound throughout Thurston County.

And then, again, in a few days, it was all over. Everyone went home, and Louis had to return to the mission school. They asked him if he would like to be on the wood crew again, and he said he would. The white man's language came back to him. He knew that he would have to work hard at everything in school and stay out of trouble. It was a new teacher, but it was the same boring old stuff. Louis tried his hardest to learn the white man's language, but when he went home, he forgot all about it. His second year at the day school was no different from his first year. He didn't go on cold and snowy days and missed a lot of school when the weather turned nice in the spring.

"This summer will be different," William warned him. "We will be staying at the winter lodge this year. We'll make a few trips down to the summer lodge, but we won't be staying there."

"How come?" asked Louis.

"We will be farming the land around the house this year, and I will need you to help me. The government has bought us horses, a plow, and equipment; and they want us to farm the land, and I said we would."

That summer was very hard on both Louis and his father. They cleared the land and learned how to plow and plant. It was a full-time job from dawn until dark. There were no more lazy days on the Missouri River checking the fish traps. This was work. Louis began to think that even the mission school wasn't as bad as this. Farming was hard work, and now the government wanted his father to have cattle and livestock.

There were more changes in store for the Hatchett family. They made fewer and fewer trips to the summer lodge, spending much more time working on the farm, and the government came and built them a new house. It had two levels or was, as they called it, "a two-story house." They showed them how to dig a cellar and an outhouse. The agency man came by that fall and promised that the government would build them a barn next year for their livestock. He was very pleased with the progress made on the farm.

Louis returned to the mission school that fall and kept going to school until he was thirteen years old. By then the farm was a growing concern, and his father needed him at home. The Y-Sapes never said anything about Louis leaving school. Louis did not convert to the Y-Sapes religion. He stayed loyal to the medicine lodge.

Many changes were taking place on the reservation in 1876. Over half of the Ho-Chunk tribe had moved out of the river bottoms. A new trading post was built close to the wooden blockhouse that was erected in 1866, along with several other buildings. This would be the new town of Winnebago. That same year, the secretary of the interior brought up the idea of moving all of the Indians in the five states to western Oklahoma. The talk of moving again was on everyone's lips. Many wondered how they could do this. After all, Winnebagos helped the army against the Sioux and other tribes of the Great Plains. In 1878, the bill was modified to include Indians from ten states to be sent to western Oklahoma. The bill failed in 1879.

Chapter 8

Louis and Olive

The English language Louis had learned at the mission school was enough to help him and his family, and the arithmetic and spelling helped too. He had learned how to buy seed and supplies from the white man's trading post, and he could count the change that he would receive back. He knew when they shortchanged him. Louis was thinking about how he used arithmetic every time that he bought something from the trading post. Maybe the Indian people should know the white man's way of life. It was so easy to rip off the Indians who knew nothing.

Louis was a young adult, and he liked to go to the new town of Winnebago and to different feasts to meet young girls. He hadn't talked to many girls before, so he was kind of awkward. Some of his buddies told him that maybe he needed some firewater to help him get over his shyness. This didn't sound like a good thing. His friends assured him that it would give him power and strength to talk to any women.

Bootlegging whiskey from other counties was a good business for some of the low-life white men who came onto the reservation, and there was no limit on payment to these people. Money was the most popular way to get a bottle, although different kinds of payments were accepted, furs, hand made jewelry and trapping equipment, could also get you a bottle. Everything had a value with these men. The top prize was the title to an allotment. The Indian agent had sent word to the Indian landowners about such men, but some Indians would still get screwed out of their allotment. This was a very sad way to lose your land, and once the title was signed, it was too late. Nothing could be done about it!

When Louis met up with his friends, they sat and talked until John Bird said, "Hey, let's get some whiskey from the bootlegger."

A few of the boys had never had a drink of whiskey before. They had heard of the stories about Indians who drank too much and made fools of themselves, and they didn't want to get that way. "Ah, come on," they said. "We don't have enough money to get drunk on anyway. We have enough to get just one bottle for all of us." Some of the boys were scared, but they didn't want to show it, so they said they were willing to do it.

"Hey, Louis, are you scared to drink whiskey?"

"I am a man. I am not afraid of anything," Louis said.

"Good," John Bird said, "then I'll go and get us a bottle, and we can all have a drink." Before they knew it, John Bird was back with the bottle of whiskey. "I will have the first drink because I went and got it," he said. He took a big slug of it and pulled the ugliest face that anyone had ever seen. Then he let out a loud war whoop. "Damn, that's good stuff!"

"By the look on your face, you couldn't tell it," said Little Bird.

They passed the bottle around, and soon it was Louis's turn to have a pull. He put the bottle up to his lips, and immediately, he could smell the poison; but he wanted to try the whiskey to see what it tasted like. He drank from the bottle, and it burned all the way down. He could see why John Bird made such an ugly face; this was bad-tasting stuff. The bottle made it around one more time, and it was empty.

"We should try to buy another bottle," said John Bird.

There wasn't any money, so they just sat and talked about how good it was. Some of the guys were acting like fools talking loudly and saying nothing, just a lot of words.

"The air looks like a ghost," said Little Bird.

"You smell like an old ghost," said Louis.

They both laughed as they walked over to a feast that was going on. They knew they could not go in, but they could hang around the outside of the lodge. While Louis and Little Bird were standing outside, three young Indian girls walked by. They all nodded and said nothing. They just kept walking. Louis noticed the one on the right. He thought that she looked his way when they passed.

"Who are those girls?" Louis asked.

"Well, the one on the right is Olive Grant, and she lives west of the Omaha Creek," Little Bird said. "The one in the middle is Laura Brothers of All, and the last one is Mary Armell."

"Do you know these girls well?" asked Louis.

"Yeah, we were in the mission school together at one time."

"I would like to know Olive. She looks nice."

"Well, if that's all you need to know, then let's go and catch up with them and talk to them," said Little Bird.

"Hey, Olive Grant, Louis Hatchett wants to talk to you," said Little Bird when they caught up to the girls.

Louis was very embarrassed by this.

"Well, what do you want to talk about, Louis Hatchett?"

Louis was shy when it came to talking to a girl, and he didn't know what to say. "Are you a farmer?" Louis stammered.

The three girls giggled. "No," Olive finally replied, "but my father farms a little."

"Well, that's not what I meant to say. What I meant was do you live on a farm?"

"Yes, I do, and what about yourself?"

"I help my father. We farm over by the hairpin turn, and we have the powwow every year."

"I know where you live, and I know your family," was her reply.

This made it easier. At least she knew of him ... maybe. "I would just like to get to know you better," said Louis.

"Well, maybe you should come over to my father's place, and we could talk."

This really made Louis nervous, but he was determined to act as if it was all right. "Yes, I can do that!"

"Okay then, how about Sunday afternoon, about two?"

"I will see you Sunday at two PM." Louis didn't know if it was the whiskey or the fact that he had talked to a girl and was going to meet her father the next day, but he told Little Bird he was tired and was going home.

The next morning, Louis was up early and did his chores. Then he went and cleaned up. His father thought that this was something different, his son cleaning up twice in one week. "Louis, are you going someplace?"

"Yes, I am. I am going over to the Grant house to meet the father."

"He is a good man. I have known him for a long time," said William. "Why are you going to meet with him?"

"I was invited over to their house by his daughter last night, and I said I would be there at two PM."

"Well, tell him I send my regards."

The work colt couldn't go fast enough for Louis. On his way, he was thinking of what to say to her father. It wasn't like the old days when you could buy yourself a wife. The Y-Sapes said, "You shouldn't do that anymore. That's not the way of church."

Standing in front of their house, Louis could feel the sweat running down his back, and his palms were sweaty too. Olive went outside to meet him. "I am glad you could make it today."

"Well, I said I would be here at two."

As they walked to the house, Louis looked over at Olive. He could see that she was an attractive woman. They both walked into the house and went over to where her father, U. S. Grant, was sitting. "Well, good day, Mr. Hatchett, and how you are today?"

"I am fine, Mr. Grant. My father sends his regards."

"Yes, your father is a great warrior. I know him quite well. And what brings you over to my house?"

"I want to marry your daughter."

"Louis!" Olive gasped. "I only met you last night, and now you want me for your wife?"

Those words shook her badly.

"I know we only met last night, but I saw the way that you looked at me, and I know."

"What do you know? Just because someone looks at you, you think that she belongs to you? You have been on the farm too long! You have been watching the cattle too much. Do you think that you can smell me and then you own me? I am not a cow!"

This was not going well for Louis. He didn't think it would be this hard to get a wife. Mr. Grant had to turn away from the young couple; he couldn't keep a straight face. Finally, he said, "I will leave and let you talk for a while; you have much to talk about."

"See what you have done, Louis Hatchett? You have made my father mad at me and you!"

"Well, I was just telling the truth—I want to marry you."

Still reeling from the ambush that she had just gone through, she looked at Louis and asked, "Where would we live if I married you?"

"At my house."

"And that's all right with your family, having another mouth to feed?"

"I don't look at it as another mouth to feed, but another person to work the farm."

"You would marry me so you can put me to work on your farm? I can stay at home and get that!"

Louis had painted himself into another corner; nothing was going right in this conversation. "Maybe I should just leave."

"You would give up that easily?"

There seemed to be no way to get out of this mess. "Maybe I should talk with your father alone," Louis said.

"I will tell him that you want to talk with him."

As Olive left him, Louis knew that he wanted this woman as his wife. He had always worked hard and did everything that was asked of him. He hadn't caused any trouble at the mission school, and he had learned how to speak English. True, he didn't know how to talk to a woman or even know how to be with a woman alone, but he would learn.

"You can go in and talk to my father now," Olive said.

"Mr. Hatchett, what can I do for you?" asked Mr. Grant.

"Well, sir, nothing has changed. I still want to marry your daughter."

"And what does she say about this matter?"

"Oh, I think she will say its okay. I think she likes me."

"Well, Olive is of marrying age, and she did tell her mother about you today. Do you drink?"

"I have tasted it before, and I didn't like it. I can speak the English language. I can write a little and do some arithmetic."

"And where will you two live?"

"At my father's house."

"You have talked it over with your father, about your bringing home a wife?"

"No, I haven't, but I think it will be all right."

"You go home and talk to your father about this matter and come back next week and tell me what he has said."

Olive could hear all that was said, but she quickly walked away from the door opening.

Then Louis went outside to talk with Olive.

"What did my father say?"

"He said to go home and talk to my father about this matter."

"And will you do this?"

"Of course I will. I still want you for my wife."

Louis could see the little smile on Olive's lips. He knew that she wanted him. Louis returned home and told his father that he found a woman that he wanted to marry and bring home.

"Just like that, you would bring a woman home, and who is this woman?"

"Her father is U. S. Grant from the west side of the Omaha Creek."

"I know who they are. They are a proud family, and I guess she will be all right to marry. Does she want to marry you? How come we never heard of her before?"

"Because I just met her last night."

"You don't want to look around some more for another woman? This seems mighty fast."

Louis shook his head. "She is the one."

William knew that it would do no good to interfere with this young couple. Sometimes these hurried marriages didn't always work out, but Louis would have to find that out himself.

Two months later, they were married at the agency and moved in with Louis's family. Olive was a good cook and helped out a lot around the house. At first it was awkward in the house with another woman around, but Olive was a great help. She carried her load of work. Living on a bigger farm meant more work for Olive. First she didn't see her family much. She worked long hours because she wanted to be a good wife.

Three years later, Olive gave birth to Edward. His Indian name would be Wa-can-jaw-goo-ga (Coming Thunder), and Edward's birth took place upstairs in their bedroom on April 12, 1885. Three years after that, Ollie was born in June of 1888; her Indian name was Ma-sch-he-gon-we-ga (Great Movement).

Not long after Ollie was born, Louis divorced his wife or moved out and took up with John Rave's wife. They moved to Wisconsin, but when Olive died in 1889 at her parents' home, Louis moved back to Winnebago to raise his two children. Louis died on May 24, 1896. He was thirty-eight years old when he died. After the death of Louis, U. S. Grant and his wife took the two Hatchett orphans into their home.

Chapter 9

Tools of Forced Assimilation

In 1889, the U.S. commissioner of Indian Affairs declared, "We must fight Indians, feed them, or educate them. To fight them is cruel; to feed them is wasteful, while to educate them is humane, economic, and Christian." He suggested using boarding schools to prepare Indian children to live in American society. At boarding schools, Indian children would be introduced to English, vocational skills, and Christianity.

Author's note: My grandfather Edward L. Hatchett was part of the government project to assimilate the Indians into the white man's society. They concluded the only way to save the Indians was to destroy them and that the last great Indian war should be waged against children. They were coming for the children. Indian agents would do anything to fill their "quota," even if it meant kidnapping them off the reservation.

Edward Hatchett was four years old when his mother died and eleven when his father passed away in May of 1896. Little did he realize when he heard the knock on his grandparents' front door in August of 1896 that he was about to undergo another dramatic change, one that would alter him and the Hatchett family for generations to come.

Standing before him when he opened the door were two white men. Behind them was a large hay wagon. "We are here to pick up Edward Hatchett," one said through an interpreter. "He has to go to the boarding school."

This came as a shock to Edward's grandparents. "You can't just take our grandson away!" Mrs. Grant gasped.

"We were told that he is an orphan and that you and your husband can't take care of him anymore."

"But that's not true!" she protested.

"We have orders to take him; he will be taken care of and given a good education. He will grow up to be a Christian man."

"We are members of the medicine lodge, and so is he," Mr. Grant protested.

"You have nothing to say about this matter. It is done."

The white men grabbed Edward and took him out the door, but Edward broke loose and ran to his grandmother. She grabbed her grandson and held on to him. Edward had a strong grip on his grandmother, but the white man tore him away from her. All his grandparents could do was just stand and watch them take Edward away.

Edward was crying and trying to get loose, but the agent had such a tight grip on him that he finally gave in. Looking back, with tears in his eyes, he gave a small wave with two of his fingers to his grandparents.

It would be many, many years before he saw his grandparents again.

This was not an isolated incident. The reservation boarding school system was a war in disguise, one of the most blatant expressions of racism in the history of North America. The war was between the U.S. government and the children of the First People of North America. The war was invented by the descendants of Manifest Destiny. Educating the Indian children was the refinement of the times. The theory was to turn the native children against their parents through education and Christianity. The boarding school era consisted of virtually kidnapping native children wholesale, and if the family protested, their ration would be cut or stopped altogether. It was all part of the cultural genocide, and this could be done by moving the children off the reservation and away from the extended families.

Once the agency heard that Edward and his sister, Ollie, were being raised by their grandparents, they took the two children and put them in different schools but not at the same time. Edward was sent by horse and wagon to the Genoa Indian School in Genoa, Nebraska, 120 miles southwest of Winnebago. The Genoa Indian School was built to educate the Pawnee Indians in 1859.

The Indian agency at the Winnebago reservation had hired the two white men to go and pick up Indian children. They provided them with a list of children and told the men, "If you have room for more, just go ahead and take one wherever you can find one!"

By the end of the day, they had a wagon full of young kids. Some of the older ones they had to tie down. The wagon left the reservation late in the evening. This was to confuse the children and make sure none of the older ones could figure out how to find their way home. By getting on the road and getting far enough away from the reservation at night, the kids were less capable of running back home. There was much crying and sobbing all night long and many attempts at escape, forcing the wagon to stop so the drivers could chase down a child or two who jumped off the wagon, give them a whipping, and then toss them back into the wagon.

It took four days to reach the Genoa Indian School in Genoa, Nebraska. The wagon pulled up in front of the administration building and told the kids to get down. Some of the younger ones started to cry because they were scared. Within minutes, a white woman, pinched face and mean looking, came out dressed in a long black dress and carrying a stick. She hit the crying youths on the head and ordered them to stop, which, of course, only made them cry harder; and she hit them harder.

Finally, an older Ho-Chunk came over and whispered in their native tongue, "Stop crying or she'll just keep hitting you!"

Edward was too scared to cry.

The first thing they did was divide them by sex. "This is how it will be for now and for your entire stay at the school," the white lady told them. "Boys on one side and girls on the other side of the line. No one will ever cross that line."

They rushed the boys off into a big brick building. Inside the building were several men with hair clippers, standing behind a chair. The interpreter told the Winnebago boys to sit down in the chairs; within minutes, their long hair was lying on the barber's floor. After all of them had haircuts, they were pushed into another large room. Inside were large tanks of water. They were told to strip down. The mean woman jumped on those who didn't take off their clothes quickly, tugging and tearing off their clothes and ordering them to stand in a line. This was really scary for Edward who had never taken off his clothes in front of strange white women before. Now all of the kids were afraid.

Next was a man dressed in a white robe. He started to look over the first child, looking into his eyes, nose, into his mouth, looking under his arms and between his legs. He examined everyone.

Next they were told to get into the tubs, where women washed and scrubbed them and then pushed them on. They kept saying, "Next, next," and soon the children were all done with the baths and left shivering and naked in the big building.

"Come this way." Walking in the direction of the voice, the children entered another room where they were given underwear and were shown how to dress themselves properly. Next came the uniforms, shoes, socks, and hats.

"You will wear this uniform every day unless told to dress in something else. Now follow me to the dining hall." Edward didn't know what a dining hall was, but he felt better with clothes on. Inside the large hall were tables set with dishes and utensils. "You will sit, and before every meal, we say grace. After grace, you will wait for the food to be passed to you. You will take a little of everything passed to you, and you will eat everything on your plate," said the mean woman in black.

The dining hall was filled with other Indian kids of all ages. There was one empty table set for the newcomers, so this is where Edward and the rest of them were told to sit. The mean woman said, "Everyone, bow your heads, and I will say a word of prayer at this table."

Not everyone knew what "bow your head" was. Most just looked and did what the next guy did. Soon the food was passed in front of Edward. He didn't know what to do about it. The older student told him to take a little and to pass it on. He actually took very little of everything because he wasn't hungry. He tried to eat the goo, and it tasted bad, but he did his best to eat it all, and it was all he could do to keep it down. Those who couldn't eat all of their food couldn't leave the table until they finished the meal.

The group was led over to a dormitory. "This is where you will sleep and clean yourselves up every morning before you do your morning chores or work details," an older student told them.

The new students were shown how to make a bed, how to wash up in the morning, and how to get ready for breakfast. Edward was put with students close to his age, but he was still the youngest of all of them. That evening before the lamps went out, he asked one of the Ho-Chunk boys what his name was and where he lived. "My name is Alex Horn, and my family lives over by the Hensley Spring."

"My name is Edward Hatchett," Edward told him. "I live on the west bank of Omaha Creek."

"I know where the Omaha Creek is. We have fished in it before. Sometimes we swam in it too."

"Are you scared?" Edward whispered.

"Yeah, I am very scared of that mean white woman. She hit me pretty hard on the head this morning, and I have a bump on it now." He showed Edward the bump.

"I hope we don't have to stay here long," Edward told him. "All I want to do is to go home and see my grandparents."

"I don't like it here either. I didn't like the food, and the clothes make me itch all over." Just like a predator, the mean white woman came into the room with the older student following her. "I want to tell you students that some of you will be here for a long time, and some of you will go home in a few years."

The older student repeated everything in Ho-Chunk so everyone could understand.

"We have many rules here at Genoa, and you will be expected to obey all of them. If you don't, you will be punished and punished hard by me or my staff. You are here to learn and to become Christian citizens," she said. "One more thing: the lamps go out at eight o'clock every night, and there will be no talking after that."

The young Indian boys just sat on their beds, and no one said anything for a long time. It was all Edward could do to keep from crying. He thought about his grandparents and missed his home more than ever. At 8 PM when the lamps went out, Edward closed his eyes and wished with all his might that he could be home in his own bed. He could hear sobbing and crying from different parts of the room. He rolled over and buried his face into the pillow so no one could hear his soft cries.

At 6 AM the bugle sounded, and the lamps went on. The mean woman was barking and telling everyone to get out of their beds and to make them. "By the time I get to the other end of this room, if you're not out of your bed, you will be thrown out of it," said the mean-mouthed white woman.

Edward just watched the others who had been there longer than he, and he did everything that they did. He got dressed, made the bed, washed up, and got ready for breakfast. Some of them had to sweep the floor, and others had to pick up litter outside of the dorm. Edward went outside to help the other students; he felt safer outside. They marched the young recruits over to the dining hall to stand in line. The older students ate first, because they had work details to do. Edward remembered what the older student had told him—"Just take a little." And he did. Again, it tasted like the same goo that they had the night before, but he forced it down and was able to leave the dining hall.

Edward had no idea where to go, so he just followed the rest of the boys as they headed to the workshops. They divided the newcomers up, and some went to the kitchen, others went to work outside, and others stayed in the workshop. Edward stayed in the wood shop. One of his first jobs was to sweep and pick up all of the sawdust and wood chips that were on the floor. He didn't know at the time, but this would be his job for a long time. This was the carpenter shop; they made and repaired desks, chairs, and all the furnishings for the school. The outside workers worked in the garden and with the livestock. Others worked in the henhouse. Still others mended the fences and worked in the barns. All this was necessary to keep the school more self-sufficient, and work was part of the training. After cleanup, the rest of the morning was spent in the classrooms learning the white man's language.

Everything was controlled by a bugle or a bell. As soon as it sounded, you went to your next work assignment or lunch or drill or class or church or to bed.

At lunchtime, the bugle sounded, and the students in the workshop went to clean up for lunch. A new student asked one of the older students in Ho-Chunk where they were to go next and was whipped in front of the rest of them. "We have told you not to speak Indian here, and we mean it," said the shop teacher.

After lunch Edward and the new students were taken into a room with the other boys and told to sit down at a desk. He didn't know what a desk was, so he just did as the other students did and sat down in one of those funny-looking chairs. Soon a white man came into the room and wrote something on the blackboard. It was his name, but Edward didn't know that. The older Indian student translated: "My name is Mr. Willard. You will always call me Mr. Willard. You will raise your hand if you need anything. You will raise your hand if you have to go and use the outhouse. You will raise your hand if you are sick and need to leave the classroom. You will raise your hand if you need help with your schoolwork; again, you will raise your hand if you need anything. Do I make myself clear?"

The older student continued translating in Ho-Chunk. "You will always say, 'Yes, Mr. Willard,' or 'No, Mr. Willard.' You will not shake or nod your head. That is not an answer. Do I make myself clear? You will come into my classroom and be quiet. You will always sit up straight. There will be no sleeping in my classroom. No horseplay of any kind will be tolerated in my class at any time. When you are called upon to speak, you will stand and face me and speak in a voice loud enough so everyone can hear you. Do I make myself clear?"

The older student paused, and then the translation continued. "Today we will learn the alphabet. We will start with the letter *A*."

The teacher sounded it out and wrote it on the blackboard.

So began Edward's first day in school. By the end of the second week, Edward could go up to the letter *E* in the alphabet. During those two weeks, two students fell asleep. One was sick, and one didn't know what to do when he was called on. All were punished for their mistakes. Because Edward had not been assigned a job or any real chores to do, he would just help pick up litter outside of the dorm and sweep up in the workshop in the morning. That was all right with the mean white woman, who was their matron and would be with them every day. Her name was Ms. Conley.

On Sunday morning, everyone had to go to church, and everyone had to pray and sing the songs. It was tough to sit on the benches for such a long time, and if you nodded off, you would get pushed or hit on the head by one of the good white men who worked for the church.

There was no translator for the church services. It was expected that all of the students would know English sooner or later. The preacher kept repeating to the Indian parishioners, "What your parents, the medicine men, and the peyote church told you are wrong; and you need to change your ways, or you will go to hell. You poor lost children of God, you need us, and we will show you the way. You need to change before it's too late. You heathens need to be saved and shown the way of God. I will help you get this done. That's why I am here for you."

The preacher would yell and talk in a loud voice, hit the pulpit with his fist, shout at the congregation, and, at times, seem visibly shaken. Then he would say, "Let's celebrate the Lord in song!" And he would lead the congregation in song while he would wipe the sweat off his face. To the young ones, this was scary, to watch this white man carry on like that in front of everyone.

Sundays were different from the weekdays. You couldn't do any kind of work, and all you were permitted to do was read the Bible or sing in the choir. Some Sundays Edward would sit outside under a shade tree with other Ho-Chunk students and talk in the native tongue about home, but it always had to be in a low voice because they would be punished if they were caught talking Indian.

By October, the days were getting shorter, and there was a nip in the air. Edward was making his way to the dorm when he looked at the trees on the far hillside, all aglow in their fall colors. He thought about the log cabin on the Omaha Creek, and a sad feeling came over him. He wanted to go home. He thought that time had come to a complete stop for him and that no one cared or that no one knew where he was. He could feel the emotion building up inside of him, but he didn't want to cry because the other students would make fun of him, so he just choked it down and felt lonesome.

When you are only eleven years old and in a strange world—a white man's world—where everyone tells you what to do and you have no one to hold you and tell you that everything will be all right, it is a lonely world. Other students had brothers and sisters at Genoa, but Edward had no one. He knew a few of the students who came from Winnebago, but he was not related to any of them. By now Edward and the rest of the Winnebago students understood the routine of the school. They knew what the bugle meant and the different bells that went off during the day. One or two of them would talk about running away, but for the most part, they didn't even know which way home was. Runaways were treated very badly. Their punishment was a severe beating, sometimes in front of everyone. When anyone started to talk about going home, all the others would try to talk him out of it for his own good!

Thanksgiving Day at Genoa was a holiday for the students. In the dining room, the superintendent stood up before all of them. "You should all gives thanks to our government for getting you here to a clean, safe place with plenty of food and shelter," he told them, "a place where you will learn the English language and learn a skill that you can use for the rest of your life. Here at Genoa, we want all of you to excel and learn so you can go home and teach others what you have learned here and make a good living."

One good thing about Thanksgiving Day was that there was a lot of food; everyone got full that day, instead of just getting something to eat.

Practice began for the Christmas program. Everyone had a part to play in it or in the choir. Edward's class sang Christmas songs. They had no parts to read, but the older students had a lot to read and learn, and the instructor made sure that they learned their parts. Whippings by the teachers can make a difference in how fast you can learn something, even when it's about the Christmas story.

"Who is Jesus?" a young girl asked the teacher during one of the rehearsals.

She was knocked to the floor and kicked while she lay there.

"How can you ask me who Jesus is?" the teacher shouted. "You don't know? He is your savior! That's who he is!"

The girl just lay there in pain. He told her to get on her feet, but finally, they had to carry her off to the infirmary. When the teacher kicked her in the stomach, he had ruptured her spleen. There was little they could do at the infirmary. She died four days later, and nothing was said about the matter. Word spread among the students, however, this only reinforced the power the authorities held over the Indian students. For a long time, there were no runaways from the school.

By February of 1897, Edward had learned most of the alphabet and could read easy words. There was a lot of talk about going home in three months. Edward hoped he was going home. March brought the first taste of spring in the air. The days were getting longer and warmer, and by the end of the month, the older students were put to work in the school gardens. They had to clear the old plants out and get the soil ready for this year's crop. Spring also brought a rash of runaways. Every time one of the students tried escaping from the school, the school would notify the local police, and the police always seemed to catch the runaways in very short time. It was pretty hard not to spot an Indian in a community where everyone else was white. The police got paid ten dollars for every runaway, so it was good business for them. The runaways always got a beating, sometimes in front of the other students. The bigger boys could handle a few whips, but soon they would cry out in agony, as the leather strap razed their backsides.

It looked like the white superintendent enjoyed whipping the Indian boys. When he was done, he would always make the same announcement. "This will happen to all of those who run away, so be warned."

Finally, the month of May arrived, and some of the students were going home. Sometimes a few would leave; at other times, it would be just one or two. The ones who left had been there for a while; their parents would have to come and get them or have someone pick them up from school. By the end of May, all of the students who could go home were gone.

Edward was still there. He would wait around in the dorm, hoping that someone would come and get him, but no one came. They moved all of the boys into one dorm during the summer months. It was easier to watch them. The nights were the worst for Edward. He would lie in his bed and think of home. He wondered why no one came for him. Sometimes he would softly cry himself to sleep. Every morning, it was the same—the bugle sounded, make the bed, get ready, the drill, the march to breakfast, and the work details. He did most of his work in gardens because of his size. Edward thought about becoming a farmer when he got older. This wasn't so hard of a job, and you got to see the plants grow and make food.

During the summer, the working days got longer. Every hour was accounted for; they wanted the students to be busy to keep their minds off home and the family. Even on rainy days, they had work for them to do—scrubbing down the dormitory with soap and water, cleaning everything inside and washing the windows inside and out. Work, work, work. On the day of rest, you had to listen to the preacher shout and pound on the pulpit with his fist. But in the afternoons, they had some free time. Edward and the rest of the Ho-Chunk boys would sit under a large tree and talk about how things would be if they were home. Sometimes it would be funny, but most of the time, it was hard to talk about home. "When I get home, I am talking Winnebago," one of the boys would say and the rest would join in and say the same thing.

In 1897, a government report on Winnebago literacy found that 420 Ho-Chunks could read and that six hundred of them could speak the English language. Who knows if these numbers were accurate, most likely, they were inflated. The government liked to deal in numbers, and the higher they were, the better.

At the end of August, when Edward had been at Genoa for a year, some of his old classmates who had gone back to Winnebago for the summer returned. He was glad to see them, but they were not glad to see him or be back at the school. "How are things back home?" Edward asked Alex Horn.

"Everyone is fine."

"Did you see my family?"

"Yes, I did see them. I told my father that you were doing fine, and he went and told your grandfather about you. Your grandfather said maybe next year, they will come and get you for the summer."

With this hope at the end of the tunnel, Edward thought he could now make it for another year at Genoa. "What else did my grandfather say?"

"That was all that they told to me. He looked well."

"I don't want to be here. This will be my second year here, and I am tired of listening to the white man. I am tired of going to his church; I am tired of his uniforms and his food."

"You are right. This is my second year here too, you know."

Soon the rest of the dormitories filled up, and it was back to school for all of them. This year there were more students from Winnebago, and now Edward wasn't the youngest anymore. Edward had moved back into his old dormitory, and so did the matron, Ms. Conley—mean and ugly as ever. Nothing had changed with her, except maybe a few more wrinkles and a few more pounds. One night after the lamps went out; Edward could hear the old familiar sound of crying into the night. He knew the feeling well, and he knew what was coming. Now that school was back in session, all of the rules were in force. Soon the runaways would be punished. First they would shave their heads and then beat them with a razor strap.

This year after the regular church services, they had the younger ones stay for Sunday school, and Edward was told to stay. The Sunday school teacher was a young-looking woman. She was nice and listened to the students. This approach to teaching the word of God seemed to work better than the hollering and fist pounding of the preacher. For the first time, someone made sense of the book they called the Bible. The stories she told them made the Bible interesting. The young students learned to trust this young white woman, some of them would say that they "liked her."

The enrollment at Genoa Indian School had increased by several hundred that fall. Sioux and Cheyenne Indians made up most of the new students. They looked scared and very homesick. They didn't like it when they cut off their hair. All they could do was to sit and look at it on the barber's floor. After the first few days of school, four Sioux boys ran away. They were caught in two days, brought in front of the school formation, and stripped down to their waists.

Then the superintendent began with the strap, grinning as he whipped them. That was the first part of the punishment. They would work extra hours and do extra details for weeks. Even the girls who ran away from school got a strap whipping. The only difference was theirs was done by the matrons. The punishment was laid down every day for different infractions of the rules. Edward couldn't help but think that the new students were Sioux and Cheyenne Indians—the ones who had defeated Custer. They knew how to fight, and they didn't like white people. It would take many whippings and disgrace and shame to bring these students into line. These students would have an especially hard life at Genoa.

With more students being sent to Genoa from the Dakotas and Wyoming territories, more beds were placed in the dormitories. This made it easier to talk at night without getting caught.

However, when the dormitory windows were closed and the heat was on, with so many students sleeping in one room, by morning, the room was full of stale human breath. This is how the spread of tuberculosis, influenza, smallpox, and mumps got started. This atmosphere was perfect breeding grounds for an epidemic. Along with a bad heating and ventilation system, badly laid-out building plans, poor building material, and very little sanitation, in some of the Indian boarding schools, more than half of the students who entered the system died of diseases. These conditions would continue until the early 1920s.

The medical care was inadequate, and so was the staff. As a result, all they could do was to make the child as comfortable as possible and wait for death.

As late as 1928, the Meriam Report stated that as little as nine cents per day was being spent on food for the native children in the government boarding school system. It is unknown how many American Indian children died from starvation. Foraging or stealing from the institutional larders helped stave off chronic malnutrition, and this was a way of life in the boarding schools. The Meriam Report also stated that in many schools, poor quality of diet presented a genuine threat to the children's health, denying students the necessary amounts of fruits, vegetables, and milk. The lack of nutrition, combined with the overcrowded dormitories and unsanitary living conditions, was positively health threatening.

There were so many deaths at Edward's school that the problem of overcrowding cured itself. Edward was one of the lucky ones. He didn't get sick, not even the sniffles. But his friend Alex Horn was very ill. When he contracted tuberculosis, they moved him to another dorm for sick students.

Another problem that plagued the boarding schools was sexual predators. The schools' remote locations, and low wages, made them a welcome mat for misfits, incompetents, and sociopaths. From day one, the native children would face this nightmare every night. There was greater safety in numbers. Some of the girls shared beds after the lights went out for protection so that if one of the predators tried to wake one of them, he would end up waking all of them. It was better to be punished for wetting the bed than to walk the dark halls at night alone to use the facilities.

Those in charge denied that it ever happened, and those who were implicated were just transferred to another school. When young girls got pregnant, it would be hushed up. But the children were mercilessly flogged for the slightest deviation from the supposed virtues of "strict chastity." This sexual terrorism continued well into the 1950s, but the charges were always aggressively denied.

By the spring of 1898, Edward's dormitory had fewer occupants, but the cemetery had more headstones in it. Edward's friend, Alex Horn, had pulled through his ordeal with tuberculosis. He was still weak and frail, but his spirits were high because soon he would be going home to Winnebago.

In April of 1898, Edward received word that his Cho-ka William Hatchett had passed away. "He was buried the old Indian way," the note said, "the way of a warrior and medicine man who was one of the few that rode with Chief Little Priest, one of the original seventy-five braves who signed up at Fort Thomson, in the Dakota Territory back in 1863." Edward just sat on his bed and reread the letter. At the time, he didn't realize he was the last man with the name of Hatchett in the Winnebago Nation. Edward still remembered the old government house where he was born. That house belonged to his Cho-ka William.

"Edward, are you all right?" asked Alex Horn.

"I was just thinking about my Cho-ka William Hatchett. I got this letter today, and it says that he passed away."

"I heard stories about him," Alex Horn said slowly. "He was a strong medicine man, wasn't he?"

"That's what I have heard too."

"You don't have time to think about your grandfather," the school matron told Edward. "He would be proud of you and all that you have accomplished here at Genoa, but now you have work and studies to attend to." The school didn't like its students to dwell on deaths that occurred on the reservation, especially if was a family member. They felt that this might make the student homesick, and he or she would try to leave.

The school year was coming to an end. Edward wondered if his grandparents Cho-ka and Ka-ka Grant would come and get him or would send money down so he could ride home with someone. Alex Horn knew that he was going back to Winnebago. His family sent money for him to go home, but Edward still kept hoping that somehow he would get to go home too.

When it came time for Alex Horn to go home, however, no one came for Edward. No one sent word for Edward to come home. Again, he would sit and wait, always looking down the road, but always in vain. Edward went to the dorm and sat on his bed and wondered why no one came for him. *Maybe they will be here tomorrow,* he thought. *Or maybe they are sick.* The thoughts were endless. By the end of the second week, Edward knew that no one was coming for him. It was all he could do to keep from crying. He had been here for two years. He had done everything that he was told to do, and he had tried to be a good student. The feeling of complete frustration and helplessness swept over him.

Thinking that no one cared about him, Edward turned to Christianity. He got more involved in Sunday school and tried harder to read the Bible. In the months that followed, he became more active with the church. He didn't know it, but he was becoming institutionalized, a product of the "kill the Indian and save the man" the Bureau of Indian Affairs goal.

In fact, U. S. Grant and family had no way of getting Edward home from Genoa. Their wagon could not make the trip nor could their team, and they had no money to send him. What they didn't know was that the Indian agent had told the school that Edward Hatchett would have no one to take care of him if he went home for the summer.

As the weeks turned into months and months turned into another year, Edward became fluent in the English language. He could solve arithmetic problems and was very good in writing. It was in one of his classes that one of the female teachers asked him what his middle name was.

"I don't have a middle name."

"Everyone has to have three names. My name is Lucy, and I will give you my name so that you can have a middle name. From now on, your middle name will be Lucia; so when you sign important papers when you grow up, you will sign your name this way, Edward Lucia Hatchett."

Edward didn't know if this was such a great gift, having a woman's name. It didn't seem quite right, but he knew that he had to use it.

"Or you can sign your name like this, Edward L. Hatchett."

This sounded better to him than the woman's name.

Edward would continue his studies at Genoa Indian School. As he became more assimilated into the system, he learned how to play a brass instrument; in fact, he learned how to play several different instruments while he was there. Being a member of the band was much easier than marching around the drill field or on a work detail. Band members had to practice with the band and practice on their own for several hours a week. This was no problem for Edward. He enjoyed playing in the band, and he enjoyed music and even marching in the band. Edward became the trumpet player in the first band. A year later, Edward would receive his first trombone. He was very pleased with that.

During this time the Chicago, Burlington and Quincy Railroad were granted permission to cross the Winnebago Indian reservation by the U.S. government. The railroad entered the Omaha Reservation and established a work camp on the west side of the Omaha Creek. Later this site would be called Walthill, Nebraska. Many of the work camps became villages on the line. In 1898, the railroad entered into the Winnebago Indian reservation. The surveyors had laid the road out many months before the track was laid. The village of Winnebago was nothing more than a trading post, a few buildings, some tents, and some lodges. The government ration building was about a mile southeast of the trading post. The best place to set up a work camp was on the east of the Omaha Creek where the land was level and they had easy access to water.

For the most part, the rail line ran parallel with the creek.

The new work camp brought many new people into the reservation. Most were working for the railroad, and others were working on getting the money away from those working for the railroad. Many canvas tents went up, and so did permanent buildings. Many Indian families had left the Big Bear Hollow and moved to town when the Chicago, Burlington and Quincy Railroad entered the Winnebago reservation. It opened up the floodgates to the white people. Some came to the reservation to help the Indians; others came to work and buy land, while others came to rip off the Indians of their land. New businesses sprang up in Winnebago—all owned and operated by white folks. Some extended credit to the Indians, while others wanted money up front.

Ration day was always busy; it was busy for the Indian agent, the Indians, and the white people who bought or traded the rations from the

Indians. It was also a busy day for the bootleggers; this was their busiest day of the month. The bootleggers dealt in alcohol, but they also ran the black market; they would sell back the rations to the Indians when hard times came around, usually just before ration day.

The Dawes Act of 1887 was amended in 1891. This authorized the government to negotiate with the Indians for the sale of all tribal lands remaining after the allotments were made to individual members of the tribe. The government often paid less than one dollar per acre for these so-called surplus lands, which it then sold to non-native homesteaders and corporations. The Winnebago Indian reservation was reduced by three-fourths of its original size. After the Chicago, Burlington and Quincy Railroad crossed the reservation, it opened the reservation to land-hungry Americans. Most wanted only to work the land and have a good life, but others wanted all the land and every bit that they could get their hands on. To them, the red man was just in the way.

With the completion of the railroad, students from Genoa could ride the train all the way to Winnebago. Soon Alex Horn and the rest of them would go home for the summer, while Edward, on the other hand, would go to work in the fields that the school owned.

In the fall of 1898, Alex Horn did not return to Genoa. He stayed on the reservation and went to the local public school in Winnebago for a while, as did some of the Indians. This was a small setback for Edward, he had enjoyed talking to his friend Alex about things that went on in Winnebago.

When Edward turned nineteen years old, he became the student who walked around with the teacher and interpreted for the new students from the Winnebago reservation. He had been at Genoa Indian School for eight years.

At night he was one of the night watchmen who walked the halls of the school, looking for students who should be in bed. One of the dormitories under his watch was haunted. He could always hear footsteps down the hall or upstairs when he was downstairs, or he would see figures or forms that would float along the hallways and then disappear. He always thought this was true because in the morning, a lot of the boys would have wet the bed because they had seen something in the night, and they were afraid to go to the washroom. In his remaining time at Genoa, Edward worked more and attended classes less. In the spring through fall, he would work in the fields. In the winter months, he would work as a watchman, a janitor, a maintenance man, or an interpreter for very little pay or no pay at all.

In 1904, the Genoa Indian School band went to perform at the St. Louis World's Fair. It was there that Edward saw the great warrior Geronimo. They had him in a cage on display. This was only done for publicity and a photo shoot, but it looked very real to the students there from Nebraska. The band placed second in all-around competitions with other bands from across the United States. This made the Bureau of Indian Affairs very happy. It was always a good day when they could show off the talent of the young Indians and explain how this was accomplished. This ranked right up there with the before and after photos of the students arriving at the boarding schools. The official's chest would swell, and he would smile big for the camera and tell the story of how this band was started with just a bunch of wild savages.

Edward was one of the older students at Genoa. He had been there the longest, and he had witnessed many a whipping and heard many a story of young girls and boys being raped by the staff. He had put many hours into the school's farm with very little in return. Even though the students who worked the "outing programs" were supposed to get paid by the employer, the school handled their accounts. Some money was passed on to the student. Edward had worked in the carpenter shop and had helped build many of the new buildings on the campus. Second to the music he loved to play, he liked to make goods out of leather. He liked to use his hands, and he liked to tool the leather and produce a finished product. He started with belts and then gradually worked his way up to making a full harness set. He was a forward on the basketball team also.

Edward Hatchett, Frank Mentz, and Peter James were all advanced students in the harness trade. The three of them judged the workmanship of the harnesses made by the other students in the harness shop. During the month of March, the harness shop was very busy. They made twenty-five sets of harnesses that would be sent to Santee Agency upon completion. Other members of his class were George Menx, John Red Owl, and Edward Crawford. They were from the Sioux Nation. Their teacher was J. McCallum.

This was what the officials liked to see—a successful and useful trade that could be used on the reservation, a positive result. It may have taken many years to get to this degree of achievement. So when the reports went into the Bureau of Indians Affairs, it always had a positive spin on it.

In Edward's final year at Genoa, he had made connections with some of his relatives. Some were very surprised when he told them that he would be home in the spring. His grandparents were still alive and still living on the west bank of the Omaha Creek. They had sent word that he was welcome to come home anytime.

Edward was nervous about going home. How would they accept him? He had been a little boy when he was taken away. His mind had been changed to think like the white man. He could speak the white man's language; he could read and write it. There were some white people that could do neither. It had been a small settlement when he was taken away. It was now a bigger town with white people living on the reservation. At Genoa, he was looked up to; he had accomplished very much.

Edward had become what the Bureau of Indian Affairs wanted him to be, a good Christian citizen, educated in the English language, able to read and write, and the perfect end product of "kill the Indian and save the man."

After graduation, Edward picked up his trunk and walked down the dorm hallway for the last time. When he got outside, he walked over to the spot where the two white men had dropped him off eleven years ago. Nothing had changed. The only change was Edward himself. Edward walked to the train station and got in line to purchase his ticket to Winnebago. This train ride would take him right to the reservation that he left many years ago in a wagon, where he and other Indian kids were tied up for most of the ride. Within the hour, the steam locomotive pulled into the station and took on its cargo of humans.

Edward L. Hatchett was part of that cargo, heading home after eleven years.

The following is a statement by the assistant secretary of the Bureau of Indian Affairs, made at a ceremony acknowledging the 175th anniversary of the establishment of the Bureau of Indian Affairs, on September 8, 2000:

This agency forbade the speaking of Indian languages, prohibited the conduct of traditional religious activates, outlawed traditional government, and made Indian people ashamed of who they were.

Worst of all, the Bureau of Indian Affairs committed these acts against the children entrusted to its boarding schools, brutalizing them emotionally, psychologically, physically and spiritually.

Even in this era of self-determination, when the Bureau of Indian Affairs is at long last serving as an advocate for Indian people in an atmosphere of mutual respect, the legacy of these acts haunts us. The trauma of shame, fear and anger has passed from one generation to the next, and manifested itself in the rampant alcoholism, drug abuse, and domestic violence that plague Indian country. Many of our people live lives of unrelenting tragedy as Indian families suffer the ruin of their lives by alcoholism, suicides made of shame and despair, and violent death at the hands of one another. So many of the maladies suffered today in Indian country result from the failures of this agency. Poverty, ignorance and disease have been the product of this agency's work.

And so today I stand before you as the leader of an institution that in the past has committed acts so terrible that they infect, diminish, and destroy the lives of Indian people decades later. These things occurred despite the efforts of many good people with good hearts who sought to prevent them. These wrongs must be acknowledged if the healing is to begin.

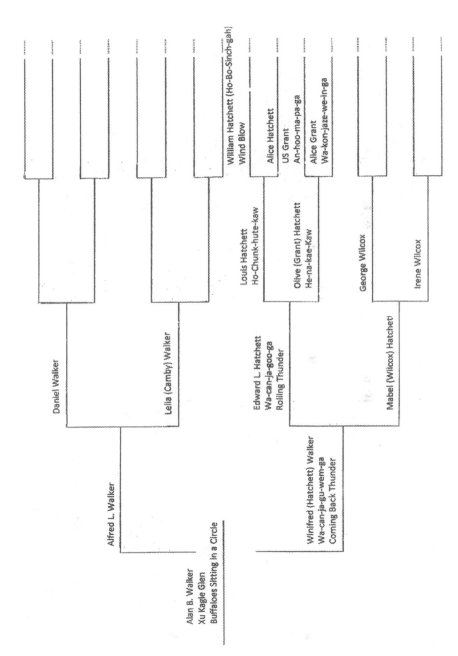

Family tree

U.S. Grant and wife Alice Grant

Wilcox family L to R. George, Mable, Joe, Irene, Ted, Eleanor, Ruth,
Flossie

Ed Hatchett with brief case

Ed Hatchett with cousin Eddie Priest

Genoa Indian School

Mable Hatchett holding Sam Sine

Church at the old Indian Mission

Hatchett farm house west of Winnebago

House on Hatchett Hill

The Hatchett family, L to R Winifred, June, Edd, Wilma, Mable,
Maxine, Kathryn

Winifred Hatchett

Terry, Alan, Mike Walker

Mike, Alan, Florence Ricehill, Terry

Alan Walker in Vietnam, 1968

Chapter 10

Home at Last

Looking out of his window, Edward could feel the butterflies in his stomach. This train ride was like going into a strange land. Everywhere there were roads, train tracks, and farms. Edward couldn't remember any of this.

"Next stop, Walthill!" the conductor called out. "Walthill!"

Edward had heard about this place from his friend Alex Horn many years ago, and now he was traveling through it. So many white people at the station. Edward looked hard to see if he knew any of the Indians standing on the platform.

"Next stop will be Winnebago," said the conductor.

Someone asked the conductor how long it would take to get to Winnebago.

"About ten minutes," was the reply.

Edward gazed at the rolling hills, but he just could not remember any of this. He did remember that it was dark when they left the reservation years ago; maybe that's why this didn't look familiar. Soon the train applied the brakes and came to a stop.

"Winnebago!" was the call from the conductor.

Edward stepped from the train and put his foot down on his homeland for the first time in eleven years. He looked around and saw several Indians waiting for the children who had ridden with him from Genoa to get off the train, but he didn't recognize anyone else.

"Edward Hatchett!" someone shouted.

He looked around and saw his old friend Alex Horn.

"I heard that you would be coming home soon, so every day I've been coming down to the train station and waiting!" Alex Horn told him.

"It's good to see you again," said Edward. "How are you?"

"I am doing fine, working every day with my father. We have a lot of farm work to do."

The two of them walked over and picked up his trunk.

"Come on, I have a team and a wagon. I'll take you home to your grandparents' house."

"Everything looks so different; I can't remember these farms. There were no farms. It was all prairie grass."

"Most of the farms belongs to the whites. There are a few Indian farmers."

They loaded up the trunk, and Edward asked Alex if they could ride through town. Edward hadn't seen Winnebago in a long time. "When I left, it was just a trading post and a few buildings."

"Sure, we can do that."

Edward looked around wide-eyed, shaking his head. "This was all prairie grass when I was taken away. There was no train depot."

"Well, believe it or not, this town now has everything you will need. It even has a jail," Alex said. "I haven't been a guest there yet, so I can't tell you about the decor inside."

Both men just laughed.

Alex Horn drove the team down the main street. Edward was amazed at the number of brick buildings that were built or that were under construction. There were many canvas tents set up and doing business. Some were dry goods. Another was a barbershop, yet another was some kind of a store. Many wooden buildings stood on Main Street; most of them were two stories. It was a thriving town.

Alex Horn turned the team around at the end of Main Street. "Whoever laid out this street knew what he was doing by making it wide," he said. Alex Horn turned the team to the right on the main north–south road; soon they made another right turn and were heading west out of town. They crossed a bridge that was built over the Omaha Creek and kept going west for a short ride.

"There wasn't a bridge here before. I never thought I would see the Omaha Creek again," Edward said softly. "It looks the same."

The wagon rumbled down the dirt road to the U. S. Grant allotment. Soon they made a right turn into the driveway.

"Stop," Edward said. "I just want to see it before we go in."

Alex Horn moved the wagon closer to the house, stopping at the exact same spot, where the agents had kidnapped Edward eleven years ago. A creepy feeling came over Edward. "It was right here where they threw me into the wagon. I tried to get out, but they caught me and tied me up, so I couldn't jump out of the wagon anymore. This house wasn't here. My grandfather had a log cabin; it was small and very rough."

Alex Horn let Edward lead the way. Edward knocked on the door. No answer. He knocked again.

"I am coming," was the reply in the Winnebago language.

Edward knew that voice. It was his grandmother's.

"Yes, what do you want?"

"I am Ku-nu Hatchett."

"You're who?" asked the old woman.

"I am your grandson, Ku-nu Hatchett."

The old woman stepped out into the daylight and looked hard at the young man standing in front of her. Finally, she knew who the stranger was and threw her arms around him. She yelled for her husband.

"Who is it that you want me to meet?"

"It's Ku-nu," the old woman cried. "*Our* Ku-nu, the one they took away from us many years ago! Yes, he's all grown-up now. He's a man."

The old man stepped out into the sunlight and looked at the stranger. "Yes, I can see that it is him. Welcome home, son! It's been many years since we have seen you. I hoped that someday I would see you before I died."

It would take several days for Edward to tell everything to his grandparents; there was so much to tell and explain to them. So much had changed in his life, but they still lived the simple life. His Cho-ka did a little fishing in the creek, and once a month, they would go and get their rations at the agency. They had some money, so they could buy a few supplies from the new stores in town.

There were no beds in the house; they still slept on the floor. It took a few days for Edward to get used to sleeping on the floor again.

It was like he never left. They still lived the old lifestyle, and he was now a white man or lived like a white man. *Pillows, sheets, and a bed would be nice*, thought Edward. But he knew that this would take time and money.

The next morning, Edward was up early, and he made his way over to the little hill that he used to play on years ago. It was grown over with trees and brush now. He made a place to sit down and just take in the beauty of it all. So many times, he had dreamed of this moment, to be home with his family. It was good to feel the warm sun on his face, to smell the new spring flowers, to listen to the birds in the trees, and to hear the rush in the cottonwood trees. No more bugles or bells, no more pinched-face matrons hollering, no more drills. It was good to be home. Edward just sat and enjoyed his freedom. Later that day, Cho-ka, Ka-ka, and Ed paid a visit to his other grandmother, Alice Hatchett. She lived with a relative in town. She was very glad to see Ku-nu. They stayed late into the afternoon until finally Cho-ka Grant said, "We better get going; we have a busy day tomorrow."

"What do you have to do?" asked Edward.

"Tomorrow we will go over and get our rations from the agency, and then we will go over to one of the stores in town and trade some of the rations," said the old man.

"They let you do that?" asked Edward

"You're not supposed to do it, but a lot of us Indians do it anyway," his grandmother Grant told him. "They don't always give us the stuff we need, so we trade for it."

"This store is run by a new white family, and they have quite a few children, some of them grown-up," said the old man. "They have one daughter that helps us. She is very pretty, and she may be younger than you, Ku-nu, but she is very nice to us."

"Do you still fish in the creek?" asked Edward.

"Yes, I do. In fact, we will go down there this afternoon and catch supper."

The old man had cut steps into the bank of the creek; this made it easy to get down to the water. He had made a favorite spot for himself as well, and he sat down and told Ku-nu that he enjoyed this spot. "You can sit over here. They really bite here."

Soon the two were enjoying the cool afternoon by the creek. At that time of the year, the creek was down to normal, and its waters ran very silently. Every now and then, a fish would break the surface and swim off. "I am so glad that you are home," the old man told him. "Your grandmother was heartbroken when they took you away. Both of us were very lonesome around here. Sometimes in the summer, I would see Alex Horn and his father. I always tried to talk to them and find out how you were doing down there. Alex always said that you were doing well and that you could handle it."

Edward stared into the water. "It was hard. They had many rules, and they were very harsh on all of us. I never thought about running away, because I never knew where I was, and I didn't want to get beaten. They even beat the girls who ran away. They did a lot of bad things to us while we were there."

"I thought that maybe we could go down and see you sometime, but our wagon is old, and the team is very old too, but we always wanted to go."

Edward felt much better just to know that they really wanted to come and see him. He chose not to tell his grandfather about how they mistreated all of them; he was an old man, and he wouldn't understand.

The old man pulled out his hunting knife to clean the catfish they'd caught. "I like to clean them here, and then you don't have a mess in the house," he said.

The old man still had his longhouse; it was north of their home. He still believed in the longhouse or the medicine lodge. Later that afternoon, while Edward was looking for his grandfather, he walked down by the creek. He could hear his grandfather talking to someone. As he got closer to the conversation, all he could hear was his grandfather. Soon he was looking at the back side of his grandfather, but he didn't see anyone else. He moved to one side and saw a snake standing on its tail in an upright position.

Edward made no sound. He just listened to his grandfather. The old man told the snake to go in peace; with that, the snake withered down and made its way toward the creek. Edward just stood and wondered how this was possible. How could a snake understand Ho-Chunk? He heard his grandfather call him "brother," and the snake understood.

Edward cleared his throat as he moved forward. He didn't want to say anything about what he'd seen, hoping his grandfather would bring it up in the conversation later.

"I was just talking to my brother. He tells me that the white man has polluted the water by dumping human waste into it, and he disturbs his nesting site with plows and fence building and that he will have to move."

Edward sat in amazement at what his grandfather told him, but he didn't doubt any of it. U. S. Grant was from the medicine lodge, and like Edward's other grandfather, William Hatchett, he had powerful medicine.

"This is one religion that the white man knows nothing about," he told Edward. "And it should stay that way. I have seen how some of the white men are. They are greedy, selfish, and always wanting more than what they need. Can you imagine if they got hold of this kind of power? It's better that it dies with the old ones like me."

Edward said nothing. He would not bring up his newfound religion or force that religion on the old man. He knew that it would just cause hard feelings between the two of them.

The next day, they got the team ready and made their way to the agency. The agency was something new for Ed. There had been no agency when he was young–just a building that gave out rations every now and then. Now there was a big office building with houses, barns, and equipment. It looked like its own little town. Cho-ka guided Ed around to the building, and they got into line and waited for their rations. Edward saw some of his old friends from Genoa. He talked to Alex Horn in English, but Alex returned the talk in Ho-Chunk.

"Why do you speak in Ho-Chunk?" asked Edward.

"Because we are not at Genoa, and our parents don't understand English," said Alex Horn. "And besides, they can't beat us here. We are home. We can do as we please."

Edward had to stop and think about that. He had been gone for so long that he acted like a white man; he almost felt guilty about talking in his native tongue. Edward visited with his old schoolmates while his grandparents got their rations.

"I heard you talk in the white man's tongue," said the old man when he returned.

"Yes, they taught me how to speak very well," replied Edward.

"That is good because now you can talk to the storekeepers for us and tell them what we want to trade for," said the old man.

The wagon bounced along the agency road. Other Indians were making their way out to the agency for their rations. Some of them were carrying their goods in a gunnysack as they made their way to town. "Most of the rations will be used to feed the Indians, but some of them will be traded for the white man's whiskey," his grandfather told him. "It's better if the women pick up the family rations; at least then, more of the food gets home."

Soon they pulled into town. Lots of Indians were on the streets. Ration day was always a busy one.

"Turn to the left by the big stone building," said his grandfather.

His grandmother told the two men that she wanted to trade the cheese and lard for some baking powder, coffee, some canned goods, and tobacco. The two men sorted the rations and found the cheese and lard.

"What do I say to these white people about trading for food?" asked Ed.

"You just tell them that you want to trade the government food for the canned goods and tobacco. They know what we like."

Both of the men walked into the store with their government supplies. "I would like to trade some of our rations for your canned goods, tobacco, coffee and baking power," said Edward.

The young lady looked up in great surprise. "How did you learn to speak so well?" she asked him.

"I was at the Genoa school for the past eleven years, and I learned how to read and write the English language," replied Edward.

"Well, it will be a pleasure doing business with you ... and your family of course," replied the young lady.

"My family would like some baking powder, coffee, canned goods and tobacco; and in return, we have cheese and lard," said Edward.

The cheese and lard were weighed, and the young lady brought the selected goods to the counter to be traded.

"How long has this been going on?" asked Edward.

"All the stores do it. We trade with the Indian people. What they don't need or want, we trade for. Its good business for both of us."

"By the way, my name is Edward Hatchett."

"My name is Mable Wilcox, and my family owns this store. Have you been in town long, Edward?"

"No, I just got back three days ago. It's been a long time since I have been here. In fact, when I left, Winnebago was just a trading post and prairie," said Ed.

"Well, the next time you are in town, stop by, and we will talk," said Mable.

This struck Edward odd. Why would a nice-looking white woman want to talk to him and about what? On the ride home, Mrs. Grant opened up the tobacco plug and took a bite. Edward had forgotten that his grandmother liked to chew. He smiled at her as she chewed away on the newfound treat.

Back at the homestead, they found a note on the door that read, "Ollie will be home tomorrow. She will be on the 1:00 PM train."

"Oh, what a surprise," said the old woman. "It's a good thing we got the rations and food from the store today."

The agents had taken his sister away shortly after they took him. They had sent her to a school in the east, and now after all of these years, he would see his sister again.

The next day, his grandmother cleaned and swept the house. "I wonder what kind of food she would like to eat."

"I think maybe a pot of soup and biscuits would be fine," said Edward. He winced as he watched his grandfather use the hunting knife he had just used to clean fish to open a can of beef; this would be done by carving a huge *X* across the top and then prying the metal apart it was a messy procedure. He wondered whether Ollie might have some trouble adjusting to her grandparents' habits. Sometimes returning home was a culture shock for the students after a long stay at the boarding school. The Grants had had very little to smile about for the past eleven years, but things had changed dramatically in the past week, and now they would not only have their grandson back, but their granddaughter too. A radiant smile broke across the old woman's face as they drew closer to the station. There were many people milling around waiting for the train. Soon the whistle could be heard coming from the south. Some of the men folk had to hold their teams tight because the horses were afraid of the train.

The train rolled to a stop and blew off a large cloud of steam. Several young girls got off the train. Edward didn't know what his sister looked like after all these years. Then one of the girls walked up and said, "A-ho, Cho-ka! Ka-ka!

Ka-ka Grant hugged her granddaughter for a long time. She was weeping as she held her. Cho-ka Grant and Edward joined them, and soon all of them were crying.

"Ollie, this is your brother, Edward. He just came home this past week," said Ka-ka.

Ollie looked at Edward for a long time; finally, she said, "Yeah, I guess that he belongs to us."

They all laughed … and continued to laugh. The ride was full of laughter and stories.

"Tell me, big brother, how many children do you have?" teased Ollie.

"Oh, about five that I know of," was Edward's reply.

"Before we go home, I need to stop at the store and pick up a few items," said Ed. He turned the team, and soon they were heading into town. Ed stopped the wagon in front of the Wilcox store and made a dash into the store. Within minutes, he was back on the wagon with a small sack of goods. The ride home was full of laughter and fun. The old wagon just shook with merriment.

As the wagon made the final turn into the drive, Ollie looked at the government house. "It was many years ago that they took me from here. I never knew if I would ever come home to this place. I used to think about this place, but I couldn't remember everything about it because I was so young then."

The old Grant house was full of great joy. The hard years were behind them, and now they could get on with living together as a family again. After the meal was over, Ed went into the kitchen and brought out the two cans of fruit, and he pulled a can opener out of the bag. He told his grandparents that this was a can opener, and he proceeded to show them how to open a can. Both of them just sat in awe and watched as Ed opened the can so effortlessly—no spilling and no mess, just a nice clean job.

When he was done, he gave the can opener to his grandfather, who looked it over very carefully and passed it on to his wife. She touched it as if it were extremely valuable. She marveled at this little tool. "It's yours to keep," Ed said. "Keep it in the kitchen."

A smile came across the old women's face.

And now it was time for dessert. As Ed passed the cans of fruit around, he told them that this was dessert, and it was always served after supper.

"Is this what they have taught you?" his grandfather asked.

"It's one of the things that I have learned," said Ed.

"Then they have done a good job," said the old man, laughing.

Edward told them he was going to the agency the next day to inquire about a business school in Sioux City, Iowa.

"Aren't you smart enough already?" his grandfather asked.

Ed looked at all three of them and said, "This is a business school; I will need it if I open my own harness shop."

They still looked very puzzled at him; they didn't understand why he wanted to go back to school when he just got home.

"This isn't a government school, although the agency will pay for it, and they will find me a room to stay while I am a school during the week."

The room was very quiet. The old folks didn't like school, and they didn't understand how he could want to go back to school after all these years.

"Well, enough said about school," said Edward.

After supper, Edward and Ollie sat outside and talked. They talked in English. The old folks didn't understand it. Ollie told her story of how they had come one day and just took her away from this place. She thought maybe that she would join her older brother, but instead, they sent her to Carlisle Indian School in Pennsylvania. "I was very scared, and there were other Winnebagos with me. We didn't know where they were taking us. They put us on a train, and we went far away. It was very hard at first. A lot of the kids got a beating for talking in Winnebago. It was a mean place, although you probably know this already."

Edward commiserated with her, telling her his tale of being kidnapped.

"Those were terrible times for both of us," Ollie said when he'd finished. "But now that is over, and we are home again. What I can't understand is why you want to go back to school."

"This school isn't just for Indian kids. It has mostly white kids in it, and it is called the National Business Training School, a college. They don't beat you. It is a different school, and it's not a government school at all. They will teach me how to run a business. Just before I left Genoa, my teachers told me about this school and said that I should go there. It's only a two-year school, and I will be home every weekend."

The next day, Ed harnessed up the team and headed out for the agency. He was told to go into the biggest building and to ask the first person he saw for information. Edward did that, and he was told go upstairs to the education office. Soon he had the right person, and they talked about the business school in Sioux City, Iowa.

"I'll need to see your diploma before we can get started."

"That's no problem; I have it with me." With that, he unrolled the diploma, and they all took a look at it.

"Very good, Ed, this is the first diploma from Genoa that I have seen," said Mr. Decker. "According to the schedule, the business school is about to start a summer session. If you hurry, you can still make it."

Ed said he would travel the next morning on the train, and he would talk with the school.

"It sounds like you really want this to happen, so I will make arrangements for your lodging, travel, and food vouchers while you are in Sioux City tomorrow."

The next morning, Ed was up early. He had a quick breakfast and headed out the door for the train station. The train jerked and moved slowly at first; then it started to pick up some speed. It rolled north out of town. This would be the first time that Ed had ever been on this part of the reservation. His family had land down by the river, over by the hairpin turn and out west. He had never heard of Homer, Nebraska, or Dakota City before; and now he would be going through both of them. In about ten minutes, the conductor called out, "Next stop will be Homer, Nebraska!"

The town of Homer was actually on the west side of the Omaha Creek. You had to cross a wooden bridge to get into town. Soon the steam locomotive was moving north again. As they rolled north out of

Homer, the bluffs faded away, and now it was all flat as far as the eye could see. The next stop would be Dakota City and then South Sioux City. The conductor said they might have a little wait in South Sioux City, in case there was a train crossing the river ahead of them or one coming from Iowa.

There wasn't a wait, and soon they rolled into Sioux City. It was a large city. Ed found the people in the city were friendlier than those on the reservation. He found his way to the campus, and he followed the directions to the enrollment office, where he asked about enrollment for the summer classes.

"We still have room for a few more students," the young lady behind the desk told him. She gave him a form to fill out.

In a few minutes, Ed handed her the filled-out paper.

"You're from Winnebago, Nebraska?" She asked.

"Yes, I am," said Ed.

"Will you be staying in the city while you attend classes?"

"Yes, I believe the agency is making arrangements for my lodging."

"Did you bring your diploma with you?"

"Yes, I did."

"I will need a payment of twenty-five dollars now and the rest during the first month. Is this all right?"

"Yes, there's no problem with that."

"We will mail to you your class schedule and a payment plan if you need one."

The school was one large two-story building. On the train ride home, Ed thought about how he would stay in the city during the week and take the train home on Friday afternoon and then catch the train early on Monday morning and go directly to school. This could work, he thought.

The steam locomotive rolled to a stop at the Winnebago depot. Ed stepped off the train and headed for home. It was a beautiful spring afternoon. As he crossed the Omaha Creek, a large snapping turtle was sunning himself on the east bank. It moved into the water when Ed got closer. *That would have been a good meal* thought Ed as he climbed up the creek bank and headed to the house.

The agency provided housing in Sioux City and funds for transportation to and from Winnebago. The following year, his grandmother became very ill. She was a proud member of the medicine lodge, and she would not go to a white doctor, and the medicine from her lodge didn't seem to work anymore. Maybe the old medicine man was getting too old, or maybe he had forgotten something, but nothing seemed to work. Ed had picked up some liquid medicine (cough medicine) and aspirin in the city. He would mix aspirin into her coffee every morning, and he also bought some canned juice. He would mix some of the liquid medicine into the juice in the evening so she could drink it. His grandmother's illness took a lot of Ed's time and attention, and soon he was too far behind in school to catch up. He decided to stop going to school for now and perhaps continue again in the fall.

As the weeks went by, his grandmother got better. Ed wondered if the mixture of the Indian medicine and the white man's medicine had been a winning combination. During his grandmother's sickness, Ed stayed close to home. He and his Cho-ka would get the rations and the supplies that they would need. Ed kept busy by chopping wood and fixing up the house and yard.

Chapter 11

Mabel Wilcox

One evening after supper, Ed told his grandparents that he would look for work in town or that if he had to, he would work in the city.

"What kind of work are you looking for?" asked the old man.

"I have a diploma in harness making, and I can do carpentry work too."

"They say that the blacksmith needs someone to repair harnesses and work some leather goods, that he doesn't have the time to do that kind of work," his grandfather told him.

When Edward got out of bed the next morning, he stoked up the fire and put the coffeepot on to boil. He made a quick breakfast and cooked two egg sandwiches and packed them in a lunch bag. He put his work gloves in just in case he might need them. He thought about working for a farmer, but that didn't pay very well. Ed had just poured a cup of coffee when his grandfather walked into the kitchen.

"A-ho, Ku-nu," said the old man.

"Good morning!" Ed poured his grandfather a cup of coffee and then sat in the kitchen for a while and talked. His grandfather told him of how glad he and his grandmother were to have their two grandchildren back home. He told Ed that he could stay with them as long as he wanted to, that this was his home too. It was good to talk, man to man, with his grandfather, and it was good to know that he had a home.

Ed walked east of the house and down the steps that his grandfather had dug out of the bank. He jumped across the creek and headed toward the tracks. Ed pushed his way through the thick weeds; he was just a little ways south of Horse Shoe Bend. Once on the tracks, he made better time. It was still early, so he took his time, and walked on the train tracks that would take him to the west side of Winnebago. The blacksmith shop was just east of the station, about a block away. Soon he was standing in front of the shop. Ed checked his pocket watch; it was almost seven-thirty.

"What can I do for you, young man?" asked the dirty shop owner.

"I am looking for a job."

"What can you do?"

"I can make and repair harnesses and do leatherwork."

The shop owner did a double take. "You can repair harnesses? Well, come in and let me show you what I have here." In the back room hung several harnesses that needed repair and the backlog was getting bigger. "Can you fix these?"

"Yes, I can make them work, and they will be stronger than new ones."

A smile came on the dirty face of the blacksmith.

"Well then, you have a job, sir," said the blacksmith.

The first thing that Edward did was put some order into the harness shop. He knew that it was easier to work in a clean and neat shop. Next he did a quick inventory on tools and supplies. He found little of both. He asked the owner what tools he had.

"Well, I was hoping that you might have some. I have a few, but not enough to do a good job."

"I have tools at home, and I will bring them in tomorrow, but I still need leather to make the repairs."

"You figure out what you need and then go up to the Wilcox store and order what you need and tell them that you work for me, Joe Williams."

By midmorning, Edward was ready to head to the store. He had his list, and he needed a break from the dusty shop. "I'll be going to the store now," said Ed.

"Just a minute there, young man, I didn't even catch your name!"

"Edward Hatchett is my name."

"How did you learn to speak so well?" asked Joe.

"I was at the Genoa boarding school for eleven years."

"Well done. I think you will work out all right, Edward Hatchett."

Edward had written down all of the supplies that he would need to get started. The Wilcox store had both of its doors propped open when Edward got there. He looked around at the different stuff that was on the shelves and sitting on the floor.

"May I help you?"

Edward knew that voice, and it was Mabel Wilcox's. "Yes, I have an order here that I need to turn in. It's for Joe Williams at the blacksmith shop. I work for him now."

"Well, step over to the counter, and I will take it down."

After the order was taken, Mabel asked Edward how his grandmother was doing.

"She is doing much better now. She is even back to chewing tobacco."

Both of them laughed.

"What type of work are you doing for Joe Williams?"

"I will be working on harnesses—making them and repairing them. This is what I learned at the Genoa Indian School," said Ed.

"That's very good! Tell your grandmother to stop in and see me. She is one of our best tobacco customers."

Both of them had a good laugh.

"By the way," she said, "how do you like being home?"

Ed told her he enjoyed being back with his family, although it would take some getting used to. Everyone still slept on the floor, and they didn't have many modern conveniences, but this would change once he got a regular paycheck coming in.

"It's good to talk with someone who speaks English well," Mabel said. "So many of the returning students and customers don't, and it makes it hard for me to understand them. Some of them just come in and point at what they want."

Edward didn't know what to say to that. "I'd better be going now," he told her. "I have a lot of work to do."

"You will come back and see me, won't you?"

"I can, now that I work in town."

One week later, when the order came in, word was sent down to the blacksmith shop to send Edward to pick it up.

"I am here to pick up Joe William's order of leather supplies," Edward told the man behind the counter.

"Oh yes, we have it here. I will need you to sign for them. You can sign your name, right?"

"Yes, I can sign my name."

"You're the Indian that they kept down at Genoa for a long time, aren't you?"

"Yes, they taught me how to read and write."

George Wilcox looked at his signature and said his name, Edward Hatchett.

With new leather supplies and a clean shop, Edward set out to repair the backlog of harnesses. Within days, the first set of leather goods left the shop. Joe Williams was very happy with his new employee. "Good job, Edward, real good job."

On payday, Joe came over with an envelope with Edward's money for the week. "What are you going to do with all that money?" asked Joe.

"I am going to buy a bed."

"There is nothing like a new bed for your tired bones."

"This bed will be for my grandparents," Ed told him.

"That's very good of you to think of your grandparents that way," said Joe.

After work, Edward went up to the Wilcox store to buy some things for himself. Mabel was there to wait on him.

"Hello, Mabel, and how you are today?"

"Very fine … just a little tired. It's been a long day, and I have been on my feet all day long waiting on the customers."

Edward shopped around and picked up some personal things for himself. "Well, that will be all for today."

"How do you like working in the harness shop?"

"Work is fine, and the pay is good."

"You don't drink, do you?"

"No, I don't like it. Plus I am a Christian. Why do you ask?"

"Well, you are different from the rest of the Indian men around here; you work and take care of your grandparents. You're an honest man and a Christian."

"This was how I was taught in Genoa, to work hard and be honest." He looked at her and asked. "Why do you ask me all of these questions?"

She blushed a little. "I think you are an interesting man, and I would like to get to know you better." Mabel delicately wiped the small beads of sweat off her forehead.

"If you would like to get to know me better, then would you go to church with me?"

"Yes, I can do that."

Edward was thinking about this white woman on his way home. Everything that was taught to him was that Indian men didn't marry white women. That was a big no-no. What would his family say about a white woman coming into the family? How could a white woman live like the Indians who didn't even have beds in their house? Edward thought about all the bad things that this marriage would have to endure, but nothing had been easy for him, since his parents passed away many years ago.

But on the other side of the coin, she was a very attractive woman—smart, kind, and she liked him. Edward had never been in love. He never allowed that kind of feeling into his life, because everyone that he cared for had been taken from him and only grief was put in their place. There were many things to consider. How would her parents feel about him? How would she be treated by other white people in the town? Indians were not even citizens of the United States.

On Sunday, Edward washed up and told his grandparents that he would be going to church. There was a silence in the room. "You don't go to the longhouse anymore?" the old medicine man asked him.

"No, I have found God and he is the way now." He didn't want to talk about church. He just wanted to leave.

"We will talk later when you get home."

There was no way that Edward could even remember the longhouse ways, which was too long ago. He had learned the white man's god, and he had accepted it. When Edward arrived at the Wilcox's house, Mabel was standing outside waiting for him.

"Are you ready to go?" he asked.

"Yes, what took you so long to get here?"

"Was I long in getting here?"

"No, I was just kidding you."

They entered the church when the bell was being pulled. Some of the members greeted them as they walked in.

"Welcome, Edward," said Alex Horn.

"Alex, I would like you to meet Mabel Wilcox."

"I know who she is. Her folks own one of the stores in town. Anyway, have a good morning, Mabel."

Mabel said "Good morning" to Alex and a few others who came to the store. There were very few whites in church and not too many Indians. After the service, Alex Horn walked over to where Edward and Mabel were standing.

"You sure know how to get the people to turn their heads and look, Edward."

"What do you mean by that?"

"Everyone in church was looking at you two this morning."

Now that Alex Horn had said it, Edward did notice that a lot of people were looking at them. On the ride back to the Wilcox's house, Edward asked Mabel what she thought of the church service.

"We don't go to church much, but it was very nice, and I enjoyed being there with you. You can come over after work, and we can talk if you want to," said Mabel. "That would be fine with me."

When Edward walked through the door at home, no one said a word to him, so he went and changed his clothes and went outside. Soon his grandfather came out and joined him under the tree.

"How was the white man's church?" asked Cho-ka.

"It was fine."

"Have you forgotten the ways of the medicine lodge?"

"Yes, I have. When I was at Genoa, if you didn't go to the white man's church, they would beat you and make you work extra hours. It was better to go to church than get a beating."

"Would you want to learn the ways of the longhouse again?"

"No. I believe in the white man's god. I have accepted it and taken the Lord as my savior. I cannot put anyone or any other religion above him. This is what they taught me."

His grandfather knew that his grandson had been turned into a white man and that there was no turning him around. Already he had ordered a bed for them and a bed for himself also; this was how white people slept. But it was better to have him home and let him live like a white man than to have him gone and be sad.

Monday at work, Joe Williams asked Edward about taking a white lady to an Indian church.

"What do you mean?"

"The word is that you have been seeing Mabel Wilcox and that you even took her to your church."

"Well, it is true that we did go to church, but it wasn't my church. Anyone can go to it."

"You know what I mean when I say your church—the church that the Indians can go to. You haven't been here very long, but Indian men don't date white girls around here. You're just asking for trouble, Edward."

"I didn't think of it as a date. I just asked her if she would go to church with me on Sunday, and she said yes."

"Well, the talk is that her dad is very upset about this whole matter. If I were you, I would lay low for a while. Now this is just me talking."

Edward didn't think too much of it. All they did was go to church and nothing more. Edward stopped by the store after work. Mabel's father was at the counter. "Is Mabel here?"

"Yes, she is, and may I ask who you are?" asked George Wilcox.

"I am Edward Hatchett."

"Ah yes. You are Edward Hatchett, the educated Indian," replied George.

"Yes, I am, we met the other day when I picked up some supplies for the blacksmith shop." He could sense the hostility in the man's voice.

"What are your plans for the future?"

"I would like to open my own harness shop someday, build my own house, and maybe have a farm."

"Well, that's a lot of planning there," Mr. Wilcox said. "And how will you get the money to do all of this?"

"I will work for it. I am not afraid to work, and I have a diploma from the Genoa school."

"Oh, I see that you have met my father," said Mabel, walking up.

"Yes, we have met."

She nodded toward the door. "We will be right outside if you need me, Pa."

"Do you like my father?" asked Mabel when they stepped out of the store.

"He is a stern man, but he comes right to the point, and I like that in a man. He doesn't beat around the bush." Edward looked away for a moment and then back at her. "I must ask you about all this talk going around town about us. All I did was ask you to go to church with me, and people are making a big to-do about it. I don't understand this."

"You have been gone too long. People talk about us because you are an Indian and I am a white girl, and in their eyes, that is not right."

"But it is all right for a white man to take an Indian woman for his bride?" Ed asked.

She raised an eyebrow. "So are we talking about brides now?"

The two of them were the talk of the town for the next few months. They went on picnics together. They took wagon rides down to the river. They explored some of the old Indian villages in the Big Bear Hollow.

They were always in church every Sunday. Then one afternoon, Edward went to the store to see Mabel, but she wasn't there. Ed was told that Mabel had to go to Sloan, Iowa, to help her aunt who was very ill and needed someone to take care of her. This seemed strange because Ed had just talked to her the evening before, and Mabel had said nothing about her aunt being sick.

Sloan, Iowa, was just a stone's throw across the Missouri River from the old Indian villages. In fact, the Missouri River was the eastern boundary of the reservation. But the only way to get to Sloan was by wagon, and you had to go to Sioux City, Iowa, and then follow the river south for about twenty-five miles or more. It would be a good day's journey.

Ed and Mabel began a letter-writing campaign. It was common for Ed to get two or three letters from Mabel in one week. Ed did well to write one letter a week, but it always had good information in it about the reservation and the people who lived on it, especially those who liked to talk.

If this separation was put in place by Mabel's parents to keep the young lovers apart, it didn't work. In fact, it had just the opposite effect on them. Their love grew stronger the longer they were apart. The days were getting colder. When the Missouri River froze over completely, the ice companies began to cut ice for the icehouses. There were gangs of ice cutters on the river. Many of the locals went ice-skating on the frozen Missouri; this gave the young couple an idea. Quite a few of the locals from Sloan went skating on the river, and Mabel was one of them. She would tell Ed in a letter when she planned to skate on the river. Ed and some of his friends made plans to be on the river that same day. It was fun to have so many young people ice-skating from both sides of the river.

Ed and Mabel found it very hard to be alone on the ice with so many people skating around, but they stole away every now and then. This made it more exciting for them, but word got back to George Wilcox that his daughter was seen ice-skating on the river with Ed Hatchett. George Wilcox began working on another scheme when Mabel moved back to Winnebago and went to work for her father at the store.

One afternoon Ed went to the Wilcox store to see Mabel. "May I speak with Mabel, please," he asked her mother.

"No," Mrs. Wilcox replied, "she went away to work in Kansas City."

"When will she be back?"

"I don't know. This all came up very quickly, and she just left this morning," said Mrs. Wilcox.

"Is there any way that I can get her address so I can write to her?"

"Come back next week, and we should have her mailing address by then."

Ed was very perplexed. This didn't sound like the woman that he knew. This sounded like a plan hatched by someone else. Edward was a determined man, and his mind was made up that this little white woman was going to be his future wife, and he didn't care who liked it or not!

George Wilcox had heard enough about this Indian man and his daughter. He didn't like the other white men in town teasing him about his future son-in-law being an Indian. That's why he decided to send his daughter to Kansas City to live with his sister-in-law, Erma.

Once the plans were made, he had announced them to his daughter … abruptly.

"We have decided that life for you would be much better in Kansas City, Missouri, than here on this Indian reservation," he had told her.

"Well, I am quite happy here," she replied. "I find the reservation life interesting. It's challenging, and I have come to understand most of the pointing and grunts when Indians come in and want something."

"We don't see it that way, and we think that you will be better off away from here."

"Let's not beat around the bush, Pa. It's Ed Hatchett you don't like and don't want me to see, isn't it?"

"Yes, it is. He is an Indian. Just because he can read, write, and knows arithmetic, some people think he is smart. Well, he isn't. He's just another stinking Indian, like the rest of them!" George roared.

"Tell me then, how many white men do you know who can do that? How many white men do you know who can read and write and speak well and make harnesses and have gone to a business college in Sioux City?" said Mabel in a raised voice.

"I have bought you a ticket for Kansas City, and you will be on that train tomorrow morning. We have made arrangements for you to live with Aunt Erma, and she has found you a job. We have paid for your first month's rent to her, and then you will pay her every month after that."

"What if I don't want to go?"

"You have no choice. You are going."

"You can run me off now, but I am almost of age; and when I become of age, I will do what I please and with whom I please," Mable cried.

Later that evening, her mother helped her pack her bags and tried to cheer her up. "We are doing what's best for you. You are just a young girl, and you think that you have feelings for this man, but it will pass, and soon you will find a nice man that you will grow old with."

Mable didn't say anything, because plans were already forming in her mind.

In the morning, George helped his daughter aboard the train and said good-bye. It was a very cold good-bye for both of them. He slipped the conductor a five-dollar bill and told him to watch his daughter and not let her get off of the train at any other station.

Mabel's plan was to write Edward just as soon as she could and tell him where she was and that it was not her doing. But would her aunt intercept Edward's letters?

Chapter 12

Kansas City, Missouri

Edward dutifully returned to the Wilcox store, as he said he would, but he could see and feel a kind of smugness on the faces of those in the room when he walked in. He asked Mrs. Wilcox if she had Mabel's address.

"I don't know if she wants to hear from you," she told him. "Things have changed in her life, and she told us in a letter that she was very happy in Kansas City."

Nonetheless, she gave him Mabel's address, and that night Edward wrote her a letter. He wanted to know why she just left town without saying good-bye or letting him know that she was leaving. It was a short letter; he didn't want to sound too pushy. Edward was lonesome. Even with his family there, he still missed her.

He was thrilled the following week when a letter arrived for him from Kansas City. Mabel wrote that her father had found a better-paying job for her in a candy factory there and insisted she had to leave right away, which was why she hadn't had time to say good-bye to him. She told him that she missed him and wanted to be with him and hoped that maybe someday he could catch the train down to Kansas City to pay her a visit. "I have not changed my feelings for you," she wrote. "My father set up this scheme to get us apart. I had nothing to do with us parting, and now I want to be with you more than anything."

Edward felt better. The letter lifted his spirits up, and now he could face the world again. Edward and Mabel kept writing letters back and forth, and he always looked forward to getting the mail.

By the time Edward had worked for Joe Williams for almost a year, his work in harness repair was known throughout the area. Around Christmas, Edward had produced many tooled belts, some of which were very fancy, others with names put on them. All of this was very time-consuming. One order had come for a fancy harness set to match the fancy surrey that the team would pull.

Edward was very frugal with his money; he spent his money on personal items, and he always helped out with the family budget. But his long-range plan had been set in place—to own his own business, to have a nice home like the white folks had, and to have nice things for his wife and family.

The letter writing to Mabel led to a plan taking shape for the young couple. Edward would travel to Kansas City in April and stay for a week where more plans would be put together. Edward asked for a week off from the harness shop and was given the time off. "Just make sure that you are caught up with all of your work," Joe told him. "What do you plan to do on your week off?"

"I plan on seeing an old school friend in Genoa."

He had to tell a fib because he knew that if he told Joe where he was going, he would tell the Wilcox family. In fact, Edward had made arrangements with his cousin Eddie Priest to take him to Walthill to board the train. He knew that the Winnebago ticket agent would tell the Wilcox family that Edward Hatchett was traveling to Kansas City. Then George would tell the sheriff and have Ed arrested on some trumped-up charges.

The Grant family had accepted the fact that Ku-nu was going to marry a white woman someday. This was tolerable because years ago, the Ho-Chunk warriors kidnapped white women and married them, and most of the time, the women were then accepted into the tribe. So his traveling to Kansas City was no surprise to them.

"So this white woman means a lot to you?" asked Eddie when they were on their way to Walthill.

"Yes, she does."

"You know what the white folks will say if you two get married, don't you? And some members of the tribe will call you a traitor."

"I don't see where it matters. Most of the Indians think that way about me anyway. Not too many of them talk to me now. They think I am white already."

"You have been gone a long time. You have changed," Eddie admitted. "But the people haven't, and they don't trust you, the government, or the agent."

Edward sighed. "It's the system that made me who I am."

"I heard someone say that you went from the longhouse to the white man's house."

"What do *you* say?"

"I go to the longhouse, because it makes my family feel good, and I believe in the white man's god." Eddie laughed. "So I am just as confused as the rest of them."

Eddie pulled the wagon up to the hitching post, and Edward went in to get his ticket. Very few people were riding the train southbound.

"When will you be back?" asked Eddie.

"In one week, but I will get off in Winnebago. I just didn't want anyone seeing me leave from town. You know how they like to talk."

"Yes, I know how they like to talk. Well, have a good trip and tell Mabel I said hello." Eddie Priest untied the team and headed north to Winnebago. He gave a final wave as he turned the team around. The train couldn't come fast enough for Edward. His mind was filled with many thoughts about him and Mabel.

He picked up a day-old newspaper to read; it was the *Sioux City Journal*; and soon the clanking of the train, the ringing of bell, and shots of hot steam could be heard as the locomotive pulled into the station. Edward took a seat in the back of the car and looked around the car, checking. He didn't see any Indians or any white people from Winnebago. "Very good," he said to himself. Soon the lurching and chugging of the train was replaced with the constant *click de-click* of the rails under the floor of the car. The first leg of his journey would take him into Omaha, Nebraska. He had never been to Omaha before. He would change trains there and head south toward Kansas City, arriving late that evening.

The city of Omaha was large and busy with people everywhere—some in a hurry, others who seemed to be just standing and looking around. The railroad ran through part of the stockyards. Edward had never seen so many cattle in one place. They were pushing, bumping into one another as they moved down the alley to be placed into a large pen. The train crept along the line, and soon they pulled into the Omaha station. It was huge, with a long platform with hundreds of people waiting to board and large glass windows with more people inside milling about. Edward bought a cup of coffee and found a quiet corner and ate part of his lunch. The Kansas City train would be loading in one and a half hours. This would give him time to look around a little.

Edward was one of the first in line when the train for Kansas City began loading. He knew there would be a lot of people going to Kansas City, and he wanted to get a good seat. Once inside the car, he took a window seat and made himself comfortable. Soon a middle-aged man approached him. "Is this seat taken?"

"No, I am traveling alone."

The businessman sat down and opened up his briefcase and started to work on some papers. His briefcase was full of papers clipped together, reports and loose papers.

The train lurched forward and slowly crept out of the station. It moved slower through the city. Edward had never seen so many houses, so many brick streets with lights, so many white people.

The businessman went right to his work. He read and then wrote some notes on a tablet and then thumbed through other stacks of paper. One of his sheets of paper fell down by Edward's feet. Edward reached down and picked it up and gave it back to the man.

"Thank you. As you can see, I am all thumbs," he told Edward. "I have just too many reports to work on." He held out his hand. "By the way, my name is Robert Reynolds."

"I am Edward Hatchett from Winnebago, Nebraska."

"*Hatchett*, isn't that an Indian name? And isn't Winnebago a reservation?"

"Yes, to both of your questions."

"Interesting, because I am wrapping up a study on American Indians and the Indian boarding schools that they attended. Did you, by any chance, go to an Indian school?"

"Yes, I did. In fact, I got a diploma two years ago from the Genoa school."

"You don't mind if I ask you some questions about the place, do you?"

"No, I would be glad to answer any of your questions." Edward told him everything—the initial kidnapping, the sexual abuse and beatings, not having enough food, and the hard work they had to do for the "outing program."

Mr. Reynolds took notes, sometimes asking Edward to slow down while he tried to write all of this down. "This is just amazing," he said when Edward finished. "I knew that you Indians had it bad, but this is just unbelievable. I cannot see how our government could allow this to happen!"

"I don't think the government knew what was going on behind closed doors."

"How did you survive all of this?"

"I had nowhere to go. We were prisoners. If we tried to run away, they would beat us, and the more you ran away, the harder they beat you. So it was better to submit and try to do as they said."

It turned out Mr. Reynolds had been sent out to investigate abuse in the Indian school system.

The sun had gone down, and the lamps were lit. Edward had talked so much that he even forgot about his bacon sandwich.

"It has been a pleasure talking with you, Edward, and I hope that you have a successful life. I am sorry for what our government did to you and your people."

"What has been done to me cannot be undone, but I hope that the next generation of Indians doesn't have to go through what I did."

"I just want to add to this, that I just came from the Genoa Indian School and I will be in Kansas City for a few days; then I am off to the Haskell Institute in Lawrence Kansas, where I am sure I will hear more of the same. And thank you, Edward, for all of your help," said Mr. Reynolds.

The loaded train pulled to a stop. The station was full of people, pushing, walking fast, always in a hurry; but amid all of the commotion and rush, Edward saw a friendly face standing on the platform. Edward made his way toward Mabel, and she rushed toward him, running up and giving him a kiss. This was the first time a girl had ever kissed him in public, so he returned the favor. It may not have been the best, but it felt good.

The two walked hand in hand up the street until they came to a small café that was open late. Edward put his hand into his pocket and found his old bacon sandwich. He smiled to himself. They talked about everything and everybody, including her father's plans to get her out of Winnebago, to get her away from Ed.

"I don't like it one bit," she told him. "I am almost of age, and I should be able to make up my own mind. I have found you a room; it's not far from where I stay."

"That's good. How do you like your job?"

"It's hard. I am on my feet all day long. The pay is low, but it pays the bills, and I have some left over."

They made their way over to the rooming house where Edward would stay for the week. After checking in, they walked over to her house. "Now, do you remember how to get back to your room?" she asked him. "And will you be able to find your way tomorrow to come and get me after work?"

He grinned at her. "I have it all down in my head."

"All right. I will see you tomorrow after work, and we will get something to eat and talk some more about our future."

Edward turned and started to walk away.

"Hey, aren't you forgetting something?" she asked; he looked puzzled.

"I don't think so."

"Come here, Ed."

He did, and she gave him a good night kiss; and again, he liked it. "This is new for me, because Indians don't kiss in public ... much."

"Well, you'd better get used to it, Indian man," she laughed and walked into her house.

She had said "our future." He thought about that for a long time. The only place that he called home was Winnebago. He wondered how they would make a living. He didn't think he could make enough at the harness shop for two people. Maybe she could continue to work for her family. And what about her family? They had sent her down here to get her away from him. So many questions, so little time. They would have to make big plans and tell no one about them.

The next day, Mabel walked out of the candy factory, into the arms of her waiting Indian man. "Hi, Indian man. How was your day?"

"My day was fine, and how was yours? Sweet, I'll bet?"

Mabel shook her head and wrinkled her nose. "We can't eat any of the candy. If you get caught, they take it out of your pay the first time, and the next time, they fire you."

They talked as they headed to the little café. It was a warm evening, and the street was filled with people walking and kids playing. Once they had taken their seats, the conversation became very serious.

"We need to talk about us," Mabel said. "I don't want to stay here and work in the candy factory any longer than I have to."

"How do you feel about moving back to Winnebago?"

"It will be hard to face my parents and other members of my family if I become your wife. Then again, it's no one's business but ours. Maybe we could move away from Winnebago and start new someplace else, like my folks did. When we left Iowa, we didn't have much, but what Pa had was enough to get started in the store."

"I don't know of any other place. Winnebago has always been my home, and I can work, maybe start my own harness shop someday."

"How would you get enough money to start your own business?"

Edward shrugged. "Maybe I could borrow from the agency. I hear that they have a credit department, and you can borrow money if you are a landowner, and I am."

"Well, that's a start." Mabel thought for a while. "Here is what we will do; between now and a year from now, you save all of your money, and I will save all of my money. You go and talk to the agency about a loan."

"What about your father?"

"I don't think he really cares if you are an Indian; it's just what the other white people in town will say if one of his daughters marries an Indian. That's what bothers him the most. Everything considered, he would probably rather have me married off than at home and having one more mouth to feed. I think that was one of the reasons he put me down here in Kansas City."

"You're probably right about not caring if I am an Indian. He does seem like an honest man."

"It's just the embarrassment for him and Ma that they should have to put up with this kind of talk. It doesn't bother me if you're an Indian." Her eyes sparkled. "In fact, it's kind of exciting."

The week flew by, and when it was time to say good-bye, the plan was set.

They stood quietly side by side on the platform, waiting for the train to come in.

"I have already started to count the days until we will be back together again," she told him. "After today, it will only be 364!"

He hugged her. "May 31, 1910."

The announcement that it was time to board the train to Omaha was a sad moment for the two young lovers. They held on to each other until the very last minute and then kissed; when Edward got on board, he stood in the doorway and waved to her.

She waved back and wiped the tears from her face. Soon the only thing that she could see was the caboose. It just kept getting smaller and smaller, and soon it was out of sight. She turned slowly and walked back to her room.

Edward slept most of the way to Omaha, and when he wasn't sleeping, he was making plans. He had to get back to work. He had to save more money. He had to see about getting a loan from the agency to buy a harness shop. If that failed, then maybe he could get a loan to start farming. He could farm his grandfather's land by the Omaha Creek.

It would be late at night when he would arrive on the reservation, and that was fine with him—less of a crowd to see him.

"I didn't hear you come in last night," his grandfather said as he walked into the kitchen the next morning when Edward was finishing his breakfast.

"You'd have to be an Indian to hear me," teased Edward.

"I used to be an Indian," said the old man with a smile on his face.

"I'll see you later this afternoon."

At work, Joe was very glad to see him. "We have a rush job on a harness set," he said as soon as Edward walked in. "I told them that you could have it done in two days."

"I'll do my best, but I will need more leather supplies, thread, and needles, maybe some more rivets. I'll turn this order in on my lunch break."

Edward was busy all morning, and on his lunch break, he made his way to the store.

"Edward, how are you today?" asked Mr. Wilcox.

"I am fine today," he said handing him the list. "I need to place an order for more supplies."

Looking over the order, Mr. Wilcox told him that he could have it filled by next Monday.

"That will be fine," said Ed.

"Have you heard any news from Mabel?" Mr. Wilcox asked.

"Yes, I did. She sent me a letter last week."

"She sent us a letter too," Wilcox said quickly. "She said that she really likes it in Kansas City and will be staying down there."

Edward knew that this was a lie, but he went along with it. He shrugged. "Very good."

Mr. Wilcox gave Edward a strange look. The news didn't seem to bother him in the least. *Maybe he doesn't care anymore.*

It was all Edward could do to keep from smiling at Mr. Wilcox, because he knew better—he knew better than all of them, but that was his secret.

At the agency the next day, Edward inquired about a loan. The secretary called Mr. Robinson, who came out to greet him. "Mr. Hatchett, please come into my office so we can talk," Mr. Robinson said.

This was the first time anyone had called him *Mr.* Hatchett, although he had always called the white men Mister.

"You say that you want a loan to start a business?"

"Yes, I would like to own my own harness shop."

"You can make and repair harnesses and do leatherwork?"

"Yes, I can. I'm presently working for a blacksmith in town."

"Where did you learn this trade?"

"I have a diploma from Genoa. I completed their harness course."

This got Mr. Robinson's attention. "I would like to see this diploma, if you don't mind."

"I will have to bring it in tomorrow."

"That will be fine, and I will have some papers for you to fill out. Also, do you own any Indian land?"

"Yes, I do. My father left me some land."

"Let me explain to you how we go about giving a loan out to individuals. We look up your allotment and see how much land you own, and then we determine how much you can pay back and how much revenue is made from your land. So the more land you own, the better you are on getting approved for a loan."

This made sense to Edward, but he didn't know how much land he owned.

The next morning Edward rolled up his diploma and placed it with his lunch. It was a large piece of heavy paper that was hard to roll up, and he would have to be careful not to damage it. Once inside the shop, he placed it well under his workbench so no one could see it. Later that afternoon, he returned to the agency to see Mr. Robinson. Edward could feel the butterflies growing in his stomach with each footstep. Soon he was at the threshold of the agency building.

"I have gone over your allotments, and you have many parcels," Mr. Robinson told him. "This is good for you."

"Good. Also, I brought my diploma today." Edward unrolled the large document; Mr. Robinson studied the diploma, checking all of the signatures and dates. He seemed pleased with what he saw.

"I will start your paperwork right away. Why don't you come back in two days and see me? You will need to fill out this form and complete a proposal and a budget sheet," Mr. Robinson told him. "You should look around for a place to set up your business. Once you figure that out, you can figure what your rent and any utilities will be."

A smile came across Ed's face. He knew then that very soon, he would have his own shop.

Mr. Robinson had a smile on his face too, because Ed would be his very first Indian-owned business on the Winnebago reservation. Ed walked back to town with more spring in his step. He knew which building he wanted. It was vacant, and it would need some repair.

Later that evening, Ed wrote a letter to Mabel. He told her of the day's events. He knew this would bring a smile to her face and that this would give her more reason to come back to Winnebago. He told her about the building he was considering and how much fixing up it would need but that this was no problem, because he could do the work himself. He didn't know how much money he would get from the agency, but it would be enough.

As he continued his letter, he mentioned that he would need to tell his boss, Joe, about his new business venture, and he wondered how it would affect him and their friendship. Ed had used the figures from Joe's harness repair bills to help him fill out the budget form. He knew how much leather cost, and he knew how much Joe marked it up. Plus even the short time he'd spent in business school helped him. In two days, Ed had all of the paperwork filled out, and he returned it to Mr. Robinson's office.

Now there was nothing to do but wait. He didn't say a word to anyone about his new business. The only person who knew about it was hundreds of miles away in Kansas City, and she wouldn't breathe a word of it to anyone. This was their secret.

Time has a way of dragging itself when you're waiting for something, and this is what Ed was going through, just marking time and working at the blacksmith's shop. Ed made the trip to the post office every day after work. Sometimes he would get a little excited when he walked through the door, only to find nothing. One week went by, and not a word from Mabel or the agency.

During the weekends, he busied himself fixing up the Grants' place. He replaced the broken screens and cut the weeds around the house. He looked forward to going to work on Monday—not that he liked his job that well, but he looked forward to getting the mail. There might be a letter from Mabel or maybe a letter from the agency.

Monday nothing, Tuesday nothing, Wednesday nothing.

He could handle not getting a letter from the agency, but where was his letter from his woman? Thursday rolled around, and Ed walked to the post office just as he always did; and to his surprise, there were two letters, one from Mabel and the other from the agency. He tore open the letter from Mabel and savored every word of encouragement. He could just imagine her standing and talking to him as he read her letter. He could hear her voice. He could see her lips move with every word that came out of her beautiful mouth. It was times like this that he didn't want to be bothered by anyone, but he was snapped back into reality by his old friend Alex Horn. "*Mr.* Hatchett!" he called out.

"Mr. Horn, what can I do for you?"

"I hear they call you *Mr.* Hatchett out at the agency."

"And why would they call me that?"

"Because you will be the only Indian in town who owns a business."

Ed wondered what else they said about him. He didn't tell his old friend about the letter he held in his hand from the agency.

"We will see. Maybe they are right, and maybe they are wrong. We will see," said Edward.

The two Genoa friends talked for a while, and then they parted ways. Ed made sure that he was alone when he opened the letter from the agency. "After careful review, we have decided to grant you a loan," the letter read. "You will need to see Mr. Robinson on Monday."

Ed's hands were shaking as he finished reading the letter. "What a day, what a day!" he said over and over again. Ed wasn't one to show his emotions, so as he made his way home, every now and then, he would stop and read both of the letters. Once he got home, he tried to tell his grandparents about the letter from the agency. He really didn't know if they understood. It was hard for them to know that their Ku-nu was going to have his own business in Winnebago. But when they finally understood what Ed was trying to tell them, a smile came over the old man's face. "You will be working on the white man's harnesses for yourself?" he asked. "And they will pay you and just you?"

"Yes, that is correct. I will be working for myself and not Joe Williams anymore."

Ed asked the old man if he would like to catch some fish from the creek. The old man liked to sit and fish; but mostly, Ed knew, he like to sit and talk about the old days, and Ed liked to listen.

This time, he told Ed of the great move from Minnesota and the hard times up in the Dakotas and, finally, the move to Winnebago. He mentioned a lot of names that were gone. They had died with the person. There had been no one to carry on the name, or the Indian schools had changed the names of the children, and now they had white man names. "You say that you no longer know the ways of the medicine lodge, and it doesn't look like you are going to learn them; and if that is your wish, I don't blame you, but let me tell you a story that happened when you were about two or three years old."

He started out by taking a big bite of the plug tobacco. "They said that a white man by the name of Ken Johansen came to the northern part of our reservation, probably up by Homer, Nebraska. That used to be in our reservation back then. He bought a run-down white man's farm. He fixed it up and called it the Omaha Creek Trading Post He bought furs and Indian stuff and gave the young bucks whiskey instead of money or goods. He was told by the Indian agent that he could not sell or trade whiskey to the Indians, so Ken got into the mercantile business. He would sell dry goods, canned goods, and cloth. He even extended them credit. This gave him invaluable information.

"He met Indians that had plenty of land, good farmland, and he also met young single women, and some of the young tough Indian bucks. He met Orville Crowson, a big young tough Indian boy. Orville was a good boy. He liked to listen to his grandfather and his uncle Joseph, who was named after Chief Joseph of the Nez Perce tribe. Orville was a bright boy. He learned fast. He could read a little and write his name. It didn't take long for Orville to take up with the white man's ways. He learned to plays cards and drink whiskey. He hung out at the trading post most of the day, and Ken liked him to be there, just in case some of the Indians might give Ken a hard time. Soon Orville was working for Ken. Orville learned how to cheat his brother Indians. At first it bothered him, but every time, Ken would tell him, 'That's just how business is done; it's called markup.'

"Leonard Crowson was a very industrious man. Even when we lived in the Blue Earth of Minnesota, Leonard had horses and cattle, and he learned the white man's language. He could barter with the white man. He enjoyed working the land, and he was a family man. He had a wife, one son, Orville, and a daughter named Joan. She was a teenager but looked more like a young adult. She had fair skin, long auburn hair, and a smooth complexion. She was named by the missionaries who were in the area long before this land was a reservation; they named her after the saint Joan of Arc. Leonard let them do that just to show them that he was an honest man and that he could live with the white man and his religion.

"Leonard had some of the best bottomland on the reservation. His land had access to water. The agency had built them a government house. They had to stay and farm the land. The family had to provide their own furniture and other household items. Their house was the first-built government home on the reservation. I think the government wanted to show the rest of us that if you farmed the land, you could get a house too.

"Leonard didn't like to have his son working at the trading post, but there were no other jobs around. Leonard Crowson didn't like this credit thing either. He didn't like loaning money or anything to anyone. At first Leonard didn't trade at the post, but times were hard, and the rations didn't always show up. Orville told his father that it was all right to trade at the post because Ken would take the money out of his pay. Leonard agreed to that. But in reality, Ken Johansen wanted Leonard's land and his daughter. His plan was to get the father in debt and keep the son drunk and on his side. It would be a challenge. Ken liked to look at Joan; he would always wait on her when she came in. He would make small talk with her and even try to flirt with her, but most of the time, she would just smile and move on.

"One day Ken Johansen told Mrs. Crowson that she could have a new bed, table, and chairs on credit; or she could come and work for him at the trading post or clean his home. Mr. Crowson agreed to this only if she worked it off on her own. Ken Johansen had marked up the furniture so much that it would take years for her to pay it off, but the deal was made. Mrs. Crowson worked every day. She cleaned his house, the trading post, and cooked for him, but the bill never went down. She also heard how Ken talked about the Indians. He made it known that he didn't like Indians. He would call them names behind their backs. He called them smelly red-faced thieves and worse.

"That year was hot, and there was very little rain. Many cattle died. The corn didn't grow. Many Indians went to the trading post for food; they were given food and supplies on credit. By spring, they had lost most of their land and were still hungry. Mrs. Crowson was still working off her bill at the store. Her son did little to help the family, and he just hung around the trading post, doing odd jobs for Ken.

"'It has been many months since you started working for me, Mrs. Crowson, and you still owe me quite a bit of money,' Ken said. 'I think your daughter should come in from time to time and help you work off this bill.'

"She said she would ask her.

"Leonard was also having his own problems, with cattle dying off and no corn to sell. He had to feed his family. This would be a very hard decision for him, but he would ask Ken Johansen for food and supplies on credit. Ken told him, 'Leonard your word is as good as gold here. You can have whatever you like. And if you don't mind, I will hire your daughter to help your wife. This will help pay off the bill sooner.'

"Ken Johansen could barely keep the grin off his face, when Mr. Crowson left the trading post. He gave out a big war whoop. This was just the beginning. Soon he would have the daughter, and there was nothing anybody could do about it.

"Ken Johansen had all of the land deeds signed or had the owners put their mark on them. Ken put his friend Orville to work, and his job was to run the Indians off on Ken Johansen's new land. The Indians resented Orville for doing this to them. Some of them were his own kinfolk; he just told them that he was doing his job. Several of the tribal members went to Leonard's home to complain about his son. 'I don't know what to tell you. I don't like it either,' Leonard told them. 'Have you gone to the agency and talked with them?'

"Nobody said anything. Leonard hated Ken Johansen. He hated him because he had his son doing his dirty work. He hated Ken Johansen because he had his wife and daughter working for him, and still the bill was high. He hated him because he owed him money, and if things didn't get turned around, he would be turning over his land and house to this devil white man.

"The months went by, and still no change. One day Ken called Orville into his office. He had all of their bills laid out on the table, plus Orville's gambling debts, IOUs, the furniture, food, and supply bills. The total came to a whopping fifteen hundred dollars. 'I can't carry you and your family anymore. I will need to have your father come in and sign over his land so I can get this matter cleared up,' said Ken.

"A few days later, when Mrs. Crowson and Joan were getting ready to leave, Ken told Joan to stay because he wanted to talk to her. Once the mother was gone, Ken told Joan to go into the bedroom. He said that he had some things to give to her.

"While she walked into the bedroom, Ken closed the main door and put the closed sign up. He hurried to the bedroom, where he pushed Joan down on the bed; she tried to fight him off, but he was too big. An hour and a half later, Joan ran home crying. She ran into the house where Orville was. He asked her what had happened to her. She told him, and he got very angry. He stormed out of the house, and he made his way to the trading post. 'Ken Johansen, you son of a bitch, I am coming after you,' said Orville when he got there.

"'I knew you would, so come in, and we will talk about it,' said Ken.

"Orville rushed through the door and was met with a double-barrel shotgun blast. The blast knocked him backward out into the dirt. He was dead by the time he hit the ground. Several Indians gathered around him. Then they sent someone to tell Leonard that his son was dead.

"Leonard got to his house about the same time a runner came to tell the family about Orville. Oh, what a blow to the family. Leonard took a rifle and made his way to the trading post. He didn't make it to the trading post. Ken Johansen ambushed him just outside of the trading post and called it self-defense.

"It would be days before the agent could get things straightened out, and when the dust settled, Ken Johansen was found innocent. They ruled that he was protecting himself in both of the shootings, and he denied the rape charge. It was a sad day for the Crowson family and the other Indians that lost their land too. Mrs. Crowson had been forced to sign over their family allotment. In a gesture of goodwill, Ken Johansen said that the mother and Joan could live on the farm for now and that they would work something out.

"Mrs. Crowson was just heartbroken over the loss of her husband and son. Then one day, Joan suggested they send for their Day-ga Joseph. Late that night, the mother thought about her brother-in-law, and by morning, she had made up her mind to have him come over and take care of the evil that lived among them. In two days, Day-ga Joseph was at the Crowson farm. He told his sister-in-law that he would sleep out in the tool shed and that he didn't want to be bothered. He would need one thing from his sister-in-law, and that was a piece of hair from

Ken Johansen's body. It didn't make any difference what part of the body the hair came from. Mrs. Crowson still did some cleanup work for Ken at the trading post, she was told that a few debts still remained; therefore it was very easy to get some of his hair. She wrapped it up in a handkerchief and brought it to Day-ga Joseph; he thanked her and said that was all he needed.

"'Don't worry any more. This evil will be taken care of,' said Day-ga Joseph.

"After two weeks, there was no change in Ken Johansen. Emily Crowson asked Joseph why nothing was happening. He told her to be patient, that he had his way of taking care of *wa-kakd* (shit). No more was said about the issue. But things were starting to change in Ken Johansen's body. He didn't feel good and had a strange odor on his breath, but he just passed it off as the bad whiskey. In a couple of days, Ken Johansen was still in bed by nine o'clock in the morning. The following day, he didn't even open the store. He sent word to have his friend James stop over. James came over later in the day and told Ken that the next day he would take him to Sioux City, Iowa, to a doctor.

"The road to Sioux City was rough and long, and the sun bore down on the smelly body of Ken Johansen. The doctor had nothing to tell Ken. 'I can't find anything wrong with you other than you have exceptionally bad breath and that you have a strong body odor,' the doctor told him. 'Maybe you should think of taking a bath and brushing your teeth.'

"This offended Ken. No one had ever talked to him like that. The odor coming from Ken's body was terrible. No one could stay in the trading post very long, and now he was in great pain. Emily told her brother Joseph about Ken. He just smiled.

"Ken no longer ate or drank any kind of liquid. He couldn't get out of his bed. It was a miserable life. Strange as it was, no one cared about the poor white man, and no one came to see him. Ken's body ached. His joints ached, and his head hurt. His breath smelled like decaying flesh. It was his turn to be called a smelly old white man.

"By the next week, Ken went into convulsions that seemed to have no end; the stench was unbearable, and the pain great. Emily went home to tell her brother about the poor white man, but Joseph wasn't there. She went to the shed, but she couldn't find him. She knocked on the shed door, but there was no answer, so she walked in. She called his name, but still no answer. Emily could smell something like rotten eggs. She found the smell coming from a small jar. She picked it up and took it outside. It was some kind of liquid. She sloshed it around and gave it a heave.

"At that very instant, Ken Johansen sat straight up in his bed and gave a big heave and threw up everything in his body. When they found him the next morning, he had thrown up his stomach, lung tissue, liver, and most of his large intestines. All of this was lying on the floor. If they could have done an autopsy on him, they would have found nothing in his upper torso.

"I am telling you this because this really happened. Day-ga Joseph was a member of the medicine lodge. Your family was brought up in the medicine lodge. You used to go to the meetings, even when you were very young. I am telling you this because you could join us again. You are a smart man. You could help us. You understand the white man's language, and this could help us." His grandfather took a deep breath and stopped. He had finished.

Ed just sat there. He didn't want to offend the old man. There was a long silence, and finally, Ed spoke up and asked his grandfather if he knew this family.

"Yes, I knew them, but all of them moved back to Wisconsin. It was too hard for them to stay here," said Cho-ka.

"Could you make this kind of medicine?" asked Ed.

"There are a few of us that can do these things, but you young people aren't following the longhouse ways. The white man's religion has entered your mind, and that is all you know. Most of our powerful medicine men are going back to our ancestral land in Wisconsin. This is why we need young intelligent men like you back in the lodge," said the old man.

"I can't give you an answer now," Edward told him. "But I will think on it." Later that evening, when Ed was lying in bed, he thought about the story that his grandfather had told him. He had heard of students telling stories like this, but he never believed them. He just thought that they were making it up or adding more to the story.

When he went to church that Sunday, he decided to see what the pastor thought. After the service, he told him about his grandfather's story. The pastor stood still for quite a while, and then he finally spoke. "You know I have heard stories like this before, but I have never seen any of it. I think they're just stories. These old longhouse members are trying to get you young people back into the old ways, but you must think in the modern times, Ed. Do you really think that people can kill someone with just a single strand of his hair? I don't put any credence into any of the old Indian nonsense."

With that, Ed felt a little better, but still not quite sure if this was the right answer to tell his grandfather. He made up his mind not to say anything, hoping it would just blow away. When Ed got home, everyone was up. His grandparents knew where he had been, and they didn't say anything. Ed greeted them with a "Good morning" and went to change his clothes. For the most part, it was a quiet afternoon. Ed did a few chores around the outside of the house and kept pretty much to himself.

Monday, Ed entered the blacksmith shop before Joe got there, put on the coffeepot, and started his work. "Now that's what I call a good employee," Joe said as he walked in, "someone who has the coffee made and is working."

"I thought I would get an early start and work through lunch today and leave a half hour earlier. I have a couple of errands that I have to do this afternoon."

"That will be fine," said the blacksmith.

Ed worked like a man possessed; he had to keep his mind on the harnesses and not on the loan. At three o'clock, Ed walked out of the shop and headed for the agency. When he got there, Mr. Robinson came out of his office and shook Ed's hand. "I have some great news for you. After we reviewed your land allotments and asked around about you and got a letter from Genoa Indian School, we decided that your business would be a great asset to the town of Winnebago. Plus, they need a good harness repairman in this community. We just need you to sign on the line."

Ed signed the contract, and Mr. Robinson gave him a check for one thousand dollars.

"If for some reason you find yourself running short, let us know. You do have a five-hundred-dollar line of credit here, but we hope that you won't need all of it."

Ed floated out of the office. This was the biggest thing that had ever happened to him. This was the biggest check he had ever seen, and it had his name on it. Ed had lined up a building that would work for his harness shop. It had plenty of room for his worktables, supply bins, and a heavy-duty sewing machine. Through contacts from the Genoa school, he had information on getting a secondhand heavy-duty sewing machine. The Sears and Roebuck catalog could supply him with needles, threads, and more for this machine. Ed was visualizing his new shop while he walked home that afternoon.

Chapter 13

Ed's Harness Shop

Edward got a rental contract on the building, made of list of things to order for his new business, and stopped by the Wilcox store to order leather and hardware he'd need to build his worktables. He did not ask about Mabel, but George Wilcox insisted on telling him that Mabel was doing really well and that she had met a young man there in Kansas City. Ed knew that this was a lie, but he said nothing.

"This is quite an order," George said, looking down the list. "I didn't know that Joe was doing such a great business down there."

"Business is good," replied Ed. He felt he didn't owe any explanation to George Wilcox or anyone else.

Now, all he had to do was to tell Joe about his new adventure, and this would have to be done soon because a lot of people had loose lips in town. He hoped that they would still be friends. "You're a good man, Ed," Joe said when he walked into work the next day. "The doors are open, and the coffee is made. What would I do without you?"

This wasn't what Edward wanted to hear, but it was good to know that some people still appreciated his efforts.

"If you have a few minutes, Joe, I need to talk with you," said Ed.

"I do have a few minutes, so let's hear it."

"I don't know if you have heard by now, but I am going to open my own harness shop here in town. I know how people like to talk, so I thought I would tell you first."

"I haven't heard a word of it in town," Joe told him. "And I can't blame a young man like you for wanting to set out on your own. You are a smart man, Ed, and to be very honest with you, I could use the extra space here. I only did this harness repair as a favor for some of the farmers, and now it has turned into a full-time job, thanks to you. I don't have any problems with you taking the harness business, and I would be glad to send you customers. When do you open the doors?"

"In one week, I will start taking small jobs. I ordered a secondhand sewing machine, which will allow me to do heavier jobs, even repair shoes and boots."

"That is very good. We could use a good cobbler in town!"

Ed made a poster about the new harness shop that would be opening soon in town. Some of the customers asked who was going to operate the new shop, and when he said he was, he got some strange looks. Some of them jerked their heads back and said, "An Indian?" And others told Joe they wouldn't go there. Joe told them that it was Ed who did all of the harness work in his shop, and they would be crazy not to use his services.

"You know, Ed, this will be an uphill battle for you until you prove that you can handle the job," said Joe.

Ed knew it would be an uphill climb. He saw how the Indians were second-class citizens on their own reservation. He saw firsthand the hate and prejudice toward his brother Indians. He himself was feeling the vehemence of a white man. This was only the beginning of his struggles to make a living in his own community and his own reservation.

Eddie Priest asked Ed if he would like to go out to the old Hatchett allotment down by the hairpin turn. Eddie knew that his grandfather was hosting a meeting in the longhouse that weekend and thought maybe Ed needed to get away for a while.

"I would like to go over there," Edward admitted. "It has been a long time since I have been there. Is the old place still standing?"

"Yes, it is. In fact, one of our cousins lives out there. I'll pick you up tomorrow, and we will head out."

The next morning was bright and sunny as the two made there way out of town. "There sure are a lot trees growing up all over the place," said Ed as they looked down from a high vantage point on their way out of town.

"Yeah, the white man or white farmers brought them," said Eddie.

"I remember when there were no trees here, no fences either, no roads, just tall prairie grass."

The two men soon came to the four corners; the two wagon roads crossed on top of a small dirt mound. In the summer, the four corners were dry and dusty, but in the rain, it was a mess; the team really had to struggle to get through the intersection.

A mile east of the four corners was the old Hatchett house. It sat about a quarter of a mile off the road. It too had a challenging driveway. "The driveway has been used." There were well-worn wheel tracks in the road. He looked up at the house. "I was born in the upstairs of that house," Edward said.

"Do you know where your father is buried?" asked Eddie.

Edward shook his head no.

Eddie turned the wagon into the long driveway. He had to hold on to the reins tightly, and he kept pulling on them hard. It was quite steep, and from there, it was all uphill. Finally, he made a left turn and pulled the wagon into the yard, and both men got out and started to walk around the property.

A man came out of the old house. "Can I help you two?" he asked. He had a weathered-looking face.

"I am Eddie Priest, and this is my cousin Ed Hatchett."

"You're family then. *Ed Hatchett* … You're William Hatchett's grandson, right?"

"Yes, I am, and we came out to visit you and see how the old house is doing."

"As you can see, it's still standing. It could use some repairs and such. By the way, I am Lo Cloud; some of the old Indians had a hard time pronouncing Lawrence, so they just starting calling me Lo, and the name stuck," said Lo.

"So you are kinfolk?" asked Ed.

"I'm William Hatchett's nephew. Our name remained Cloud, when William changed his to Hatchett after a great battle that he was in. My family never changed our name. We just stayed Cloud," said Lo. "I hope you boys can stay for lunch. We have some *wa-sha* (corn) soup that we had dried from last year. We Clouds use deer in our wa-sha. Some other Indians use any kind of meat. I think it tastes better with deer meat."

The three of them sat down at the table. Soon Lo's wife came out of the kitchen with a large pot of wa-sha and fry bread. "It really smells good, Mrs. Cloud." The two cousins had said it in unison. They both laughed.

Lo introduced his wife to Ed and Eddie. He told them that he and his wife had been together for twenty years and that all of her family had moved back to Wisconsin. She didn't want to leave this area, so she stayed, and they got together. He went on to say that they had no children, but from time to time, they took in some of their kinfolk's children. Lo told the two that when William died, no one wanted to live in his house. "I guess they all wanted to live closer to town. We needed a place to live, so the remaining Hatchett family said we could live here. It is quiet and tucked away from the road.

"I like to think that my Day-ga is still here in this house. He built most of the outbuildings and all of the fences," said Lo.

After the meal, the three of them walked around the old Hatchett allotment. It needed some repairs and some fence mending. "I think there is a lot of history on this property," said Lo.

The two boys agreed with him.

"I was born upstairs in this old house, and I lived out here for a while, I guess, until my father ran away with John Rave's wife to Wisconsin," said Ed.

A silence fell on the group for a while as they continued to walk around the property.

Ed asked Lo if he knew the man-eating snake story.

"Yes, I have heard about this story. They said that William could talk with this reptile. Some say that he could conjure up this monster, and still others say that this was his payback weapon. Anyway no one has seen this snake in a long time. They say that this snake lived just down in that valley," he said, pointing east. "Your grandfather was a powerful medicine man. He could do many things, and I hear that he had no enemies. Why would anyone want to make trouble against a powerful man like him? I guess that is why some of the people on this reservation don't like you, Ed, because you have this rich inheritance, but you don't follow the medicine lodge and its way of life."

"When I left here," Ed said, "all I knew was the Winnebago way of life, but at Genoa, they told us that it would be to our advantage to learn the white man's way of life, and the sooner the better. I found that it was better to learn the white man's ways and to let go of the old Indian ways. Many of our young Indians took many terrible beatings for talking in the native tongue. I was very young, and I didn't know what to do, so I watched and learned the white man's ways and his religion. It's the only way that I know now," said Ed.

"You could relearn the longhouse ways, couldn't you?"

"I suppose I could, but that's not what I believe in now."

The three men sat under a large oak tree, where they talked about the old days. Lo knew many of the old stories, and he told the two cousins about them. Some were funny, others were true, and some were just unbelievable. It was four o'clock in the afternoon when they went into the house and sat down with Lo and his wife. She served them coffee and fry bread. After the coffee, everyone sat around the table, telling old stories again and talking of those who had passed on.

Lo told the boys about the Hatchett drum. "My father built it with your father, when Louis was just a boy," he told Edward. "I was a baby then, but the story is one that we were all taught. They cut down a huge cottonwood tree and used the bottom part to make the drum circle. It took weeks to do all they did—burn out the center, carve it, and soak deerskins to stretch across the opening. And when they finished, the Hatchett drum was big enough for something like eight singers to sit around it."

"What did they sing?" Edward asked.

"William Hatchett's song," Lo said. He stared off into the distance. *Every warrior has his Own Song* and your grandfather was quite a warrior. It's a song about how brave he was and how he could see spirits rising from the battlefield before it became a battlefield."

"Who made up the song?" Ed asked.

"That I don't know." Lo shrugged. "So much of the past has been buried with our ancestors."

"What happened to the Hatchett drum?"

"I don't know the answer to that either. Some say that when the old man died, they buried the drum with him, but I don't believe that. Others say that he had it destroyed, and others say that it was just too old, and it fell apart." He sighed. "So much history is fading." He turned to them. "You two boys need to learn the Hatchett song and to make sure it stays in the family. Songs like this should always be passed down to the next generation."

Ed told Lo that there was a longhouse meeting this weekend. Lo sheepishly admitted he knew, but he had other things to do. "I know that this is not the Indian way. I know that I should be right there, right now. Since we became farmers, though, I don't have the time to go to meetings that last all weekend. I guess I am getting a bit like the white man too. Do you boys belong to the medicine lodge?"

Both of them shook their heads no.

As the two cousins made their way down the driveway, they looked to their right at the valley where the man-eater snake used to live.

"Do you believe that story about the snake?" asked Ed.

"I do," said Eddie.

The team and wagon rumbled down the old dusty dirt road that so many Indians had traversed. It was one of two main roads going to the river. Other than a few government houses and a few hard-scrabble farms, not much had changed. Some of the Indians still lived the old way like those few that lived down in the Big Bear Hollow. Most of them made their monthly trip to the agency to get their rations and pick up supplies and tobacco in town. Some of the younger Indians liked to live in town where they could find work and even ride the trains to Omaha or Sioux City, Iowa. They liked to think of themselves as the modern Indians. Most could carry on a good conversation in English; others talked with a broken accent.

"Let's go through the agency on our way to town," said Eddie.

"That's fine with me."

The agency was a group of government houses, large barns, outbuildings, and the official office of the superintendent of the agency. The agency employed many white and Indian employees. The agency was set up after the reservation was put in place. It handled all of the affairs of the Indians: rent, housing, rations, education, and much more.

"When I left here, there was no agency. There was an old ration building, and that was it. Believe it or not, this road was here then," said Ed.

"Yeah, it feels like it," said Eddie as they both adjusted their seats after going over a huge rut.

The two men rumbled through the agency, turned to the right, and headed toward town. As the two got out at Ed's harness shop, they noticed a sack under the seat of the wagon. "What do you have in the sack?" asked Eddie.

"I don't know. It isn't mine."

Ed pulled the sack from under the seat and found it had some fry bread and gooseberries in it. Lo must have put it there. "Well, it looks like we have our supper already made."

They looked at each other and smiled. Ed laid out the floor plan for his new shop, and soon the two of them were hard at work. When they broke for supper, they gave thanks to God, Lo, and Lo's wife for the humble supper that she had prepared for them.

"I would like to place the heating stove right here," Ed said, pointing to his right. "I will need to pick up some dishes, a coffeepot, and some silverware, just in case I might have to stay here overnight, like tonight."

"What do you mean stay overnight?"

"I just don't feel right about going home tonight while they are holding a longhouse meeting. I will stay here in the shop. I brought some bedding here the other day."

"It was a good day," Eddie said when he got up to leave. "I really enjoyed going out to the old house. I had never met our cousin Lo. He is quite an interesting man."

Ed wrote to Mabel and told her of visiting the old Hatchett farm down by the hairpin turn and about all of the work he and Eddie had done on his shop. It had been a good day. Ed surveyed his harness shop; he liked the progress that they had made, blew out the lamp, lay down on his bedroll ... and thought about Mabel.

The shop needed a sign. Ed made a simple sign that read Ed's Harness Repair and Leather Works. He had painted it on a board. He thought if business was good that he would have a sign custom-made for him. After several hits from his hammer, the sign was in place. The sight filled him with pride. A few of the local Indians came by and looked, but they never said anything to him. Some of them were curious, and others were just plain jealous. Ed just kept working. He wanted to be ready to open on Monday.

On June 28, 1909, Ed's Harness Repair and Leather Works opened its doors for business. Ed had put on the coffeepot and waited. A few orders came in, but it was a slow day. By the middle of the week, business picked up, and soon Ed had work on back order. Alex Horn stopped by on Thursday. "Nice place you have here, Mr. Hatchett."

"Thank you, Mr. Horn."

Then the two just started to laugh. "How are the white people treating you?" Alex Horn wanted to know.

"Sometimes better than my own people."

"Well, that can be expected; you are the first Indian to have a business here on the reservation, a business that most of the white people think Indians shouldn't have."

"Maybe in the future, I should get a white partner."

Again, both of them just laughed.

"You mean Mabel, don't you?"

"In fact, I could use her right now. I need a good bookkeeper. Maybe then only half of the white people would be mad at me."

"I think that if you and Mabel get married, there will be more than white people mad at you two."

That night's letter to Mabel was filled with excitement, telling her how he looked forward to getting the new sewing machine. This would let him repair boots and shoes, something that was really needed in Winnebago. He went on to tell Mabel that he really needed a good bookkeeper and asked her if she knew where he could find one.

Business really grew after the heavy-duty sewing machine was put in. He had Eddie Priest work for him from time to time, and he thought about hiring a part-time or full-time employee. He hadn't realized just how much shoe repair was needed on the reservation. Joe Williams sent new customers to see Ed if they needed leatherwork done or harness repair. Sometimes Ed's hands would get stiff and sore from pushing and pulling the large needles. He always looked forward to the weekends to rest a little.

Mr. Robinson stopped by to check in. "I knew that you were the one. In fact, we all knew that you would do fine. Keep up the good work, and if there is anything that we can do for you, let me know."

This was a nice pat on the back, and it was good to know that he still had a credit line left. Bill paying was all part of doing business, and one bill that Ed needed to pay was for his supply of firewood. He thought about gathering it himself, but he really didn't have the time, and there were plenty of Indians who sold firewood.

The plan was made to bring Mabel back to the reservation on May 31 of 1910. She would then be of age, and there was nothing that her father or her aunt could do about it. This would be a very touchy situation; Mabel might not even be able to walk into her father's house. Edward might be the only friend she had in town. Going against all odds, the young lovers made their plans via the U.S. mail service. They talked about everything that might be a roadblock. Making money seemed to be taken care of for now. Their wedding day would take place at the county courthouse. They even talked about who would be the best man and the bridesmaid.

When the fall weather rolled in, Ed had his firewood in place, the heating stove fired up, and a new coffeepot on the stove. The summer business had been steady once the farmers and the locals accepted him, and they knew that he did a good job. The fall harvest was hard on equipment, so Ed geared up with more supplies. He was hoping that he might pick up more shoe repair too. He felt that people would get their shoes and boots fixed before cold weather set in. He couldn't believe how good business was. Sometimes it was hard not to tell his cousin Eddie that he really was making good money on the reservation. The only person who knew his secret was Mabel, and she would never tell anyone.

January and February were very cold and snowy. Business was slow, but there was enough coming in to make the loan payments, pay himself a salary and put a little away, and count the days on the calendar until May 31 when Mabel would be back. It was hard to get his grandparents' rations. The lines were long, and everybody wanted their food and needed more blankets because they were cold. The families who lived in the earthen lodges were quite comfortable in the cold weather. They were the same families who lived in teepees in the summer—the traditional families. Ed never forgot his grandmother's tobacco. He still traded some of their rations with the stores in town. He liked the look on her face when he brought home the chew; she always got the first pull of the plug.

Sometimes on the long and cold weekends, Ed would take his grandmother over to her friends to play cards or gamble. Sometimes the games would last well into the night. Other times, he would take his grandfather to a longhouse meeting, which would last two days. Other days they might go to a clan feast. Sometimes these lasted many days, and a lot of people would show up.

March was cold and windy, and the leather business was slow, but Ed knew that in a matter of weeks, the farmers would bring in their harnesses for repair and their work boots for resoles. It would be just be a matter of time before he got busy.

In April, the harness repair work picked up, and Ed was putting in longer hours at the shop. He even went in on Saturdays just to keep up with the workload. Indians were bringing in their shoes and boots for repair. Most of them accepted him and his business, glad there was somebody who could repair their footwear. One time a group of Indians brought in some heavy canvases to have Ed sew them together. They were making a sweat lodge and needed the two pieces sewn.

Others would have leather bags made or different kinds of belts that could be used on dance regalia. As the word spread that Ed could sew heavy canvas on his machine, other Indians from the Omaha tribe came in and had their tents repaired. Some even had him sew a whole new tent. Canvas was easier to work with than leather. He didn't mind doing this. It all paid the same. Because some of Indians paid him in trade, he always had mushrooms when they were in season, milkweed for soup, eggs, and even live chickens. Ed enjoyed going to work; he never knew who would walk through his door and want something different sewn up or patched.

And the countdown on the calendar was progressing nicely.

Chapter 14

The Marriage That Made History

Every time Ed looked at the calendar and saw it said "May," his pulse rate would pick up. May 31 would be here before he knew it. Mabel was having the same reaction. She had secretly purchased her train ticket to Winnebago. Her plan was to pack her bags and go out the door as though she was going to work, but instead, she would head down to the train station. She would not say anything to her aunt she would just leave.

The night of May 30, Mabel tried to get some sleep, but sleep was not possible. Finally, she got out of bed at 4:45 AM. She decided to just leave a letter for her aunt with some money to bring her up-to-date on her rent and any food that she had eaten. One thing she was not putting in this letter was a thank-you. She had been railroaded by her father and aunt, and she felt that no thanks were in order!

The letter was short: "I am going back to Winnebago. I am of age, and neither you nor my father can stop me. I have enclosed money for my rent and any food that I have eaten. Sincerely, Mabel."

At 6 AM, she left her aunt's home, leaving the letter on the kitchen table. Mabel felt free! She walked faster as she got closer to the train station. She inquired about the train leaving for Omaha and was told that it was on time and would be boarding in half an hour. She would have a small wait in Omaha for the train to Winnebago. When she boarded the train, she clutched her bag tight and made her way into the coach. She took a window seat and waited for the train to take her out

185

of her father's imposed sweatshop. The train lurched, chugged, jerked, and began to roll down the steel road that made its way north, Mabel was filled with excitement.

She was on her way!

Mabel dozed off for a long time and woke up just outside Omaha and then waited a half hour for the train to Winnebago. Stop after stop on the local, she finally heard the conductor shout, "Next stop Winnebago!" She found it hard to believe this was really happening. She had sent many letters to Winnebago, Nebraska, and she had received so many letters back. The northbound train picked up speed, but almost as soon as it did, the engineer backed off on the throttle and began to coast. They had arrived.

Mabel could see the platform on the station, and yes, she could see him standing right there, waiting for her. Her heart raced, the butterflies in her stomach all took flight. When her feet hit the platform, she felt a little wobbly, but she ran to Ed nonetheless. The two hugged and kissed. This turned many heads, but they didn't care.

"I am home," said Mabel.

"Yes, you are," replied Ed with a smile.

Their first stop was Edward's new shop. She loved the sign that hung above the door. "This is such a great spot for your shop!"

"Come in, and I will show you your new workstation or desk," said Ed.

Once inside, the young lovers embraced and kissed and talked, and embraced and kissed some more. "I guess we should go over to my father's store and let him know that I am back in town," Mabel said finally.

"Do you think they baked a cake for you?" asked Ed with a grin on his face.

"Well, did you?" she asked him. Then she winced. "I am scared. I don't know if I can enter their store, let alone their house."

As they made their way through town to the Wilcox store, every head turned and looked. They pulled up in front of the store, and Ed tied the team to the hitching post and helped Mabel down from the wagon.

"How do I look?" asked Mabel.

"You look like you just saw a ghost," said Ed.

Mabel walked up the steps and entered the store, and Ed followed her in; and at first, no one paid much attention. When Mabel walked over to the counter, her mother looked up. "Mabel," she gasped, "what are you doing here?"

Her father suddenly appeared from the back room. He did not look happy to see his daughter. "Yes, Mabel, what are you doing here?"

"I am home, and Ed Hatchett and I will be getting married on June the fourteenth, and I would like to know if I can stay here until then?"

Both of her parents looked flabbergasted and floored. "Do you think that you can just walk in here and tell us that and that we have nothing to say about it?" asked her father.

"It's my hope that we will get your blessing."

"I think not."

"It doesn't make any difference anyway. I am of age, and so is Ed."

George Wilcox knew that she was right, that there was nothing he could do to stop this wedding from happening. There was silence for a while, and then her mother spoke. "I suppose you will need a place to stay for a few days?"

"Yes, I will."

"You can stay here if it's all right with your father."

They all looked at George Wilcox. He looked out the window for a while, as if he didn't see them. "All right," he said finally, "but this is just until you get married, and don't think we will be going to the wedding. We have too much to do around here."

Mabel walked over and gave her mother a big hug and kiss. She walked over to her father and did the same. He returned the hug a little, but no one was saying "Welcome home, daughter." This was as good as she was going to get, she thought.

George Wilcox walked back into the office and continued with his bookwork. Mrs. Wilcox was very glad to see her daughter and was not surprised to know that she would soon marry Ed Hatchett. "Ed, I understand that you are doing very well in the harness shop," said Mrs. Wilcox.

"Business is good, but I could use a good bookkeeper," he teased. "Do you know where I can hire one?"

"Why, yes, you have one hanging on to your sleeve. She is a fine bookkeeper."

Now that the tension was gone, Mabel and Edward enjoyed the afternoon. Ed was invited to come to supper that evening. Ed knew that he could never bring his grandparents to the Wilcox home. They were just too Indian for these white folks. They would have a hard time communicating with them, and they would never understand how a woman could chew tobacco.

But on the other hand, Mabel would have to learn how to live with the Indians, because that's where her new home would be, living with Ed and his grandparents. Word spread like wildfire in the small community that a white woman was going to marry an Indian man, a good-looking white woman!

At first Ed didn't notice, but his harness and shoe repair business was slowing down. Some of the white folks didn't approve of this up-coming marriage, and they began to boycott his shop. It gave him time to catch up on his work, and it gave them some time to go shopping in the city. There was still some tension in the Wilcox home. Mabel had offered her services to help in the store, but her father declined the offer. He felt this would disgrace him in the eyes of his white brothers. Mabel would work in the harness shop after they were married. This would help Ed with the paperwork. Mabel noticed that some of the white women in the community no longer talked to her. They wouldn't even say "Good morning."

June 14 fell on a Tuesday, just two weeks after Mabel arrived home, and there was no reason that they chose this day other than they wanted to get married. The day started early for the two of them. They picked up James Mallory. James was an old schoolmate from Genoa Indian School, who would be Ed's best man. The trio left Winnebago at seven AM. Ed had borrowed a surrey from Joe Williams in order to make the trip go faster, and it looked better than an old work wagon.

James asked Ed in Winnebago how long it would be until they got to Pender. Ed said in a polite voice, "Jim, would you say that in English? Mabel doesn't understand Winnebago."

So Jim repeated the question in English. Mabel thanked Jim for doing that.

Ed said he thought they'd be there by mid-morning or maybe before lunchtime. Two and a half hours later, they pulled into the courthouse square.

In the county court clerk's office, they met Ester Tarrcent, the county clerk. They told her that they wanted to get married. She produced an affidavit and told them where to fill in the blanks. The clerk told them that the judge would finish with court soon, and he would be free for a few minutes, and she would ask him if he could marry them then. Ed and Mabel finished the affidavit and the marriage license and the certificate of marriage.

James Mallory and Ester Tarrcent were witnesses for Ed and Mabel. The judge agreed to do the simple ceremony in his office, so the five of them gathered there, and within five minutes, Edward and Mabel were husband and wife.

Ed gave the judge money for his services; a few more signatures, and Mr. and Mrs. Edward Hatchett left the courthouse.

"What's for supper, Mrs. Hatchett?" Jim Mallory asked Mabel on the ride home.

"Milkweed soup and fry bread," said Mabel, and all of them laughed.

"Do you know how to make fry bread, Mabel?" asked James.

"Not yet, but I will learn."

"You found a good woman, Ed."

Ed took Jim home, and then he and his new bride went home to his grandparents' house. Mabel had met the Grants, but she never thought that she would be living with them. Now she would learn how to eat real Indian food, maybe even chew a little tobacco too.

Ed and Mabel walked into the house, and Ed told his grandparents that they were married. They both looked at them and said, "That's good, Ku-nu," and went back to playing cards.

There wasn't any wedding cake. In fact, their wedding meal was fried ham and eggs with fry bread. The Grant house only had one bedroom, but Ed had bought a full-size bed that sat in the living room in a corner. They had no electricity, but a lot of people didn't have electric lights either.

Ed was so used to making coffee and his own breakfast, but now he had someone there who was willing to do that chore. Ed dropped

Mabel off at the store while he returned the surrey. Mabel made a fire in the stove and put a pot of coffee on, and then she began to look over the pile of papers that Ed had left. She sorted the mess, and soon she had set up her own bookkeeping system.

When Ed returned, he could smell the fresh coffee brewing and was greeted with a smile, a hug, and a kiss … and Mabel explaining how she would go about setting up the books. Later that morning, Mabel walked over to her father's store. She had the marriage license with her and a new wedding band on her left hand. She showed them the paper and the ring. Her mother said it was very nice. Her father said he hoped things would work out for them. George Wilcox knew deep down that his daughter had married a good, hardworking man. He didn't like it that he was an Indian, but on the other hand, this was one less mouth for him to feed. On the other hand again, however, his daughter was the first white woman to marry an Indian, and he didn't like that at all. He hoped his other three daughters wouldn't follow their sister's path.

Mabel packed her belongings and told her folks that she would be in town every day working at the harness shop. If they needed her to work in the store, she could do that too. Her mother thanked her. Her father said nothing.

The young Hatchett couple became the talk of the town. Mabel soon found out just who her real friends were. The white women in the community treated her with insults and talked behind her back. Most of the white men teased George Wilcox about his new son-in-law. The boycott on the harness shop didn't last long because when the farmers needed leather repair, they brought in their gear. The harness shop provided a good living for the couple, enough to buy some livestock, a few chickens, and pigs. The old folks liked this because these kept them in fresh meat, eggs, and bacon. At the same time, the agency was offering farm equipment, teams of horses, and a home if any Indian would farm his land. Mabel and Ed talked about this program, and they talked about other things. Then one day, the agency wrote Ed a letter asking him if he would be interested in working for the government in Washington State.

Ed talked with the Winnebago agency about the job. They wanted someone who had experience owning and operating an Indian business. He would be using his own experience in business and showing the tribal members how to get started. This sounded good, but Mabel didn't want to leave Winnebago. She didn't want to go that far from her parents, and she wanted them to farm and to keep the harness shop. It was settled then—they would be staying on the reservation and farm, and they would keep the harness shop open until they didn't need it or until they could hire someone to run it for them.

Mabel had to make adjustments living with the Grant family. The old folks pretty much stayed to themselves and left the two young lovers alone. It was a learning experience for both parties. Mabel tried to learn some of the native words, and she tried to help out with the cooking, but she didn't understand the Winnebago diet and foods.

Business at the harness shop began to slow down. Everyone was talking about the young Hatchett couple. Even the Indians didn't like this, and they said this isn't the Ho-Chunk way of choosing a wife. She wasn't Ho-Chunk, and she wasn't even Indian! This made a lot of them mad and others very jealous. Some of the Indians blamed the Indian school system for doing this to their people. Others said that Ed should have gone back to the longhouse and learned the Indian way.

No matter, Ed had confidence that his business would pick up, because he was the only one in several miles who did harness repair. It would just take some adjustment for the people of the community to get used to it. In time some would, while others never would accept the fact that a white woman married an Indian man and lived with the Indians. Many untrue stories were told about Mabel and how she was becoming a squaw. Most of the stories were very cruel and nasty.

Chapter 15

Farm Life

Some of Ed's land was located west of town, an area referred to as the west end, which was closer to Thurston, Nebraska, than Winnebago. This was where Ed and Mabel made their first home and farmed. They received the horses and equipment that the agency promised and a one-story farmhouse as well. Ed hired help to run the harness shop while he began his new life as a farmer.

By March of 1911, the farmhouse was completed, and they were moving in. It was then that Mabel told Ed that a new member of the Hatchett family was on the way. She was pregnant and due sometime in August.

Life on the farm was tough. There were no outbuildings, fences, corrals—not even an outhouse. But there was a lumberyard in the town of Thurston, and Ed made several trips to pick up materials. Between tilling the land and building a barn, Ed and Mabel had little time for anything else. Friends very seldom came over. When Ed needed help, he would go to Winnebago and hire a hand or two to work for three or four weeks at a time. He was only able to get sixty acres put in that year. The soil had never been tilled before, and it was very hard to turn it over. Equipment broke down, horses got tired, and it often rained for days on end; but the cattle, hogs, and chickens still needed to be taken care of. Farming was hard work. On the other hand, no one was giving them a hard time about a "white woman married to an Indian."

The long hot, humid summer days were difficult for the young bride, but she worked by her husband as long as she could. By late July, the creek that ran through their farm had dried up, so Ed had to pump water every day for the livestock. Mabel was very close to her due date, and she was very uncomfortable. On August 23, Ed harnessed up the team to take Mabel to the Indian hospital—a long and bumpy fourteen-mile haul. Up and down they went into the creek beds so the horses could get a quick drink of water.

Finally, they made it up the last hill west of Winnebago, and Ed picked up the pace a little bit, knowing that time was getting close. The agency road was better than the county roads, and he managed to make the last turn and pull into the hospital in time. Wilma Geraldine Hatchett was born on August 24. She would be the first of five daughters born to Ed and Mabel. Her Indian name was Wa-can-ja-ska-wega, which means White Thunder. In 1911, it was the hospital policy to keep the mother and newborn in the hospital for ten days. This gave Ed some time to stay at his grandparents' house and work in his harness shop. Ed went over to the Wilcox store and told George that he was a grandfather. A little smile broke out on his face while he told his wife that they had a new granddaughter. Later that afternoon, they went out to the hospital.

The Grant family too was glad to see Edward and happy to hear about Wilma. Ed put in long hours at the harness shop. Shoe and boot repair was in big demand. When ten days passed Mabel and baby Wilma were ready to go home, Ed left word that he would be back in two weeks. Ed, Mabel, and little Wilma went home to their farm, and all their hard work paid off. The farm began to prosper, and they were better prepared for winter that year. They dug a cellar and had many jars of food in it, plus potatoes, onions, carrots, and other goods.

The next summer, things were moving along very well for the young family when Ed suddenly developed a stomachache. At first he thought it was just his egg sandwiches that he had for lunch, but by suppertime, it was worse. Later that night, he was in a lot of pain. The next day Mabel put the harness on the team and laid a small mattress in the back of the wagon. She helped her husband into the back of the wagon, laid Wilma down with Ed in the back, and off they went to the hospital.

None of the work wagons at that time had any kind springs on their axles, so the ride to the hospital was very hard on Ed. Once she pulled into the hospital yard, she jumped off the wagon and ran inside to get some help. After a quick exam, they discovered that Ed had a ruptured appendix. He was rushed into the operating room, and they did an emergency operation on him to remove his appendix. After the operation, the doctor told Mabel that Ed would not have survived another hour without the operation.

It took several weeks for Ed to make a full recovery, but by harvest time, Ed was back on his feet again, although he still had to hire a hand to help him with the harvest. By Thanksgiving Day, everything was in, and they had a lot to be thankful for. The new virgin soil gave Ed a bumper crop of corn and hay that year. It seemed as if anything he planted came up bountifully. The west-end farm was productive and profitable. That year at Christmas, Mabel found out that she was pregnant again; Ed hoped that maybe this time, it would be a boy, but insisted he would be happy with whatever the Lord gave them.

The following year, they decided to buy a farm of eighty acres south of Winnebago, about four miles from town. It had a creek that ran year-round, and the land was fairly flat, and it was close to the main road. They decided to build a house and barn on the property along with other buildings, living there would make it easier for the kids to get to school and for them to get to the hospital, stores, and Ed's harness shop that he had neglected. (The man he had hired to work and run the shop hadn't done a good job of it.) This would be a good move for them. Ed would lease out their present farm to their neighbors for an additional source of income.

They finally decided to build a two-story frame house that would sit on a full basement. The main floor had a kitchen, dining room, a parlor with piano, French doors, and a large picture window. The upstairs had four bedrooms with plenty of closet space. The basement was set up for the hired hand to live in; plus Ed had purchased a gasoline generator that powered the whole house. The Hatchetts were one of the first on the reservation to have electric lights.

Ed's hired hand, Will Davis, stayed with the Hatchetts in the spring and fall of the year to help with the harvest. He slept on a cot in the basement and was available most of the time. He did work for other farmers, but that was on a day-to-day basis.

The barn was built to hold four teams of workhorses on one side and eight milk cows on the other. It also contained a large hayloft and a huge corral, with a calf pasture and a pig shed. This was a major undertaking, and when it was finished, it was an impressive working farm!

On August 3, 1914, the Hatchetts' second daughter was born. They named her Kathryn Jerrine. Her Indian name was Wa-can-ja-penga (Good Thunder).

When U. S. Grant died the following April, they held a meeting for him in the longhouse, after which Edward buried his grandfather on a small hill just north of his home, where other family members had been buried. Ed arranged to have a tall headstone put up to mark his grandfather's grave. This headstone had a cross on top, which was the sign of Christianity. Ed did not tell the members of the Snake Lodge about the headstone. Later when asked if he had placed a marker up for Cho-ka, his reply was, "Yes, I took care of it. I placed a headstone on his gravesite." He knew that members of the medicine lodge, who referred to Christianity as "a religion without a god," might come back and take the headstone down and destroy it if they knew about it.

Farm life had treated the Hatchett family very well. Even though Ed was not a U.S. citizen because he was an Indian, he could borrow money from the bank, to purchase more land and equipment and horses. Getting the fields ready to plant in the spring was quite the project; Ed hired more help for the planting season, and it was a major concern when it came to harvest time. Mabel and several of the wives had to make lunch for all of the hired hands, setting up several tables outside and feeding everybody.

Maxine Lois was born on November 12, 1918, at the Winnebago hospital. It was a cold and windy day, but still it was a nice day to have an addition to the family. Maxine's Indian name was Wa-can-ja-zen-ga (Yellow Thunder).

Wilma stayed at the Dutch Reform Church mission during the school year, because there was no way to get her to school from the farm, and Kathryn joined her when she was old enough. After a while, Ed and Mabel decided to build a home in town so Mabel and the girls could stay there during the week while Ed stayed on the farm and did the chores or came to town after he got all of his work done and worked at the harness shop. It was always nice to have extra income coming into the house.

Ed provided a good living for his bride. He bought her a mink coat. They had fine china for the dining room and enjoyed the benefits their hard work had earned them. Of course this made some of the white people and Indians very jealous.

The Hatchett farm kept growing in size. Ed added more cattle to their herd. Mabel always had plenty of chickens and a large garden to tend to and plenty of canning to do in the summer months. As Wilma and Kathryn matured, they were very helpful in the kitchen and with chores. Everyone had a job to do every day. This was a working family farm, with electric lights.

On June 12, 1921, Alice June Hatchett was born. Her Indian name was Wa-can-ja-cho-wega (Blue Thunder). This birth took place at the new Winnebago Indian Hospital, which was built on the south end of town. It was a three-level brick building with an elevator in it—the first elevator ever in Thurston County. There was a clinic on the first level of the building, along with a dentist's office and laboratory. At the time, it was the state of the art for a hospital. On the Hatchett farm, Mabel established a house rule that Wilma would take care of Maxine and Kathryn would take care of Alice June while Mabel was working on the farm. This gave the two eldest daughters quite a bit of responsibility, the system worked well.

The new Winnebago school "bus" that picked up children in the rural areas was actually a team and wagon driven by George Bird. It was a slow and painful ride for everyone, but with the system in place, Mabel and the girls didn't stay in the house in town anymore. Instead, they moved out to the farm and stayed there year-round, renting out the house in town, although to catch the bus, the girls had to walk about a mile and then wait. During the fall and spring, it was all right, but in the winter, it was very cold standing and waiting for George to show up.

On June 2, 1924, the Indian Citizenship Act, also known as the Snyder Act, was signed into law by President Calvin Coolidge, granting citizenship to all Native Americans born within the territorial limits of the country. The privileges of citizenship, however, were largely governed by state law, and the right to vote remained denied to Native Americans in some states until 1948.

The possibility of becoming a citizen of the United States did little for some, meant a lot to others, and still others grumbled it was the government's way of taking the rest of the Indians' land and assimilating them into the American melting pot. There was no celebration or dance held for this event; for most, it was just another day. Some of the locals asked each other, "Do you feel any different now that you are a citizen?" Most of the answers were the same: "I feel just as I did yesterday at this time, no better and no worse." Most Indians didn't know it, but now they had to pay taxes, and if a war broke out, they could get drafted.

Edward's Grandmother Alice Grant, one of the last traditional longhouse members who believed in the medicine lodge and its members' healing powers, died on December 19, 1924. Ed was at the Grant house while the medicine lodge held its funeral for Alice Grant; and when it was over, Ed buried her next to her husband, U. S. Grant, on the little hill just north of their house. Ed placed a smaller headstone at his grandmother's grave site. The medicine lodge members who helped Ed bury his grandmother never said a word to him about the cross on top of U. S. Grant's headstone.

The passing of the Grant family was a milestone in the medicine lodge religion. The Grant family had one of the last actual longhouses on the reservation. It would fall into decay, and in a few years, it would be totally gone, never again to be seen on their home site. The younger generation paid little attention to the longhouse and its teachings. Most of the youth by this time enjoyed living the way of the white man, which they had learned from the boarding schools. It was part of the burial rite to have a spirit house built over the grave. This was done on U. S. Grant's and his wife's graves.

The peyote church came to the Winnebagos around this time and became incorporated and chartered as the Native American Church of Nebraska. This pulled many members from the medicine lodge, resulting in its dramatic downturn and the beginning of the end of the medicine lodge in Winnebago, Nebraska.

On February 7, 1926, Winifred Patricia Hatchett was born and given the Indian name Wa-can-ja-wem-ga (Coming Back Thunder). Ed and Mable had no sons to carry on the Hatchett name. Like her Sister

June, Patty was born in the new Winnebago Indian Hospital system. When Mabel and Patty returned to the farm, the other girls were staying at the Dutch Reform Church mission for the winter, a result of the inadequate school bus system. Later in her school years, Patty would stay at the mission during the winter months, and like her older sisters, she would return to the farm when better weather arrived.

As Patty grew older, she was given chores just like the rest of girls. Wilma and Katherine were always in charge of cleaning up the house. One of Patty's jobs was to wipe down the tables and chairs. She would rush to get it done and do the dusting, and then she would go and tell one of the two bosses. They would always give the same answer: "Well, get it done"… even if was already done. She learned the hard way that it was better to take her time and just keep her mouth shut.

When Patty started school, the school district still had the team and a hay wagon to pick up the kids in the rural areas, and she and her two sisters still had to walk about a mile to catch the school wagon. The driver was an old man who never pushed the team to work hard. They would loaf along to and from school. Sometimes one of the kids— Josephus Baker—would jump out of the wagon and taunt the old man that he could run faster than the horses until the man whipped the team up and got them going a little faster. Everyone on the wagon laughed as the old man tried to keep up with Josephus.

When several members of the tribe asked Ed to be on the tribal council, he accepted the position and thought this demonstrated a change in the people's attitude toward him. He soon found out that this was not so. Most of Ed's suggestions were voted down or just plain overlooked. He soon realized that this was just a waste of his time. When the elections came around again, Ed's name was not on the ballot.

On the Hatchett farm, they had two riding horses—Nell and Barney. Nell was very gentle while Barney was still green. One day while Wilma was riding Nell, she pulled too hard on the reins, and Nell stood up on her hind legs, and Wilma went sliding off her back. She went crying into the house and told her mother that she slid off the horse, but fortunately, it turned out only her pride was hurt.

They also had a rooster with long spurs who liked to chase anyone who came into the yard. One day when June was playing outside, the rooster came after her. She ran for the house, but the rooster was catching up to her. She grabbed a stone and, with all of her might, threw it at the rooster, and she scored a direct hit on the rooster's head.

At first the rooster just stopped and sat down on its tail; soon its head started to turn in circles, and then it fell on its left side while its head was still turning. June ran inside and told her mother that she killed her rooster. Mabel went outside, and sure enough, the rooster was lying on its side with its head still turning in a circle. Soon it stopped, got on its feet, and walked on. From that day on, that rooster never chased anyone in the yard again, especially June.

Mabel had a small toy Manchester terrier dog that sometimes followed them into town. She always stayed on Mabel's side of the wagon. The problem was that when they got into town, the other dogs from town would chase after her and try to fight her. Tootsie May was a smart dog. She learned how to leap up onto the wagon tongue, and from there she would jump onto the horse's rump and ride there. She would smile down at the town dogs that tried to get to her.

Chapter 16

Starting Over

The Depression hit the country. All over the United States, farmers were losing their farms because with the price of corn and other grains crashing, they couldn't keep up with their loan payments. Ed and Mabel had borrowed money from the bank to purchase land and equipment over the years, but they had always kept up on their payments to the bank and therefore felt safe.

"It's George Price," Kathryn called to her mother as she watched the car pull into the driveway. Mabel and Kathryn walked out to greet him.

"How are you, George?" Mabel asked cheerfully. "We haven't seen you in a while!" When she saw the expression on his face, her expression changed. "Has something happened?" she asked.

"This part of my job I hate," he said as he walked toward them. "I have known you, Mabel, for a long time. I know that you and Ed have worked very hard on your farm, but the bank is short of cash, and we are calling in our loans for full payment. Times are hard, and we need to do this. Please accept my apologies, but there is nothing that I can do. I am just the messenger."

With that, Mr. Price handed the typed foreclosure papers to Mabel and left. Tears welled up in the women's eyes when they read the letter. It said they had exactly thirty days to pay the bank the balance of their loan, or they had to collect their personal items and leave the farm.

When Ed made his way back to the house for lunch, Mabel gave him the letter. He looked it over and said nothing. After lunch, Ed and Mabel went out to the screen porch to talk. They decided to ask Reverend Waldurmuller for advice.

The pastor told them to keep working and when the thirty days was up, to just leave everything. Mabel didn't agree with the pastor, but she got an unkind look from Ed when she said so. Ed believed that whatever the pastor said was all right and that they should do it. Ed would need to finish up some work at the harness shop before closing the door for the last time.

Before they left Winnebago, they turned right and went out to the old U. S. Grant house. It had been empty for a while, but it was still very solid and would just need some repair on it to make it livable again. It brought old memories from the past, it was still in the family, and it was vacant. This would be the new/old Hatchett farm again.

It was a quiet ride back to the farm; and when they got there, Ed did the chores, and Mabel and the girls prepared the supper. It was very quiet during the meal. Everyone knew what was in the letter. Ed could not sell any of his grain, cattle, or pigs, not even any of the chickens—the eggs, yes—also the milk and cream; but that would just add up to gas money for the car.

The following weeks were very sad for the Hatchett household. On the thirtieth day of May, they left, taking only the clothes on their backs. Mabel again told Ed that some of the stuff was theirs and that they should take it, but Ed stood by what the pastor had said. They arrived at the Grant house and immediately went to work cleaning up the old homestead. Mabel insisted on bringing their bed. She said that after having five kids, she would not sleep on the floor. They also brought pots and pans for cooking, a few plates, cups, and glasses. They greatly missed the farm, but on the other hand, there were no more chores—no chickens to feed, no garden to tend, no cattle or pigs to feed.

Without a job, Ed went to work for the CCC (Civilian Conservation Corps). He was put in charge of a crew, and this paid a little more. Most of the crews were made up of Indians, although there were a few white men in some of the camps. The CCC boys built different structures on and off the reservation. This put a lot of men back to work. They had to stay in the camps, but on payday, they got to go home and see their families and pay bills. Wilma and Kathryn, who each married and had their own homes, came out to the Grant house and helped clean and cut weeds. They also had to dig a toilet and clean out the old well so they could have some drinking water. When the time came for their farm and furnishings to be auctioned off, they were allowed to bid on any of the items. It seemed strange to bid on your own stuff, but they managed to pick up the kitchen table and chairs, plus some living room furnishings.

They didn't need much to furnish the Grant house. The Grant house had one bedroom, a living room, an eat-in kitchen, a large screened porch, and a large attic. Patty slept on a cot in the living room that she had to make up every day. The next spring, Mabel sent away for some spring chicks. They built a small chicken coop, and Ed built a small barn. The girls and Mabel had cleared enough land for a garden. Gradually, the old Grant place looked like a small farm. The money Ed made from the CCC paid for lumber, wire, and tools. This was the rebuilding stage of their lives—start small and grow.

Even though the United States was still in a slump, the Hatchett family was able to purchase cattle and farm a very small plot of land, just enough to feed the livestock during the winter. Talk of war in Europe was on the radio. Every day it sounded worse than the day before.

During the spring of 1940, Ed was able to plow and plant his small acreage. He managed to get everything in, even the Indian corn. But then on the first of June, it started to rain, and it did not stop. Kathryn and her husband were staying at the Hatchetts' home, and they were concerned enough about the rising water to bed down in the back porch. The water began to creep into the yard. By sunset it hadn't moved much, so everyone went to bed. Later that night, when Kathryn got up and stuck her head out the door to check, she let out a scream that woke everyone in the house. The water was lapping against the screen door. Water began seeping into the house. Then it started rushing into the house.

Ed went out to move the Hereford bull to higher ground. When he returned, he couldn't get the screen door on the front door to open. There was too much debris pressing against the screen. Ed moved the debris away with his foot and pulled the screen door open. When he did, a large rush of water came into the house. Patty screamed in fear, and everyone began placing everything up as high as they could on the furniture and on the bed, hoping that the water wouldn't get that high.

When they did all that they could do, they held hands and made their way to the hill about seventy feet away. The bull that Ed had moved earlier was already in water, so Ed had to move him again to higher ground. It was wet, muddy, and dark; but somehow they made their way to the road. The O'Gormans lived just up and around the bend from the Hatchetts. It was a hard walk, but they all made it. Once inside the O'Gormans' home, they told them of the flood. The O'Gormans made room for the overnight guests, but there wasn't much sleeping going on.

At daybreak the men folk walked back over to the Hatchetts' house. It had dirty floodwater surrounding it; the door was ajar. Ed made his way inside. The lamp that Mabel had lit the night before and set on the table was still burning, even though the table was bobbing up and down as it floated in the room. There was nothing anyone could do but just sit and wait for the water to go down. Later that day, the water was back inside the creek, but much debris—trees and branches, parts of barns and outbuildings, tires, trash, dead animals—had come downstream. Cleanup would take a long time.

The Red Cross set up a large tent in Winnebago, offering help to those that needed it. The Hatchetts turned in their request for assistance, but they were denied any kind of help because, they were told, they "had a farm and Ed worked so they had money." From that time on, no one in the Hatchett family spoke well of the Red Cross.

The next week, the agency came out and told Ed to move everything out of the house, and they would return the next day with a pump. It was a high-pressure pump, and they started in one room and worked their way around to all of the rooms. Then they pushed all of the mud out of the open doors. They told Ed to leave the house open for a few days to let it dry out. In the meantime, Ed and the family cleaned up the yard and restored order to everything. In two days, the house was dry, and they moved everything back in. There was still a lot of cleaning to do inside of the house. Mabel and the girls washed down all of the walls and floors; washed out all of the cupboards, shelves, and closets; laundered some clothes; and threw out those that were beyond repair.

The town of Winnebago had to be cleaned up too. There were lots of trees and old buildings left in the lower streets, and flood debris was everywhere. The Omaha Creek flood of 1940 was the worst in many years. Railroad tracks were washed out, and many bridges were destroyed. The train station at Winnebago was swept away, along with the ticket agent, who was never found.

After the flood of 1940, Mabel did not want to live on the Omaha Creek. She got very nervous whenever it stated to rain, especially if it rained for days. Ed still received money from land that was leased out to the white farmers. They decided to stay for a couple of years and try to save some money. After all, they didn't pay any rent, nor did they have any loans to pay off.

June graduated that year from high school. She had a room at the mission, and later that summer, she enrolled in a nursing school in Omaha. She would graduate in two years and go into the army and be stationed in the South Pacific as a nurse. Patty was the only daughter left at home. The school bus didn't run out her way, so she and her two nephews, Sunny and Hay-na Lewis, had to cross the Omaha Creek. Ed had put a long plank across the water. And then they would make their way up the other side of the bank to the railroad tracks. In the winter, once the three of them crossed the creek, Patty had to make a trail for the two younger nephews, and she pushed a trail to the railroad tracks. The tracks were always open and easy to walk on. They walked south until they got close to the schoolhouse. Then Patty would have to make a trail going east into town, and then they could all walk on the sidewalk to school. The winter months were the worst, but in the spring during the runoff, they would have to walk on the road, and that took a long time.

Once in a while, the cattle would get out of the pasture, and they would be on the road, or they might be over at Mrs. Fisher's property. Sometimes they might even be as far away as Wilma and Hank's (Wilma's husband) house. Patty would be dispatched to round up the cattle and bring them home, and then she would have to fix the fence or find out where they got out. Life on the farm was not an easy thing for a young girl.

Patty was in the tenth grade when the Hatchetts bought a farm south of town and started all over again. The house was a two-room shack when they took it over, but Ed added a living room and a bedroom and a back porch. They had to carry water and use an outhouse until as late as 1965, when the Indian Public Health Service dug a well for them and put in a limited amount of plumbing.

Patty's space was in the living room on the couch. Everyone went to church every Sunday, no exceptions! It was a hard life, but it was better than most. In the summer, the well would dry up, so they had to haul water from the spring down at the bottom of the hill, about two miles down and steep, and this was no easy job. They would load large barrels onto the wagon and drive the team down to the spring. Once at the spring, they would drive the wagon around to the tank; then someone would dip a bucket into the tank and then pass it up to the wagon, where someone else would dump it into the fifty-five-gallon barrels. This would go on until all four barrels were full. Then they would tie a large cloth around the top of the barrel so it wouldn't slop out. During the dry spell, this was done twice a day, every day.

The CCC and other work projects had stopped, and now Ed was back to being a full-time farmer. The long days and short nights paid off. They saved enough to purchase an additional forty acres, which they called Lower Mary's. They still planted Indian corn and had a large garden, several fruit trees, and many buildings for grain, chickens, and tools.

A few months after the Hatchetts moved to the farm, Mabel moved her brother, Ted, and her mother into a little house that sat down over the hill close to the timbers. Ted was a part-time farmer and did odd jobs here and there. He liked his liquor every now and then. He would hitch up the team and go down to the B & H Bar in Winnebago. Sometimes he made it home, and other times he didn't. During the times that he didn't make it home, he would leave the bar, head for home, and get down by the hospital when, for some reason, he would drop the left rein and the team would go around and around in circles until the local law would go and tell Ed and Mabel about her brother. They would take their grandson Hay-na Lewis with them, and he would jump on the wagon and grab the reins from the then-sleeping Ted and pull the left rein free. As they all headed home, Ted would wake up and say, "Hey, Hay-na, what are you doing here? You're a good boy."

Mabel and Ed eventually took her mother into their home. By that time, she was old and dying, and none of her other children would take care of her. Despite all the insults and negative words she and her husband said about Ed and Mabel; she spent her last days on this earth in their home!

It is hard to believe, but even after so many years, some of the Indians still didn't like Ed Hatchett because he was a Christian and because he had married a white woman. After losing so much in the Depression, he was starting over and once again doing well, and this made some of them very mad. Some of the talk going around was that Ed had gotten a lot of help from the agency; some even said that Mabel's family was helping them out. None of it was true. It was just plain sweat equity that was helping them out. But the hate never stopped.

One night a visitor from the medicine lodge came to do harm to the Hatchett family. Mabel heard a noise outside and saw him, and then she smelled the bad odor that he carried with him. She got up and closed all of the windows and woke up everyone in the house. Everyone just sat in the dark while the spirit moved about in the darkness outside. Some thought they saw a glow down by the barn, and then it was gone. The next morning, Ed and Mabel washed down the door handles, even on the car, the windows of the house, and doors on the barn. This was to eliminate any "medicine" power that may have been placed there. No one was going to harm them.

Patty enjoyed not having all of her older sisters bossing her around and giving her chores to do, but she had to listen to her mother all of the time. Sometimes she had to work harder because she and her sister Dee Dee did the water run when the well went dry. First they rounded up the horses, put on their harnesses, and hitched them to the water wagon. Then once at the spring, someone had to be on the ground and the other in the wagon to dump the water into the barrels. Once the team and wagon made it back up to the farm, they had to drive the team down to the stock tank. They would pull the water wagon as close as they could to the tank and then would have to start dipping the buckets into the barrels and dumping the buckets of water into the stock tank. This was not a pleasant job. Being the youngest had its advantages and disadvantages.

Chapter 17

Winifred Patricia Hatchett

Patty was getting restless on the farm. She liked school because she could meet all of her friends and talk about the boys in their classes, and after school, Patty worked at the local café waiting tables. In her last year, Patty had met an Omaha boy who lived at the mission. He was in her classroom until he joined the army. His name was Alfred Walker, and they had spent many hours together.

Patty graduated on May 19, 1944, at 7 PM in the high school auditorium. Patty had no plans to go to college. She had plans, but she made sure no one knew what her plans were. She and Alfred had been keeping the post office busy for a long time, and it was in one of those letters that Alfred had proposed to Patty. He wasn't a very romantic guy, but he didn't have long; he would be shipped overseas after his leave was up. They made all of their plans through the mail. No one knew about any of this, not even her mother and definitely not her father. If he had known about this matter, he would have sent her away.

Alfred and Patty were married on Monday, June 26, 1944, just five weeks after her graduation. Was this a ploy to get out of her parents' house, or did she really love Alfred? It didn't matter because she moved back in with her parents after he shipped out. A month later, Patty found out that she was pregnant—two months out of high school and already pregnant, with the father nowhere around. Alfred was shipped overseas to fight in WWII.

Patty gave birth to her first son, Michael Roger Walker, in March of 1945. When Alfred came home, the three Walkers moved down to Macy, Nebraska, to live with his parents. Alfred had money coming from the army, and they found a sparsely furnished house to rent. Patty tolerated his drinking at first, but the party just kept going day after day, week after week, until the money ran out. One day when Alfred went out to see a friend, he told his wife when he returned they would go and get some food for the house. The day turned into late afternoon—still no Alfred. Then evening fell, and she knew that Alfred was out drinking, and the only thing to eat in the house was a small piece of salt pork and a little flour. Patty cooked the salt pork and made gravy out of the fryings with the flour. It was enough for Michael. He was the only one who ate that night. After too many days like that one, she left Alfred and moved herself and Michael back to her parents' home on the hill.

Soon Alfred was at the farm, wanting Patty to come back home with him. She invited him to stay for supper, and he accepted the offer. During the day, two chickens had gotten loose and been hit by car. Instead of just throwing them away, Mabel had cleaned them up and cooked them for dinner. When Alfred found out, he threw a fit, yelling that he didn't see how anyone could eat something that was killed on the road, making it sound as if it were a sin to do so.

Patty packed up her things and left with Alfred that evening. Mabel packed a few things for them to eat. It was a hard decision for Patty. She knew how hard it would be for her and Michael, but she left any way. Once Alfred had his family back home, he beat Patty and told her she had monsters for parents. How could anyone eat something that was killed on the highway? The abuse and drinking would continue. She endured it all to keep her marriage together, and she claimed that she still loved the man.

Alfred Walker reenlisted in the army, claiming that there was no other work for him and other vets, but the army wouldn't put up with his drinking and not showing up for duty. He received a bad-conduct discharge. A trip to Detroit for a job in the auto industry was also short-lived because of Alfred's drinking, and they moved back to Nebraska.

By late July of 1946, Patty was pregnant again, and life with Alfred was miserable. Patty put herself and Michael on welfare because they needed something to live on, and although Alfred was gone much of the time, he always came by the day the welfare check came. When her second son, Terry Wayne Walker, was born on April 2, 1947, Alfred stumbled home two days after they got home from the hospital.

Alfred's addiction to alcohol controlled his life. He never did get or keep a steady job. But while he was unable to support a family, he sure knew how to make one. When Patty found out that she was pregnant again and Alfred was nowhere to be found, she'd finally had enough. She packed what few belongings they had and moved home to Hatchett's Hill, where she made plans to divorce Alfred as soon as she could raise the money for a lawyer.

On August 19, 1948, Alan Brent Walker, Patty's third son, was born on a Thursday afternoon at 5:25 PM. Shortly after Alan was born, Patty started the divorce proceedings. As usual, Alfred was nowhere to be found or didn't want to be found. Ed and Mabel helped Patty find a lawyer, and they paid his fee for her. They wanted this menace out of her life also. Patty asked for no child support from Alfred, knowing he would never pay it anyway. All she wanted was to be left alone. Patty and Alfred were divorced on May 11, 1949; Alan was six months old at the time. They had been married four years, but it had been a lifetime for Patty.

Patty and her three boys moved into a very tiny two-room apartment. They were very poor at that time, but so was everyone else. The house was owned by Annie Armell, who rented out the two apartments upstairs.

The Walker family had a table and chairs and a run-down couch. Patty had her bed, and the three boys slept on a studio couch that folded out into a bed. Patty cooked on a two-burner kerosene stove fueled by a one-gallon glass jug that had to be filled every two days or so. The stove was very small, but it did the job of cooking for the four of them.

During the next few months, Patty worked at different jobs on the reservation. During a summer job for the Bureau of Indian Affairs, she met Joe White, who worked for the road department at the BIA. We lived twenty miles south of Sioux City, Iowa, that's where most of the jobs were. While walking down Pierce Street in Sioux City, Iowa, she saw a sign in the window of S. S. Kresge Dime Store for a clerk position. She was hired, but the food supervisor was short a girl at the fountain, so she was placed there. She had the early-morning shift, and one of her jobs was to type the new menus every day. When the store manager found out that Patty had worked in an office, he started dictating letters to her in the back of the tearoom in the afternoon. Eventually, she was assigned to the office.

Sometime in 1950, Joe White moved in. Now it was really crowded in the little apartment. Joe worked in Sioux City also; they would leave early in the morning. Mike was the only one of us who went to school then. So Terry and I had the run of the apartment, along with our babysitter, Florence Ricehill. Florence was a tough older Winnebago woman who chewed tobacco, cussed like a man, but she was good to us. We walked to downtown Winnebago with Florence, getting to know the friendly lady who ran the bus station. We visited the post office with its large lobby with benches and Horack's general store, where they had the Dutch Cleanser containers in the large glass storefront that I thought looked like a ghost. I was afraid of them and always tried to walk fast past that store and not look at them.

One Saturday night, Mike went to the movies with one of his friends. Mom gave him some money, and off they went. About a half hour later, there was a knock on the door. Alfred had come back with Mike. Alfred told my mom to get Mike cleaned up because he was taking him back to Macy with him. Alfred was drunk. He stood in the doorway, weaving back and forth, talking loudly. Mom stalled for time, and finally, Joe White got up, grabbed a claw hammer, and took off after Alfred. Alfred took a step backward and fell down the stairs. When he hit the landing, he said, "I am going to tell my brother."

That was the last time Alfred came to visit.

In the summer of 1951, we moved out to Joe White's allotment about a mile east of town. Joe had purchased a small two-room shack down by the river, added two bedrooms and one porch to the old shack, and put on new siding and a new roof. It didn't look the same; it actually looked like a real house sitting in the woods. Mom wouldn't let me ride in the back of the stock truck with Terry and Mike and our furniture, because she said I was too small. It's hard to believe that we had a stock truck full of furniture. Mom and Joe bought a heating stove, a fridge, and a propane cook stove. We were really living in high style. We actually had our own bedroom and beds, no more sleeping three to a couch like dogs.

The following year, additional improvements were made on the Joe White house: a two-car garage was built, a small step was made for the front door, and several trees were brought up from the river and transplanted around the house. There were many places to explore and check out. There were many new animals to watch and to stay away from. We even enjoyed burning the trash. Mom burned it in a fifty-five gallon barrel that had the top cut off. We had to take cod-liver oil, and no one liked it, and we were all glad when we finished the bottle and threw it into the trash, we went with Mom when she took out the trash. She lit the fire, and when we heard the cod-liver oil bottle blow up, we clapped our hands. She never bought it again.

Growing up in the country was fun and exciting. There were always new places to explore, a new hill to sled down, huge snowdrifts, very muddy roads in the spring. It seemed as though anything would grow; all you had to do was put it in the ground. There were all kinds of wildlife in the woods. One day when the three of us were exploring in the woods, Mike saw a snake lying across the path. We all got scared. Mike jumped over it and kept running. Then Terry jumped over it, and he just made it. Then I came down the trail and jumped, but I landed on it, and it really scared me. It felt soft and wiggly. Years later, I was riding my bicycle, and a large bull snake was sunning itself across the driveway. I didn't see it until I ran over it. It coiled up as if it was going to strike. I didn't go back into our driveway for a long time.

On August 15, 1953, Public Law 83-277, sometimes called the Kansas-Nebraska Act, was signed by President Dwight D. Eisenhower. The act repealed the federal law that had prohibited Indians from buying alcoholic beverages. (The 1933 repeal of prohibition had not applied to Native Americans.) My stepdad, Joe and his buddies no longer had to wait until Dick Carne, the local cop, got off work so Dick could go into the bar and buy a bottle of alcohol. Joe could now go in all by himself and buy what he wanted.

For the drunks in town, this was a blessing. No longer did they have to find a "runner" (a white person over twenty-one years of age). Now they could just walk into the B & H Bar and buy their own drink or get something to go. The downside of this law was that Indian alcoholism rates skyrocketed.

When I started school, our grandmother took care of us. Mom and Joe would drop us off in the morning about six AM. Grandmother would then cook us a farm breakfast, eggs and sausage and bacon and toast, and we would catch the school bus at seven. The bus dropped us back at my grandparents' farm after school, and our parents would pick us up from there. The bus was now a real bus—not the wagon my mother had ridden in. One time on our way home, I was sitting by myself, and one of the girls opened the window behind me, and my ball cap went flying out the window. When I told Mom and Joe, they blamed me for losing my cap, and after supper, we all drove out to where it happened and we got out of the car and looked. We didn't find it. They told me it was my fault for not taking better care of my cap.

The next morning on the bus, the girl who had opened the window handed me my ball cap. She apologized and told me that her family went out as soon as she told them where to find my cap.

My grandmother was a very loving, caring person, easygoing and always willing to help. Grandfather had been very stern with his own children, but was less stern with us. We could do anything as long as it wasn't breaking stuff or fighting or carrying on. They were still running an active farm, however—with horses, fifty to sixty head of cattle, chickens, and a pig called Sallie Sow, who always seemed to run away. We were expected to pitch in and help with the chores.

Probably because I was the youngest, I was the one who tried hardest. When I was about five, I remember my grandparents always talking about how *hard the work was* on their farm, how there was always something to do. Grandpa and I did a lot of woodcutting with a bow saw. We would take turns sitting on the log and one of us sawing the end that hung over the sawhorse. We did this most of the summer, but that didn't seem like work. So I was always asking my grandma for a job to do, but it had to be "hard work." All my older cousins laughed about how often I'd ask and how hard Grandma would think and think to come up with a job for me.

One of Terry's friends lived across the cornfield from us. After school, we would go over and play with him. His name was Davey Burk, we would steal some of his mom's cigarettes, we would go into the woods and have a smoke … until Joe's Day-ga Bill White saw us and reported us to Mom and Joe. We were then sent to bed without any supper and told to stay away from Davey. This lasted about two weeks, and we went back over to Davey's house.

Sometimes Terry and I would call each other *Hay-na* (second-born son) and *Ha-ga* (third-born son). We told Davey that those were our Indian names, so he wanted one. We thought about it for a while, and we named him Davey Baby. I don't think he liked the name because he kept asking for another Indian name, but we just kept calling him Davey Baby.

Our Indian nicknames were about the only Indian thing we knew. Even though we had a lot of white farmers on the reservation, most of the children in my elementary school were Indian, and most were still steeped in custom. They talked about different ways of digging roots for medicine and the food they ate at home, which was totally different from what we ate. We ate white people food. They still did a lot of hunting—especially the poor Indians—and they still dried and prepared food the old way and tanned skins and used them. (If ever we needed a skin, we'd just go buy it.)

It was hard to be loyal to our Indian culture when every time we looked around, we saw that the whites had all the power. We lived on a reservation where everyone who had a position, be it a judge or policeman or mayor, was white. All the businesses were owned by white people. The Bureau of Indian Affairs superintendent was white. A total of 80 percent of the school kids were Indian, but there was no Indian on the school board.

And then there were the ancient tribal differences that made the Indian kids surrounding us less than welcoming. Most of them were Winnebagos, and we were Omahas. There was a lot of rivalry, a lot of bitterness. The fact that my grandfather had married a white woman didn't help matters.

One day when we were at my grandparents' farm, I noticed something new in the front yard: a tombstone. It looked very old. "PRIVATE WILLIAM HATCHETT," it said on it, "Omaha Scouts, Company A, Winnebago, Nebraska. *Every warrior has his own song.*"

"What's that?" I asked my grandfather.

"Your great-great-grandfather's tombstone."

"Is he buried down there?"

"No," Grandfather laughed, "don't know where he's buried, but somehow his tombstone got separated from his grave. One of your uncles found it and brought it to me, since he was my grandfather."

"What was he like?"

My grandfather shrugged. "A famous warrior, I guess. Least that's what it says."

"What does that mean?" I asked, pointing to *Every warrior has his own song.*"

My grandfather rubbed his chin, trying to recall. "I think they made up songs about warriors back then, songs about their accomplishments in battle, that kind of thing. And there was a song about him and his courage. And ..." He squinted into the distance, as if trying to remember something. "And when they sang it, they played it on a big drum that could be heard for miles around." He grinned, proud of his memory.

"So my great-great-grandfather was a famous Indian warrior?"

Grandpa waved me away with a laugh. "Maybe, but that's not important. What is important," he said, eyeing me sternly, "is that you're Christian. That's all you need to know. You need to follow the Christian teachings."

The three of us had to wear bow-ties with our white shirts to church every Sunday. There was a whole ritual involved. On Saturday night, we'd go with Mom up the hill to Grandma's. Mom would set Grandma's hair in bobby pins. Then in the morning, Grandma and Grandpa would drive down to our house, and Mom would comb out Grandma's hair, and the three of us would ride to church with our grandparents.

One Sunday Mom said that we didn't have to go to church. I was so happy. When my grandparents drove up and Grandma went inside to get her hair combed out, I ran outside with a smile on my face and stuck my head in the car window and told my granddad, "Mom said that we didn't have to go to church today!"

He looked at me sternly. "That's nothing to be smiling around about," he snapped. "You go in there and get your church clothes on! You're going to church with us now."

He was really mad. I kind of slid down the car and made my way out of there fast. I went into our bedroom and stayed there. I told Mike and Terry what had happened, and they stayed in the bedroom too until our grandparents left for church. This church thing was a funny thing, because our cousins didn't go to church at all.

"You boys, when you get older, you need to get out of here," our stepdad was always telling us. "I mean off this reservation. If you stick around here, you will get a girl in trouble, and then you will have to stay. You can go on to school or join the army, but you need to get out of here."

We would get this speech about four times a year, so I guess he wanted it to stick, but if it was so important for us to leave, why didn't he leave or stay away after his hitch in the army? And our mom had no intention of leaving either.

In the summer, we rode our bikes up the hill to Grandma's house. It was a hard hill to pedal all the way up, so we usually pushed our bicycles up most of the way, but the ride down was so fast we didn't have to pedal at all. We rode our bikes all over the place. We rode them down to the river, which was about a five-mile ride. It was fun going down Big Bear Hollow. We had to be careful because most of the time, it was rough. Once down on the bottom, the roads were all sand, and that made it hard to ride on, but we managed to get to the river. The ride back was a tough one. I don't know of anyone who ever pedaled all the way up Big Bear Hollow. It was just too long and too steep of a hill. Very few Indians had new bicycles. Most of them had hand-me-downs or used bikes. They were all the old type. By this I mean no gears or hand brakes, just regular pedal brakes and a single speed.

The Bureau of Indian Affairs relocation program was introduced to the Winnebago Indian reservation in 1956, although the program had been in the BIA since 1948. In 1950, the average Native American on a reservation earned $950 per year. The average black person earned $2,000 per year, while the average white person earned almost $4,000—over four times more than Indians. In 1952, the Urban Indian Relocation Program was initiated to entice reservation Indians to move to seven major cities in the United States, where the jobs supposedly were plentiful.

The relocation program peaked in 1957, and by 1960, a total of 33,466 Indians had been relocated throughout the United States. The relocation program continued until 1979. A few of the Omahas and Winnebagos took advantage of the program, but most Indians living on the reservation didn't care to leave or didn't even know about the program. To them, this was their home, and they didn't care to leave it or their families.

In the mid-fifties, the state of Nebraska decided to pave or blacktop the rest of Highway 73. The state had stopped the blacktop at the agency; it was a gravel road down to Decatur, Nebraska. This was an exciting time for the three of us; we would watch for hours as they tore up the road and then graded it and did it all over again the next day. We also made money by standing around and watching. Some of the workers would pay us to go down to the well and get them some freshwater, and we never had money before, so this was really good for us. We soon learned which of the men not to trust because not all of them paid for their water. Most did. Those that didn't would always tell us, "I will pay you next Monday," and they never did.

When we got older, Joe bought horses and kept them at my grandparent's farm. They were a lot of work. The fences always needed fixing, and in the winter, one of us would have to stay with our grandparents so we could feed and water the horses. We had to make sure that they had grain and salt too.

Getting them water was a job. First you had to walk down to the pump and break the ice in the tank or cut into the ice so they could drink. Then you had to hook up the trough to the pump and keep pumping, waiting until all of them had a drink.

Then you unhooked the trough and put the three-gallon bucket under the pump and pumped it full. Then you carried it back to the house because that was water for the house.

Grandma still had chickens that she fed and watered. In the morning, after she picked up the eggs, she would go outside and fill a large wash pan with snow and place it on the Airtight woodstove and let it melt down; then she would take the water out to the henhouse, and that was their drinking water for the day. The chicken house was a few degrees warmer than the outside, so the water didn't freeze right away.

My grandparents had a single-barrel 410 shotgun. This was the first gun that I ever shot. I used it to hunt rabbits and squirrels, which I sold in town to some of the old Indian women for a quarter a piece. Sometimes at church, a few of the older ladies would ask my grandmother if I could bring them a fresh squirrel.

In the spring of 1959, Joe purchased the old Grant house, and we started to tear it down. Everything had to be taken apart carefully. One afternoon, Aunt Dee Dee (Maxine) and the kids came out to see how much we had taken down. While she was talking with Mom, Joe said, "If I had my electric skill saw, I would have this building down in no time."

Aunt Dee Dee asked him, "Where would you plug it in?"

No more was said about the electric saw. We pulled the boards off the two-by-fours and got all of the nails out of them and cleaned them and then stacked them in the pickup truck. This project went on all spring. That fall we set up a nail-pulling and board-cleaning shop in the side garage. Mike, Terry, and I had the job of pulling out the nails and cleaning the boards and stacking them in a neat stack in the garage. First were the sheeting boards and then the roofing boards and then the hardwood flooring. We had lumber stacked all over the place. In the backyard, in the garage, behind the garage, some of it was covered with a canvas; most of it was just outside in the weather.

The next summer, we started another project that Joe took a long time to complete. It was the addition to the house. I might have been in the fourth grade when we started, and I was a senior in high school when I dug the lines for the water and sewer, and there were still a few odd and ends that needed to be finished. Joe would say, "That's good enough for now." And it never got finished, or that was as finished as it was going to get. This made my mother very upset, because there were a lot of things that were never finished in the house.

Most people traveling through the reservation didn't know that they were on an Indian reservation until they read the sign that stated 'Entering the Winnebago Indian Reservation.'

The town of Winnebago looked just like any farming community in Nebraska. It had three grocery stores, two cafés, two gas stations, a bar, a post office, and an International Harvester dealer right on Main Street. The hospital was on the south end of town, and the high school was on the north end of town. There were four churches in Winnebago and an old bank that was now a Laundromat. The town also had a motel. The village had a town hall and a fire station. There was also a hardware store, a law office, and a movie theater. The village of Winnebago had its own police force, jail, and judge; most of the citizens were Indians, and most of the inmates were Indians.

When farmers came to town looking for workers, they would go to the north side of the International Harvester building. There was a huge long log that lay by the building; any Indian men who were looking for work would go there and sit. This became known as the employment office.

Chapter 18

The 1960s

June 14, 1960, was Ed and Mabel's fiftieth wedding anniversary. The actual celebration was held on Sunday June 12 at the Dutch Reform Church basement. Several months before June 12, Mom said that she would pay us a weekly allowance of twenty-five cents for doing chores around the house and helping her out. We were delighted to get any kind of money, since we'd never had an allowance before, but this only lasted about two weeks. Then the money stopped.

We were told that our allowance was going to help buy a cake for our grandparents' fiftieth wedding anniversary. Sadly, after the celebration was over, so was the allowance.

The celebration lasted all afternoon, and there were many gifts and cards. Many people—both whites and Indians—came to Ed and Mabel Hatchett's fiftieth wedding anniversary. I don't know if anyone there remembered their wedding day or if anyone was still alive from that time, but gone were all the name-calling and the talking behind their backs. Gone also were the "ugly Americans"—the women who had treated Mabel so cruelly. The two had outlived all of them, and now they were reaping their just rewards.

In the fall of 1960, Uncle Marvin and Aunt Dee Dee moved to Utah. Uncle Marvin worked for the BIA in the soil conservation program, and Aunt Dee Dee worked for the Winnebago Indian Hospital in Winnebago. They lived at the agency right next door to the office. It came as a shock to everyone that they would leave Winnebago. Prior to the big move, they had moved a shed out to our house; this would be used to store their goods that didn't make it on the first trip. They had a late-model Plymouth station wagon that was loaded; it was pulling a U-Haul trailer. Uncle Marvin was driving a Jeep with a small trailer behind it. They left the agency late in the evening. The small caravan drove all night, and by late the next day, they were in Utah. Aunt Dee Dee went to work the next day at Intermountain Indian School in Brigham City, Utah, the same school where Aunt Wilma worked.

Every now and then, Marvin would make a trip back to Winnebago to pick up more of their stuff. This went on for a few years. Sometimes he would bring his car and rent a trailer; other times he had a bread truck. Once he had a pickup truck. He made several trips to the reservation, making us think that maybe he missed the place. But he finally managed to move all of their stuff.

Uncle Marvin and Aunt Dee Dee moved their family into a home in Willard, Utah. Aunt Wilma had an apartment on campus at the Intermountain Indian School. Late in the fall, Ed and Mabel would journey out to stay for the winter with their two daughters. This worked fine for a couple of weeks, but then Ed would want to come home. They could usually only talk him into staying until after Christmas.

After Christmas, Grandpa wanted to go home *now*, and that was it! One year Uncle Hank drove them home in January. It was bitter cold on the ride across Wyoming. Ed and Mabel had to cover up with blankets. Hank's old 1954 Ford, even with the heater blowing on high, couldn't keep them warm. They stopped quite a bit for coffee on that ride. The next year, it was the same story; they would go out in the fall with the intention of staying until spring, but they would return in the middle of the winter. Ed just didn't want to be away from his farm.

It was when I entered the fifth grade that I met my best friend. His name was Gene Stout. He had two brothers and one sister. They lived on a farm about seven miles west of Winnebago. Their one-room country school, Pleasant Valley, had been shut down forever, and now they were being bussed to town. Many of the rural schools had been closed; it was just too expensive to keep them open with just a handful of children. When I first saw Gene, he was standing on the monkey bars, and he was going to leap out and grab the second or third rung. He never made it. His foot got caught in the ladder, and he fell straight forward, banging his head on the steel ladder. I am surprised that he didn't split his head open, because he really banged his head hard. He got off the monkey bars and rubbed his head and had a tear in his eye, but he toughed it out and went on like nothing had happened. I stayed at Gene's house, and he stayed at ours. We did lots of things together and got into trouble together, but that's all part of growing up.

In the fall of 1962, I entered the eighth grade. There were twenty-five of us in my class. I think that most of us just wanted to get out of grade school and move on into high school. I was in the eighth grade when I had my first taste of alcohol. Some group would have a dance at the town hall most every Saturday night, so Gene and I and about four other guys would all chip in and get a quart of beer. Then we had to find a runner, one that we could trust who wouldn't rip us off, because there were a few of those guys around. Once we got our brew, we would take it behind the town hall, and all have a good pull. Gene told me to always take as much as I could because he and I put most of the money in, so I did as I was told. The quart only made it around two times before it was empty. Once in a while, we would get some flavored sloe gin. We really thought we were something.

On May 20, 1963, our big day, the members of the eighth-grade class who passed into high school were seated in the front row of the gym. We stood up as our teacher read our names. Once all of us stood up, we had to turn around and look at the audience. Then we were officially in high school. My brother Mike graduated from high school that year, and in the fall, we took him down to the Haskell Indian Institute in Lawrence, Kansas, a land grant college set up by the U.S. Congress for Native Americans.

Mike's choice of college once again made me wonder about my Indian heritage—my roots. Terry, Mike, and I knew we were three-quarters Indian—my mother was half-Indian and my grandfather was all Indian, but no one seemed to know many of the details of what that meant or who our ancestors were. Focusing on the tombstone in my grandfather's front yard, I sent away for any information the Bureau of Indian Affairs had on Private William Hatchett.

I got back a packet of information. My great-great-grandfather William had started out as William Cloud but later changed his last name to Hatchett. He had been a scout for the U.S. Army. He had been the scout tracker, the person who rode in front of the column in advance of the cavalry to find the enemy's whereabouts. He was famous for his valiance in battle and much decorated.

I couldn't get over it. I really *was* descended from a warrior!

On March 5, 1964, my mother got a call that our father, Alfred Walker, had been killed in a car accident south of Macy, Nebraska. She called Mike, and he came back from Haskell, and the three of us went down to the old Walker farmhouse. It was very old, and I can't remember who lived there then. The word was that before Alfred's father—our grandfather—died, he put a medicine bundle someplace in the attic of his house and that if anybody messed with his house or tried to burn it down, something bad would happen to them, so the old house was left alone.

I had never been to a peyote meeting before. Although Alfred himself was not a member of the Native American Church, his father, Daniel Walker, was. The community turned out. The men folk butchered two pigs, and the women of the community started to cook the pigs. It smelled really good while they were cooking. This was the first time that I had ever attended a funeral on the Omaha Reservation. There were many people at the wake, and many members of the Native American Church showed up for the meeting. Alfred was buried in the Macy cemetery on a cold and windy Sunday afternoon, next to his parents. My mother was asked to sing in the choir for his funeral. It was kind of strange, but Alfred had told my mother many, many years ago that's where he first spotted her—singing in the church choir.

The story that we got was that Alfred was helping someone change a tire, and he stepped back and got hit by a car. The young driver never stopped. He just kept going. Another driver saw the accident and chased down the young driver and made him come back to the accident scene. Alfred died at the accident scene.

After the funeral, my mother got in contact with an attorney. He told her not to sign anything until he had a chance to look at it. He told her that the insurance company would try to settle this as soon as they could and for the smallest amount of money. My mother never signed anything, but Alfred's wife signed, and she thought that she would get a thousand dollars. She didn't realize that she had to split this with Alfred's three sons.

One of the few encounters I had with Alfred Walker was when I was in the sixth grade. I was walking downtown before school with some of my friends when he saw me, and he came over to us. I told my friends that I would catch up with them later. Alfred had already been drinking, and he was asking me a lot of questions about Mike and Terry and how we were doing. When he saw the new watch I'd gotten for Christmas, he tried to take it off my wrist. The woman with him stopped him. She told him no. He just stood and glared at me. Then he asked me if I had any money. I told him no, and I told him that I had to go to school. I walked fast and caught up to my buddies.

When I first entered high school, it was fun, and I did pretty well. I thought it was easy, but by the time, I got into the tenth grade, I dropped out. I just stopped going to school. I was "too cool" to go to school … until my stepdad got hold of me and told me, "You'd better be in school tomorrow." So I went back to school the next day. It was tough. I had to make up a lot that I had missed, but I did, and I was able to graduate with my class.

In the summer of 1965, we needed a new toilet hole dug; Terry was working down at Macy, so I got the job of digging the new hole. I got tired of our needing to dig a new toilet hole every other year, so I decided this one was going to be deep. I laid out the size, and I started to dig. By the second day, I was in over my head, and soon I needed a ladder to get in and out of the hole. The hole was about nine feet deep, and I was getting tired of throwing the dirt out of it; plus it was starting to roll back into the hole. Mom told me that was good enough, and my response was that I didn't want to ever do this again. This was going to be the last toilet hole that I ever dug.

In the spring of 1967, we finally got plumbing, and guess who got to dig the water lines to the house?

The summer of 1966, I worked on Highway 77, south of town, putting in cement culverts. Sometimes I had to work with the big crew, whose job was building forms and pouring cement, making square waterways. It was fun, especially on payday. Work was hard, and sometimes we put long hours in; but most of the time, we worked eight hours a day and no weekends. One day when the foreman had business with the main office, his assistant, Albert Robinson, was put in charge for the day. Robinson was an Omaha Indian from Macy, Nebraska.

One of the men from Decatur, Nebraska, a white guy, said, "I am not working for an Indian." He quit on the spot and walked off the job site. I was shocked. I thought that racism was dead. I had a lot of white friends. In fact, my best friend, Gene, was white.

That August, I got a call from Booth and Olsen Construction. They offered me a job on their form crew to go to work in eastern Iowa at Cedar Falls. This work was really hard; plus they worked long hours, usually from sunup to sundown, plus half a day on Saturday. The money was awesome; I had never made so much money in my whole seventeen years on this earth. I made more than my high school teachers, but it was short-lived. I had to go back to school.

My last year of school, I just wanted to be out of school. I wanted to be off the reservation. I wanted to be in the Marines, fighting the war in Vietnam. I wanted to be a *warrior*, like my great-great-grandfather. That fall, Terry was out of school and was classified as 1A with the draft board. One day he and I went up to talk to the recruiters. We both talked with the Air Force recruiters. They were more interested in Terry than in me. Then I talked with the Marine recruiters and pretty much made a commitment to the Corps. I just wanted to be sure that I could handle it. I didn't date any girls that last year in high school. I didn't want to think about someone back home. I had a job to do, and I wanted to give it my full attention.

I found some pictures of Marines in WWII and hung them on my side of the room; I bought a cool-looking poster. It was a Bell CH-46 Sea Knight helicopter that had its tailgate down. The bird was actually in the air, it was backed into a steep hill, and the Marines were charging off the tailgate in full 782 gear (equipment that Marines carry in combat). Under the poster, it said, "We deliver." This was my best poster.

It was seven o'clock in the morning. The spring breeze that rustled through the budding walnut tree that shaded part of the porch found its way into my bedroom. It felt good to lie there and listen to the warm spring morning. In the distance, I could hear the calling of a blue jay, the sounds of a huge farm tractor straining under its load as it pulled a four-bottom plow, slicing its way through the rich black soil, and I could smell the pigs' yard from the neighbor's farm.

In two weeks, I would graduate from Winnebago High, and then the party would begin, but it would be a short party, because that Friday

I had to be in Omaha. I couldn't wait to get out of there and off the reservation. I wanted to get to Los Angeles. I wanted to see the ocean and a lot of other places that I'd only seen on TV. I didn't think Gene would make it at the University of Nebraska, but his folks wanted him to go there. I was sure glad my parents weren't like that. They were just glad to see me make it through high school. I wouldn't have to worry about a job for the next four years; I would be working for Uncle Sam. They said that Marine boot camp was the roughest boot camp of all of them, but others had made it through. I was certain Terry was having a ball at the Air Force boot camp in San Antonio, Texas.

On the big night, everybody was all dressed up in their Sunday-go-to-meeting clothes. We slipped on our white robes and lined up for the march down to the stage. I could feel everyone's eyes on me. The sweat ran down my back, but no one could see it. We finally got to our chairs and sat down. I stepped up to get my diploma. With a handshake and a few words from our principal, it was over. My best friend, Gene, was almost in tears. I was just glad to get out of there. My thoughts were on the Vietnam War and how soon I could get over there.

Afterward, I ran down to my grandparent's apartment in the projects so I could change clothes. (They had moved into town after my grandmother had a stroke in the fall of 1966.) I told my grandfather I had to meet Mom at Uncle Donald's wake in Sioux City and would be there most of the night. In minutes, I was out of the apartment and heading for Sioux City.

I entered the smoke-filled room and didn't recognize any of the Indians. They were all from Sioux City. I sat with Mom for a while to make it look good and told people that I had just graduated that night from Winnebago High School.

The traditional Winnebago burial way is to have a wake and stay up with the body for four days and nights. On the fourth day, they have a feast. During the four days of the wake, the immediate family does not get involved with the preparation of the food or other activities that can be done by others. A person is asked to be in charge of the burial and all other arrangements. He is usually a close friend or a relative. This is the Indian way. All of the people are volunteers and friends. The last meal is cooked outside and served to the immediate family first, after the water and tobacco have been passed around. Everybody has to take a puff of the tobacco and a drink of the water from the same cup. Then the food can be served to the family first.

Donald died in the hospital. The cops had found him the night before and threw him in jail even though he was hurt. He kept trying to tell them that he needed help, but they kept ignoring him. One of the inmates told the cops that Donald needed medical help, but still they did nothing until he passed out and fell on the floor, and by then, it was too late.

On the fourth night, the next day, they would lay Donald to rest in Winnebago's Boot Hill, an old cemetery where there was no caretaker; and usually in spring, someone set a fire, and that burned off the weeds but left the headstones blackened.

When it was time for me to leave, I told Mom that I would be home later. She told me to be careful. I said I was always careful. She just nodded her head.

Fifteen minutes later, I rolled into North Sioux City, South Dakota, to the Big R (Reynolds) as everybody called it. In South Dakota, you only had to be eighteen to drink, so everyone went to North Sioux City to drink. A lot of my classmates were already there and looked funny in their suits and dresses, talking about the coming summer jobs they planned to have, and then it would be off to college in the fall.

The party went on and on, and it was getting late, and they were talking about going down to the tower. Jody Simmons jumped in my car. We drove out to the IBP (Iowa Beef Packers) tower west of town; I think both of us knew that everyone else was at the tower at the river. This girl was trying to suck my tongue out of my head. What a chick! We left the IBP tower at 4 AM and went down to the tower at the river. That's where the party was.

We made it back to town and drove up to the school, dropped off all of the juniors, and then headed back to the river for a few more cold ones. Later, Gene, John, and I headed for South Sioux City to get some breakfast at the Crystal Truck Stop and then talked about how school was, all of us knowing it was time to go home.

I took John home first and headed out to the Stout farm. I told Gene that I would stop by before I took off for boot camp. Back home, I took a shower and got dressed. I put on some forty-five records and sat down for a while. Friday morning, I would be heading down to the Omaha

Armed Forces Entrance Examination Station office. I just sat there for a while. It was quiet. I was thinking about how the old house used to be, how it had been real small, and now it had plenty of room, and I was the last kid at home, and I just had a few more hours. I didn't think I would miss home. I had always wanted to be gone from there.

That afternoon, I drove out to see Gene. I found his mother doing some wash. She told me that it was in the nineties, very unusual for the month of May. Gene came out of the house, and we moved away from his mother.

"What did your folks say about the past few days?" I asked him.

"Nothing, not a word."

"You're kidding?"

"No, they didn't say a word when I walked in this morning."

We talked some more, and I said I had to get going. Gene wished me good luck in the Marines, and I told him that I would see him sometime in late summer or the fall. On the ride back to my house, I could see the farmers out in the fields preparing the soil for the planting. When I return, it would be time to harvest the corn and get ready for cold weather.

Chapter 19

Becoming a Marine

On the first leg of our train ride to San Diego, we stop at Kansas City, Missouri. It's dark by the time we get there. The conductor tells us that we will be hooking up with a train that will take us west. All we have to do is just stay on the train. He also tells us that we can't drink on this train!

The train ride is exciting. We talk about boot camp and ask one another questions about it. It turns out the only thing we all know about boot camp is that we have to go through it and that it will change us for life.

Earl is from Storm Lake, Iowa. He has a Marine tattoo on his left arm. It's really just the initials *USMC*, and it looks homemade. We ask him who did it, and he tells us that he did it; the *US* is on the forearm, while the *M* is on the side of his wrist, and the *C* is under his wrist. He tries to act like a badass, but he looks like a hillbilly. My roommate is a farmer from O'Neill, Nebraska. He doesn't say much. Guy Redowl, the fourth Marine, is a Sioux Indian from Valentine, Nebraska.

Sunday morning, the train pulls into Fullerton, California. The conductor tells us there will be a short delay while they change engines, and then we will start the ride to San Diego. I feel my stomach start to knot up when they announce the final "all aboard," and the train starts to leave the station. On the way down to San Diego, the tracks take us by the ocean. I see people out there riding the surf and lying on the beaches. The ocean looks so big. It never ends, and it just keep going and going.

By mid-afternoon, we are standing on the platform at the San Diego train station, and nobody knows what to do. The green Marine Corps bus pulls up, and they tell us to get on the bus, sit down, and shut up. The bus moves through the city of San Diego. I don't have any idea where we are. After a few minutes, the bus pulls up to a large building, and then all hell breaks loose.

"On the yellow footprints, you maggots!"

And I thought they would let us go downtown and come back on Monday. No way. They take recruits anytime of the day or night. I've seen the yellow footprints in the movies; now I am on them, and the shit is hitting the fan and blowing all over me.

Holy shit, these DIs (drill instructors) are mean. They are hitting us, yelling at us, screaming, punching, and kicking us all over the place. We are in receiving barracks when they tell us to fall outside and get into formation. They march us over to the barbershop. We get our first Marine Corps haircut, and everything comes off. We really look funny without any hair on our heads. When we're done there, they march us over to the chow hall and tell us to eat everything we take.

"We don't waste food in the Marine Corps."

After chow, they march us back to receiving barracks and take away our civilian clothes and give us one pair of trousers, a pair of tennis shoes, a cover (cap), and one bright yellow sweatshirt to wear. We pack up our civilian clothes and ship them home.

The first night, we don't get any sleep. They keep us up all night working. We polish the floors: we do it again and then again. When we're not working, we stand on the stairs and read the Marine Corps Handbook. The only thing that keeps me sane is that on the very last page of the handbook, it states, "Remember others have made it." And that is true. One is my cousin who made it through boot camp. I remind myself that Dewayne Rave was a Marine a while back, and Ed West was just through boot camp a little over a year ago. I know that I can make it.

About the only good thing about boot camp is mail call. I get a letter from Mom, who tells me that our dog Skip ran away and never came home and that ever since I left, he wouldn't eat and would just lie around. One Saturday morning, the old man took my car out for a spin, and when he came up the road, Skip jumped up and down and ran over to the driver's side, his tail wagging; but when he saw it was just the old man, he wilted and lay back down. One day they let him loose, thinking maybe he would like to run around a bit, but he left and never returned home. Mom said that he went looking for me and probably went into the woods and died.

We spend a week at the rifle range on Camp Pendleton, and Private Shedder kills a mouse. Our DI just happens to walk by and asks in his DI voice, "Who killed my Marine Corps mouse?" Immediately, Private Shedder stands up and says, "Sir, I did sir." The DI tells us that after chow, we will come back and give this mouse a Marine Corps burial. After chow that evening, Platoon 285 assembles outside of the chow hall, and we are marched over to the butts' area. There Private Shedder finds his kill. The rest of the platoon stands at attention while Private Shedder digs a hole for the mouse. He digs and digs until the DI tells him to stop. The hole is about two feet deep and about three feet around. Then Private Shedder is instructed to place the mouse in the hole and bury it. The DI tells Private Shedder to fall back into formation when he is finished, and then he tells us, "No one—and I mean no one—can kill a Marine Corps mouse without permission! Is that understood?"

"Sir, yes, sir," is our reply.

Just before lights out, we're lying in our bunks, and the DI calls us to attention. He then says, "Forward march!" And we march in our beds. He then calls for a column right, and we make a column right in our beds. It is kind of funny, but no one laughs. It's just another way to see if we can follow orders.

August 15 is graduation day for Platoon 285. No more doing push ups in the dirt and doing squat thrusts forever when we make a mistake. I wonder what happened to Earl from Storm Lake, Iowa, who started with us but was put in a motivation platoon. Redowl says he saw him carrying a sledgehammer and wearing a helmet without a liner in it, and that means Earl was in the brig.

That afternoon, in our squad bay, the DI tells us about MOS (Military Occupational Specialties) and explains what they mean. He tells us the majority of us will be grunts and will probably go to Vietnam. That's fine with me, because that's why I joined the Marines—to see if

I could become a Ho-Chunk warrior like my great-great-grandfather William Hatchett.

I make it through basic training. I didn't want my folks to know how much I missed them and wished I was home, but I got over that. Tonight we are all United States Marines. I hope the world can handle it, because the most dangerous thing on the face of this earth is a Marine and his weapon.

At Camp Pendleton, we are put into a training company of about one hundred men and told we can get liberty on the weekends. A few of us go to Disneyland, which is kind of disappointing, but we still have a good time. It feels good to get off the base for the first time in three months. When you're in boot camp, you don't get any time off; every day is a work day or training day.

In second ITR (Infantry Training Regiment), we all learn basic Marine infantry; but after the second ITR, we're split up. Some of us are going to be mortar men, rocket men, and machine gunners. Still others will go on to a more advanced school, such as demolition school, communications school, and aviation school.

I am sent to mortar school for two weeks and then get to go home for twenty days' leave. Nobody sleeps the night before our first leave. The next morning, everybody is up. Most of us don't go to chow. We just wait for the first sergeant to cut us loose. Everywhere you look, you can see a smiling face. This will be my first airplane ride, and I can't wait. The adrenaline races through my veins as the jet taxis to the runway. A smile breaks across my face as the jet roars down the runway, and we lift off. I can feel my body being pushed back into the seat. I look out the window. Just think, I'll be in Omaha in two hours.

It's great to be home. I put on some of my old records and turn up the volume and kick back. I think to myself, *I made it. Nothing can go wrong.* Later that day, I go down to Lincoln to the university to pick up Gene. We stop on the way back to pick up some refreshments. We make it back to Winnebago in time for the football game. It's good to be home and talk with some of my old classmates. It's only been a few months, but I've gone through a lot. I put weight on and filled out more.

I meet up with Ed West, who will be leaving about a week before I leave. Ed has been in the Marines about eighteen months. He has been in commutation school back east, and now he is ready to go and fight the war, in the rear with the gear. Ed has a top secret clearance, so he will never be out in the bush. He will stay at the communication bunker.

Too soon, I am at Eppley Airfield on Omaha, Nebraska, saying good-bye. I tell Mom not to worry, that I will be all right. The old man tells me to write and call when I can. I would like to hold both of them and tell them how much I love them, but I don't have the time. I don't look back, just keep walking. I look out of the window and say good-bye to Omaha, Nebraska. I don't know if I will see it again. I know Mom and the old man will stand there until my plane is out of sight and then look some more.

Staging battalion at Camp Pendleton, we have officers and NCOs with us, and it's like a real Marine company. One of our classes is about getting captured and interrogated; the setting is like a Vietnamese village.

I ask my squad leader, "Do Vietnamese villages look like that?"

He says, "Yeah, they do, but there's more huts." This will be his second tour of Vietnam. The first time, he was fresh out of boot camp like me. He was a grunt (Marine infantry). But now he is a cook and going back for the money. The last week of staging battalion, I run into Ed West again. He will be leaving in the morning. He is ready to go over.

Ten days later, our company is getting ready to ship out.

The night before we leave, there's no liberty. We pack all of our military clothes and are told to take only a few civilian clothes for R & R. We pack two sea bags. One will be left in Okinawa, and we will take the smaller one with us to Vietnam. The next morning, we're up at 0400 hours; and loading onto the buses, we will be going to Norton Air Force Base, California. At Norton, they run us through the mess hall, and soon after, we are seated in a Flying Tigers jet. The captain comes on the intercom and tells us that we will be landing in Anchorage, Alaska, for a fuel stop. Then we will fly down the coast of the Soviet Union and then on to Okinawa.

That's as far as we'll be going for now. The jet will continue to Vietnam with Marines who are ready to go to Vietnam. Upon arriving on Okinawa, we go to Camp Butler, where all Marines have to report. It is there that we leave the larger sea bag. In thirteen months, when we come back from Vietnam, we will pick up our larger sea bags and go back to the world.

From Camp Butler, we are taken over to Camp Swab. After getting off the cattle cars, they put us into a formation and tell us that we will be here for a while. During the orientation, a drunk Marine comes out of the barracks. A fight breaks out between the sergeant and the drunk Marine. Somehow they get the drunk back into the barracks, where he breaks away and runs into a window; glass flies all over the place. He is cut badly, and blood is pumping all over the place. In a few minutes, the corpsman arrives and gives him a shot. It knocks him out, and they take him away. After it's all over, the sergeant says to us, "See what the Saki will do to you?"

Our stay at Camp Swab is about four weeks. Every day we ask when we are leaving, and we get the same answer: "Don't know." The club has slot machines, and the drinks are cheap. You don't have to be twenty-one. I could get used to this place.

In the morning, the *Na-son* (cleanup women) comes in to clean up the barracks and wash any of our clothes; they sew them if needed. It's something to have them walk into your cubicle when you're getting dressed and ask if you need any clothes washed or mended. I always try to get dressed before they come into the barracks.

There's one thing that I will never forget. It's the smell of hot tar. They are always repairing the roofs of the barracks. They even work on Sundays; the air is always filled with the smell of hot tar. Then one day, they tell us to saddle up. We're going to Vietnam. At Kadina Air Force Base, Okinawa, we are loaded on a C-130. Our sea bags are tied down to the tailgate; and we form a single file, turn, and face toward the center of the plane and take a seat. They don't have real seats. There is webbing stretched over some kind of tubing, and that's your seat. The crew chief tells us to get as comfortable as we can because it's a long ride. Soon the tailgate closes. We are packed in like sardines. They point to the head (the toilet) and tell us that's as good as it gets on this plane.

It's dark inside the potbellied olive drab bird. The bird shakes and vibrates; soon the noise of the engines and the high pitch of the turbo props are almost too much. I wonder if it's going to fly apart. Can the body take all of this vibration? The wings look like they are going to start flapping up and down like a chicken trying to fly and everybody knows that a chicken can't fly.

Then the brakes are released, and we lunge forward. I think everyone has his fingers crossed. Once airborne, everyone gives a sigh of relief. We move in our chairs and try to get more comfortable. They tell us the ride to South Vietnam will be about six hours. In the fifth hour, they tell us that we will be landing in Da Nang Air Base, South Vietnam. It's dark outside. I try to look around and see if there's any shooting going on. I don't see anything but dark. The potbellied bird touches down. A sergeant tells us that we will be taking a chopper ride out to sea to the USS *Tripoli*. That's where we will be staying for a few days. The chopper lands and we all board it. Some of the windows are in, and some are blown out, but it's pretty cool to be in a CH-46 that is heading out to the South China Sea.

Soon we see this big flattop out in the ocean. The chopper sets down on the flight deck, and we hurry off. We make our way through the ship's narrow passageways. Soon we crowd into an area called a "birthing compartment," where we're told to grab any bunk and relax, and in the morning, they will start working on our paperwork.

Marines from the field come over and talk to us Boots, as we are called. They tell us that we are in the Second Battalion, Third Marines and that this is Foxtrot Company. After two days, we take a chopper ride to Hoi An combat base where we are given M-16s. They have a small rifle range for fan firing. *Now* I feel like a Marine.

Chapter 20

Into the Bush

In the distance, we can see some yellow smoke. The bird circles the smoke, and soon we set down. Everybody rushes off the tail end of the bird. I feel as if I just got off a carnival ride. I need to get my equilibrium back.

We are led away, and soon we meet all kinds of Marines, the CO, the company Gunny, platoon leaders, squad leaders, members of the squad; and I can't remember half of them. The squad leader tells me that we are operating somewhere in the Happy Valley area. One of the first things that the squad leader does is he takes my pack and gives me a huge gunnysack type of pack. I am now the lowest member on the team, the last ammo humper; I am, a "boot"—just to list a few names that they call new guys out in the bush. Because I am a boot, I get to pick the first meal from our C rations; after that, I go into rotations just like the rest of the guys.

PFC Harris comes over and tells me that he is no longer the last ammo humper. He tells me that he has been in the company about three weeks. Harris is a black Marine, and the rest of the team is white, and now the company is complete—they have their token Indian. Within the hour, I am given the nickname Chief. I am told that our FO (forward observer) is an Indian also.

The company is set up in a cemetery. It has large mounds where the dead are buried; I find a mound and roll up in my poncho. Sometime before my watch, it starts to rain. The water runs down into my poncho, even though I am lying on an angle with my head above my feet. It feels like I wet my pants. I feel uncomfortable. Someone from the CP (command post) makes his rounds. He sits with me for a while. He asks me if I am new. I guess they can tell us new guys. He asks me what part of the world I am from. I tell him I am from Winnebago, Nebraska.

"Never heard of it."

I tell him it's about eighty miles north of Omaha.

"I have heard of Omaha."

The next day, they show me how to load up my pack with mortar rounds and my gear. We start to move out. I have a hard time getting up, and the gunner gives me a hand. On my feet, I can feel the pack digging into my back through my flak jacket. We move out in single file. I am the last man on the mortar crew. Doc Hughes is behind me, and he jokes with me. "If you fall, I will pick you up, Chief."

We move along a rice paddy dike for quite a ways. I am drenched in my own sweat. It runs down on to my glasses. At first I try to keep them clean, but after a while, I don't have any dry shirt left on me. The straps on the pack dig into my armpits, and already I can feel the sting from a rash developing.

They pass the word to tie up the trousers around your boot tops because we'll be going into a deep paddy soon. I slosh through the rice paddy. I sink deep into it. The walk gets hard, and the rest of the gang doesn't slow down. We come up to a rise, and we take five; they pass the word to take off your boots and socks and try to dry them out. It feels good to sit down and take the pack off. I rub my feet and legs. Mud covers my new jungle boots; I bang them together to get most of it off. I get a chill from the warm moist air because I am all wet with sweat. I must have an old helmet, and it smells like BO now that it's all wet with my sweat.

I notice that I have blood running down my leg. I pull up my trousers, and there is a long black leech on my skin. He comes off when the sunlight hits him. He slides down my leg and drops to the ground. The corpsman sees what has happened and comes over to take a look. He wipes the wound with some disinfectant and puts a Band-Aid on it. I ask him why he did that.

"So it won't get any infection in it."

The radio cracks with orders to get ready to move out. Soon we're saddled up and moving again. We walk through more rice paddies; only this time, I tie up my trousers tighter than before. I don't need any more leeches. By mid-afternoon, we're out of the rice paddies and in some brush; it feels good to walk on solid ground again. I'm exhausted.

The second night, I am put on an LP (listening post). Now I understand why they all had smiles on their faces. The new guy gets to go on the LPs, OPs (observation post), etc. They take two new Marines and place them at night in front of the company perimeter. Then they give you a radio, and every thirty minutes, someone will say, "If everything is okay, key the handset twice."

At daylight, they bring us back into the perimeter. They ask me how it went last night. Corporal Milo tells me that all new guys have to take their turn doing this, and they're not picking on me.

I am tired from not getting enough sleep last night, but it doesn't matter. We're moving out. I don't think I'm going to like this job, short nights and long days of humping. Today is a carbon copy of yesterday—brush, rice paddies, humping, and more sweating. There is no change of clothes out here; you wear your clothes until they fall off. Already my clothes are beginning to smell like sweat and BO; nobody says anything about a shower or getting cleaned up in the morning. I would like to brush my teeth once in a while, but I don't even have a toothbrush with me.

No sign of the enemy. We take a long lunch break. Every time we take a long break, we set up the mortar tube and have it ready to fire; just in case Charlie (short for Viet Cong the enemy) comes for lunch.

A few nights later, one of our ambush sites gets lucky and opens up with a twelve-gauge shotgun, M79 grenade launcher, and automatic weapons. They kill four rice carriers. Yelling and screaming, "I got one, I got one," they drag in their victims into the CP area and search them. No weapons, just a lot of rice for the VC (Victor Charlie, the enemy). The next day, the bodies are still lying there. They look old to me. This is my first look at the enemy, and they don't look so tough to me. Some of the grunt cut off their ears and string them around their necks. I wonder what they would say if I lifted their scalps and tied them around my waist.

A few weeks later, someone spots movement out in the tree line. Everyone looks. The CO puts a call into S2 Intelligence; their response is, "There are no friendlies in that area."

The CO calls for mortars up. We move forward and set up our tube. The company has a reporter with us; he is from CBS. He lies down in front of the mortar tubes and clicks away; his camera is recording all of the action. One by one, the mortars find their mark; a total of thirty-eight rounds are dropped on the NVA (North Vietnamese Army), and a spotter plane confirms that he can see thirty bodies on the ground.

We keep moving all day long. My sweat doesn't bother me anymore. Even my wallet is soaked. I didn't think my body had that much water in it. Boots never know when they will pull an OP or an LP because we are expendable, and we don't know enough about the bush to be an asset to the company.

On Thanksgiving 1968, we are somewhere in the Happy Valley of South Vietnam. We're still looking for Charlie. I wonder if he spends as much time looking for us. Sometime in the afternoon, we take five and set up the tube, but then they pass the word to saddle up and move to a large clearing and wait for the chopper to come and pick us up.

No one knows where we are going, but wherever it is, we get to ride on choppers. The birds circle the base of Hoi An, and we land. The word is that we will be treated to a Thanksgiving dinner and a night off. This is quite a break with a real turkey dinner and all of the fixings. We don't get any bunks or huts, but we're not standing watch, and we get to sleep all night long. The next day, we saddle up and head for the helicopter pad and head out to the bush. Once they find a good drop zone, they land, and the first Marines unload. When the second load of Marines comes in, the enemy open fire. The Marines on the ground scramble to make a hasty 180-degree perimeter.

They pass the word that our bird will be coming into a hot LZ (landing zone). Someone pushes my head down. We're hit! Oil, hydraulic fluid, is squirting all over us. The sounds of bullets passing through the chopper sounds like bullets fired into water.

The pilot pulls out of formation and heads back to the fire support base, making a hot landing at Hoi An. We're whisked off the wounded bird and onto another. They pass the word to lock and load. This will be my first firefight. Actually, I can't wait. I want to make my first kill, but I want to see him first and then kill him—the real Ho-Chunk warrior way.

During our absence, gunships were called in to give us cover and to soften them up. By the time we land, the rest of the company has formed a 360-degree defense perimeter. We are rushed over to the CP (command post), and we set up. But there is no fire mission. The enemy had melted in the jungle. It was probably the VC. They like to do that to the Marines. Patrols are sent out, and they find four confirmed kills. I get a real look at the enemy, not just rice carriers. The typical VC, I am told, has the black pajamas on and carries an ancient French rifle—no grenades, no extra ammo. There is no way they could have much of a firefight with us.

We move out, again chasing Charlie. We move into the jungle. Once under the triple canopy, the humidity jumps up to 90 percent. It's stifling. The vegetation is thick, and it grabs and pulls on your gear, weighing your body down and making it harder to walk, and slices your exposed arms with its razor-sharp leaves; buried deep in the overgrowth is a pagoda. It has a rusted rail fence around it. On the rusted gate sits what looks like a swastika, but I am told that it's a Buddha sign and that Hitler reversed it and called it the swastika.

Our helicopter ride takes us to a secure base south of Da Nang, south of Marble Mountain. The compound is called the triangle because its perimeter is shaped like a triangle. We are told that we will be here for an indefinite period of time. They have moved the battalion HQ (headquarters) off the USS *Tripoli*, and the battalion commander has set up shop in the triangle. He has a sign put up outside of his tent; the sign says Rent a Battalion. Life at the triangle starts at six o'clock in the morning with hot chow, and then at seven, we have a company formation. Day patrols are sent out; night patrols are set for the evening. One of our areas of responsibility is a leper village. It's not too far from the triangle and a good place for the VC to hide.

I go with the first platoon to the Tu-Cal Bridge, which has been blow up three times by the VC. The first night I stand watch in a foxhole, it pours, and it's cold, and I am miserable. In three days, I pulled back to the rear and was put on mess duty.

A few nights later, another Marine and I get drunk and decide to have some fun. What the hell. Why not steal a jeep and head into Da

Nang or over to Dog Patch? We find a jeep, get in, and immediately get stuck, since we're not used to driving on sand. The next thing I know, my coconspirator takes off, leaving me with the jeep. Since I see no other way out, I confess. I tell the Skipper that I took the jeep for a joyride. My punishment is to walk point—head out into the unknown ahead of my company.

This is my punishment; little does anyone know, I view it as a reward, not a punishment. It's one of the reasons I wanted to go to Vietnam. I am, after all, the great-great-grandson of William Hatchett; and according to what I learned from the Bureau of Indian Affairs, when the cavalry moved out in the morning, William Hatchett was already out there—riding point!

The next day, I am volunteered to walk point for the company and lead them out on a day patrol. "How you feeling today, Chief?" Captain Smith asks me.

"I am fine, sir."

"I hear you volunteered to walk point."

"Yes, sir, I did, and I don't mind it one bit."

"Very good, because today you will take us through a leper village. Don't let them touch you. Keep your eyes open and keep in contact with the lead element behind you."

I enter the leper village, and the people want food. They look sorry. I look hard at them, but I don't see any open sores on them. We search for Vietcong but don't stay long. The Skipper tells me to head out and back to the triangle.

VC and NVA activity is picking up in the bridge area, so we send more patrols out, night and day. The grunts make more contact with the VC. The Tu-Cal Bridge compound has an unmanned machine gun bunker, and they ask the mortar section if anyone would like to stay in the gun bunker twenty-four hours a day. I tell them that I can handle it. The bunker sits about five feet above the perimeter. I move all of my gear into the bunker. The old man had sent me a transistor radio. I can pick up the Da Nang AFRVN (Armed Forces Radio Vietnam). This is my post. I am in here twenty-fours a day. The only time I leave is to go to the head or when we have a fire mission. I like it. I feel safe in this sandbag behemoth; at night Marines from my squad have to stand duty in the bunker while I sleep.

One day they load us up in trucks, and we head north; the scenery looks the same wherever they take us. We roll along; then we slow down, and I can see streetlights, paved sidewalks, and paved streets. It almost looks as if we could be back in the real world. This is Hue City, they tell us. This is where the Fifth Marines had a bloody battle with the NVA just a few weeks ago. We don't stop, and the convoy moves north to a place called Ca Lu.

On the first of April 1968, we start Operation Pegasus. We are told that this operation will open a route to Khe Sanh. We push into the bush and start to climb up the huge hills; our movement is laborious. Grass and small trees tug at our 782 gear; our canteens and gas masks always find something to grab on to and pull us one way or the other. The uneven ground throws our balance off.

The third day of Operation Pegasus, Decker, Rush, and I are up and ready to go. Rush and I went through training in the camp Pendleton; then off to Vietnam. We are talking about being halfway through our tours, when the first shell comes crashing down on us.

All of us hit the dirt. My foxhole is just right at my feet, and I fall into it. The second shell hits right where we were standing. I can hear screaming and yelling, loud crying, more screams from Marines. There's carnage and mayhem all around me.

Decker has his shinbone sticking through his pants, and he is in a lot of pain. The corpsman gives him a shot of morphine. Human bodies lie strewn about, bodies that just a few seconds ago were of Marines. I get up and try to help with the first aid. I move over to where Lance Corporal Rush lies. He's in two pieces. His upper torso is lying a few feet from the trench. His stomach and parts of his rib cage are gone. His legs are in the trench. One of his crew members has no head. Another is in the trench crying for his mother. I go over and try to give him first aid. His head is split open from his forehead all the way back to his neck, his brains leaking out of his wound.

The corpsman comes over and takes a look and throws up. The wounded Marine cries for his mom. Finally, the corpsman gets a bandage on him. We try to pull him out of the trench. He cries out in pain. We finally pull him out of the trench, and he dies. The only member of that team that lives is wounded in the neck.

One of the sergeants who went through staging battalion with me is medevaced out. He isn't hit, but he is crying. He needs help walking. He has messed his pants, and he is totally out of his mind. He is loaded aboard the chopper, never to be seen again.

We get all of our wounded and killed in the choppers, and we move out. I keep thinking of what has happened; it goes through my mind time and time again. That round was just a few inches from my foxhole; if it had landed only three inches more, I would not be here. I am promoted to gunner on the mortar team.

Operation Pegasus is a success. Route 9 is now open to Khe Sanh. We move onto Route 9 and set up on a wide-open spot on the road. My squad is sent down to a pontoon bridge. It's located in a deep valley. They tell us to build a bunker and a mortar pit. We build it on the east side of the bridge. I don't know how we can defend this bridge; we are the ones that will be shelled and have nowhere to go.

Easter morning of 1968, I leave the bunker and look around for my squad. They are all standing up by the bridge. I walk up to join them and ask them what they are doing. They tell me that they are holding Easter services. It isn't much, but it's all they have. I am asked to join the group. We all take turns reading from the New Testament. Soon our platoon commander asks us the same question. We tell him that we are having Easter services and are just about done, and we ask him if he would like to say the closing prayer. He does, and that is Easter for us on the pontoon bridge somewhere on Route 9 in Vietnam.

On one of our walks in the beautiful country of Vietnam, we get into a firefight with the NVA. They are dug in and not moving an inch. One of our rocket men pulls out a LAW rocket, takes aim at his target, and squeezes the trigger. A loud boom and blast is heard, followed by an ear-piercing scream. The LAW rocket has blown up in his hand. All that is left is the bloody bone of his wrist. That Marine is out of this war and also out of the Marine Corps. We call in for a fixed wing, and we napalm them. There are no more dug-in NVA.

The NVA do not back down from a fight. One night they throw several rocket-propelled grenades at one of our patrols. They knock out one of the tanks, and it goes off the road and down a steep cliff. Lance Corporal Hernandez, although seriously wounded, stays with the tank, hanging on for his life as the out-of-control tank picks up speed and races down the steep hill. There are wounded Marines inside the tank, and it is his job to keep them safe. The war is over for Gil and so is his stint in the Marine Corps.

We are losing a Marine or two, killed in action, every day, sometimes more. On one patrol, we run into an NVA patrol that has a very good sniper. He kills two Marines. The word is passed for mortars up. We climb the hill and make our way into a bomb crater, where they tell me where they want the mortars dropped. The fire mission starts, and we unload round after round on the enemy.

One of our scouts climbs up to the top of the bomb crater and looks around and asks, "Where is that sniper?" He is shot in the heart. He grabs his chest and slides down into the crater. His final words are, "Oh God, I am hit."

Our company Gunny says that he will call in a medevac. The Gunny clears out of the bomb crater, and we never see him again. Time goes by, and the CO wants to know where the Gunny is. One of the grunts moves into the next crater and yells to us that the gunny has been hit in the head by the sniper.

Enemy action picks up tenfold. Every company in the battalion has firefights with the NVA; the contacts are major events, not the four or five shots we would get from the VC down south.

I wonder if I am a Ho-Chunk warrior yet.

Chapter 21

Foxtrot Ridge

I have been in the bush for more than six months. I am no longer the boot, and except for a few close firefights, it's been a good experience. Six months ago, I was a lowly ammo humper; now I am a squad leader in Foxtrot Company.

We have been sent to the top of a ridge. We clean out the mortar pit and clear the fields of fire. The elephant grass is about three feet high. Our mortar pit is right on the perimeter. This does bother me a bit. Mortars don't carry enough bullets to sustain a long firefight with the enemy.

I don't see how we can secure this ridge; we don't have enough men to cover it. The foxholes are too far apart, and the ridge is quite long. A crew service weapon should be inside the perimeter, not on the perimeter itself. Two weeks ago, when we were here, it was very quiet. We didn't see anything.

The first night goes by without any incident.

The next day, everything is quiet. The day patrols go out and find nothing. At 1905 hours, a young Marine spots an NVA column. Everybody stares off in the direction of his pointing finger. Both mortar tubes are put on a fire mission, but they put us on hold. The CO opts for artillery and air strikes. With the sun sinking low in the western sky, we look harder into the twilight. Suddenly in the shadow of the still evening, there's movement—lots of movement.

A column of NVA soldiers moves across a faraway hill. Once again, we're put on another fire mission, but it's too big for us. They must know that we are watching them. They have no fear of us. They just keep moving toward us. Artillery and eighty-one mortars are called in. This scatters them, but they will regroup and continue.

Adrenaline is rushing through our veins. For the new Marines on this ridge, this is the first time that they have seen the NVA. It doesn't bother me because they are still quite a ways out there, and no one has passed the word, and we have seen the NVA before. The night passes without any incident. Everyone is glad to see the sun rise. The word is that we will be staying on this ridge. We do a few work details. The company sends out day patrols. They come back and report nothing that could be bad news for us. It's been known that the NVA will not make contact before a major operation, that sometimes they will let our patrols just walk right by them. They don't want to tip us off.

The supply chopper comes in with c-rats, mail, water, and ammo. We have some Marines leaving the company because of an illness or maybe R & R. During the day, it's peaceful and quiet up here on the ridge. Some parts of the ridge are very steep, but the slope in front of us is very gentle. We work on clearing fields of fire in front of us, but for the most part, we just sit and wait and look.

This day goes down into history as uneventful, just another day in the Nam. Uneasiness has settled over the company. I look at my men. Some of them have never been in a firefight. I don't think any of them have seen the enemy up close.

I get the 2200 to 0200 watch. I play the transistor radio my stepdad sent me very low, but it's hard to pick up AFVN because we are so far north. The night is very still and quiet. It is strange how cool and damp it gets in the night. The rest of the squad is sound asleep; at 0130 hours; someone from the CP comes up to my mortar pit and asks, "Is everything okay?"

I ask if there's any word on NVA coming our way. He hasn't heard, and he continues his rounds. At 0200 I wake up PFC Dan Kendall; he looks around, probably wondering where in the hell he is. He finally gets all of the cobwebs out of his head and rubs the sleep out of his eyes. We sit and talk for a while because I'm wide awake and can't sleep. It's getting late, and I need to get some rest. I lie down next to the mortar pit and think about home. When I was young and we used to go camping, we always stayed up late and talked and laughed.

Dan wraps up in his poncho liner and sits over the mortar pit with his legs inside the pit. In a second, there are explosions all around us. Dan jumps out of the mortar pit and asks me if I am okay. Lieutenant Dido runs over to me and asks if I fired any mortar rounds.

"No, I don't know what that is."

He disappears into the dark toward the CP group. Again, the explosions go off. This time, some go off in the mortar pit; it's incoming hand grenades. The CP is only seventy-five feet from my position; I run up to the CP and tell the Skipper, Commanding Officer Jim Jones,* that it's incoming grenades. I catch the last transmission from one of the LPs. He says, "There's movement out here, lots of movement, NVA!" A few seconds later, the LPs are dead. An enemy soldier jumped into their position with a satchel charge and blew up all of them. The last word from the CP is to hold fire on the mortar.

The nightmare has started. I run back to my squad. By now everyone in the company is awake. We get our mortar ready to fire; all of us get into the mortar pit. We are very fortunate that we have a claymore mine in front of us. It isn't long, and we can hear voices and movement in front of us. We can hear them dragging up equipment. We can hear their canteens clanking on their belts. We can hear them lock and load their weapons.

More of the elephant grass is pushed down. It seems like its right in front of us. My squad tells me to hit the claymore. I tell them very softly that we need to wait a little more. I am so scared. If someone were to say, "Let's get the hell out of here," we would; but no one has told us to leave. More movement in the grass, soon they will be right in our faces. I don't want my squad to know that I am scared. I think everyone is. In fact, Homes, my A gunner, lies down in the mortar pit and starts to cry.

I hit the plunger on the claymore, and nothing happens. I do it again and still nothing. I start to pull the wire in, and I find it has been cut. My heart falls out of my chest. I know we will all die tonight. Death is just a few feet from our mortar pit. I pray to God to let us live until morning. That's when help will be here. I pray again and again.

A flare is sent into the sky, and the whole hill rises up right in front of us. Hordes of enemy soldiers charge at us. The NVA soldiers are shooting farther up the hill. They think we are farther up. Instead, we are shooting them in their bellies. They don't even know that they are being shot at. They fall into our mortar and outside of it, and soon we have more than ten bodies lying around us. I put my empty pistol magazines in my pocket so I can reload them later. Now I am out of bullets. I am loading my magazines as fast as I can. I can hear people dragging up behind us. I push the last bullet into the magazine and quickly push the magazine into the .45-caliber pistol.

I pull the slide back and turn around, and I am looking into the muzzle of an AK-47; before the NVA soldier can squeeze his trigger, I put a .45 slug into his forehead, and I hit his buddy in the face with the next bullet.

The battle rages on. Artillery from Co Roc rains down on us. Hand grenades keep coming our way. Automatic rifle fire and machine gun fire is all around us and coming at us. We run out of ammo. I tell my men to strip the AK-47s from the NVA soldiers and use them. We find a few grenades and throw them at the advancing enemy. This goes on for almost an hour.

The second wave attacks with more vigor and speed. More bodies fall on us. The enemy is charging so hard that they don't even notice us sitting in a hole; they don't even notice that their comrades have been shot. The night air is filled with exploding shells. Flares burn overhead. This helps visibility a little. There is movement all around us. I tell my men to just sit tight and wait. We have no help coming until daylight.

It stops as fast as it started. The sounds of heavy labored breathing and low moans come up from the hillside. Not all the enemy soldiers are dead, but we don't have time to check them. The lull in the fighting gives us time to catch our breaths and to reload. We find that we are just about out of bullets. From nowhere, a grenade lands in the mortar pit; we all jump out. Dan Kendall takes off; the rest of us jump back into the pit, only to find that Homes has been wounded by the last grenade. More grenades are thrown into the mortar pit; we all jump out and then back in.

Then out of the dark, a lone figure comes running at us. We cut him down. He falls outside of the mortar pit. I tell my guys to take his weapon. They roll him over and get the shock of their lives. He's a Marine. Where did he come from? What the hell is he doing out in front of us? Questions that I don't have the answers for. We take the dead Marine's ammo, weapon, and grenades. This will help for a few seconds. We move dead NVA's out of the mortar pit and get ready for the next attack. We are down to just three Marines, and one is wounded. We can hear more movement coming up from the hill.

Puff the Magic Dragon is overhead, kicking out his thirty-minute illumination flares and using his Gatling guns on the enemy. It's just a continuous roar when he fires his guns.

The human wave comes at us again; we can see their faces wrench in pain as our bullets find their targets. We can't sustain another attack. We pull Homes out of the pit and lay him on the ground. I pull the pin on a grenade and gently toss it down the hill. Within a few seconds, we hear moaning and thrashing around after the explosion. I pull the pin on my last grenade and let it slide down the mortar tube; it goes off, taking the firing pin with it. If I can't use it, neither can the NVA!

Gil and I pull Homes at a very low crawl; we pull him toward the middle of the perimeter. NVA! We lie down, playing dead, and they jump over us. We continue toward the middle. As we get closer, we can hear enemy soldiers talking. We lie still for a while. The sound of the battle rages on with blinding flashes and shells still falling around us. The enemy soldiers move on. We pull Homes a little more and hear fast-moving footsteps. We play dead again, and the NVA sail right past us and head up the hill.

We drag Homes toward the CP, only to find out that we are on the outside of the perimeter. They have cut us off; no one told us about this. The second and third platoons have formed a new perimeter just above our mortar position. We head for the north side of the perimeter. We find Marines still in their holes. I tell them what has happened over on the other side of the hill. The Marines begin to pull out except for one. He's not from the company. He's a combat engineer attached to our company. He lies in the foxhole and cries. He doesn't want to pull out. He thinks he is safe there. He cries so hard that his whole body shakes. I tell him again about what has happened.

"You're an Indian," he says. "You're used to it."

I tell him I don't have time to waste on him, and I am not going to risk the lives of the rest of us over him. He looks at me and shakes his head and cries some more. The next day, we will find him where we left him—only dead.

We move out at a low crawl and make our way around to the back side of the ridge. Marines open fire on us. I identify myself as Chief with sixty mortars. They know me and let us through. It's steep, but we manage to make it back into the perimeter. It feels good to be in with the rest of the company. Soon I get word that the Skipper wants to talk with me. Jones asks me who is alive on the LZ. I tell him I don't think anyone is, and they are staging for another attack. He makes plans to bombard the LZ.

Huey gunships arrive and pour hot lead on the advancing NVA. They hover over the LZ, and it looks to me that they are right over my mortar pit. But a stream of green tracers rises from the overgrowth, and the gunship turns and leaves us. We hold on and pray; we hold on to our precious ammo and try to make every shot count. Still the artillery and RPG rounds impact into the perimeter. The NVA still attack our lines, in teams or individually, and they are met with white hot lead.

I split up my crew. I keep Homes with me. We drag him over by the other mortar pit. The corpsman wraps his wounds and says that's all he can do for now. We set a zero charge on the mortar rounds and almost set the tube at a ninety-degree angle; the Skipper, Jim Jones, tells us to hold a few rounds back and to point the tube toward the north perimeter.

The AK-47 rounds crack overhead. RPG rounds swoop in and impact all around us. More artillery rounds come crashing down, with the swiftness of lightning. I feel the explosion, realize I'm hit, and feel my body being tossed about like a rag doll.

I don't know how long I am unconscious, but when I wake up, I am standing on a prairie. I have no idea where I am. It's not Vietnam. It's very peaceful. I can hear birds singing, but I can't see any. I can hear a brook, but I don't see it. The sun is bright, but it's not hot. The air feels cool against my skin. I feel at peace. I am not in any pain, even though there is blood coming from my left eye and shrapnel wounds on my arm and back. I can feel something warm running down the left side of my neck. I wipe it away. It's blood coming from my left ear and the left side of my body. I am the only Marine here. I don't know where the rest of the company is, and I don't know where I am.

In the distance, I can see three riders coming my way. They are riding hard. I am not afraid. Soon the three riders are standing in front of me; they stop, and we make eye contact.

They are Ho-Chunk warriors from a bygone era. Their mounts are not breathing hard. There is no sign of sweat. I don't understand. The horses should be breathing hard and sweating profusely, but they stand still as if they had been here all the time. Then one of the riders dismounts and walks over to me. He has a chiseled, weathered face. His army blue coat has been modified with Indian designs, and he wears an eagle feather.

William Hatchett (Wa-Bo-Cinch-ga), my great-great-grandfather, walks up and looks at me. "My grandson, I knew that you would live," the old warrior says.

I ask him how he knows me.

He tells me that many years ago, when he walked the earth, he saw me in one of his dreams and that he saw men with slits for eyes trying to kill me, sneaking up on me and my men. "I tried to tell you that two of them were behind you, but my medicine didn't work. Tell me what happened."

"I got my pistol reloaded. I heard something behind me. I turned, and I was looking into a muzzle of an AK-47 rifle. I shot the enemy soldier in the forehead, and I shot his buddy in the face."

The chiseled face smiles. "You did well. You have proven to be a Ho-Chunk warrior. My medicine wasn't strong enough to let me go into the future to protect you."

"Where am I?" I ask.

"You are in the spirit world."

"Am I dead?"

"No. You are only a visitor. It was my wish to bring you here."

"Can I stay?"

"If I let you stay, then you can never go back," he tells me. "You have to go back. You have things to do. You have a story to tell."

I reach out to touch him, and suddenly I come to, and my arm is in the air, and a corpsman is working on my wounds. I am back in the battlefield in South Vietnam, and the war is still raging all around us.

The corpsman puts a large head dressing on my left ear and eye.

"Are my legs and arms still attached?" I ask.

He assures me that I do have everything, and that makes me feel better.

A new day dawns, but the battle continues around me. After almost eleven hours, we are still in contact with the NVA. We move around in the CP but stay close to the ground. The sun is high in the sky. Burned bodies surrounding the perimeter are giving off a terrible stench. More explosions go off in the direction where Echo Company has gone. We start to find our dead and put them in ponchos and drag them to the LZ.

General Davis of the Third Marine Division flies out to the battle site. His chopper touches down, and the general steps out, with razor-sharp creases in his starched uniform. He walks around the LZ and looks at my mortar pit with dead NVA in it. He praises the company for what a great job they did. He tells us that from now on, this ridge will be called Foxtrot Ridge and that all of the men of Foxtrot Company will have a letter entered into their records stating that they served with Foxtrot Company on May 28, 1968, in the Republic of South Vietnam.

I can't help but think that this would please my great-great-grandfather.

THE END

* Author's Note: 1st Lieutenant James Jones was the XO (Executive Officer) of Golf Company, the only XO in the battalion, since all of the others had been killed or wounded. 1st Lieutenant Jim Jones took over Foxtrot Company when 1st Lieutenant Bo Dishman went on R & R for a week. When Jones was sworn in as Commandant of the Marine Corps in 1999, they tired to locate all the survivors of Foxtrot Ridge for the ceremony. Jones went on to become Commander of the U.S. European Command, and Supreme Allied Commander, Europe. When he retired from the Marine Corps as a four star general, he remained involved in national security and foreign policy issues and is presently President Obama's National Security Advisor. He still calls me Chief.

EPILOGUE

Mabel Alice (née Wilcox) Hatchett was born on February 13, 1890, and passed away on September 25, 1969, at the Lyons, Nebraska, nursing home. She had suffered a stroke in the fall of 1966 and never fully recovered. She was a deeply religious woman. One time I asked my grandmother if she was afraid to die. Her response was, "No, I am ready to meet my creator." I thought *what a positive answer.* She was a strong-willed person, and she made every tongue wag on the Winnebago Indian reservation in June of 1910 by marrying Edward Hatchett, a full-blooded Winnebago Indian.

At the time of her death, I was stationed in Guam aboard the USS *Proteus.* I was given ten days of leave to attend her funeral. I made it back to Winnebago in time. Many of her friends and the community turned out to help my family in our time of sorrow. The day of her funeral was a warm September day. Her services were held in the same church that she and Ed had attended many, many years before.

A few weeks later, I received a letter from my mother telling me that Granddad had passed away exactly three weeks and three days after Grandma died. Along with him went the name Hatchett, since there were no boys in the Hatchett family. Ed was born on April 12, 1885, in his grandfather's house.

Together, my grandparents made history when they were united in marriage at the Thurston County Courthouse on June 14, 1910. This marriage between a white woman and an Indian man was the first in the state of Nebraska. They endured name-calling. Edward was typed as a turncoat by his own people. Mabel was scorned and snubbed by her own kind. They also endured the loss of everything during the Great Depression and the flood of 1940, but through it all, their love for each other never wavered.

Ed and Mabel Hatchett have been gone from the Winnebago Indian reservation for over four decades. Today, if you mention Hatchett's Hill, people will know what you are talking about, but very few people knew who they were.

In the spring of 1972, my stepfather, Joe White, suffered a heart attack. After several months at home, his doctor told him on a Friday that he could return to work the following Monday. While Mom was cutting the grass that Saturday afternoon, Joe went in to take a nap on the couch. He never woke up.

The last warrior song given to the Hatchett family was in 1865, and it was given to William Hatchett for his bravery and duty to this country. The St. Cyr boys of Winnebago, Nebraska, Curtis and Hay-na boy, are doing me the honor of putting together a warrior song about me. I am very thankful to the St. Cyr family for doing this for me. Like my great-great-grandfather, I just wanted to serve my country, because *every warrior has his own song.*

GLOSSARY

Cho-ka:	grandfather
Chu-shgay:	nephew
Chu-wee:	aunt
Day-ga:	uncle
E-jah-nic-nah-ke-gah:	He Is Always There (William Cloud's father)
Ha-ga:	third-born son
Hay-na:	second-born son
Ho-Chunk:	Winnebago tribe
Jda-Gee:	father
Koo-nee-ka-ga (Ka-ka for short):	grandmother
Ku-nu:	firstborn son
Mah-oonah:	God
Ma-ka bag:	medicine bag
Ma-sch-he-gon-we-ga:	Great Movement, Ollie Hatchett's Indian name
Mi-xa-da:	white man
Na-nee:	mother
Sheench:	ass (a person's behind)
Shoonk:	dog
Wa-can-ja-cho-wega:	Blue Thunder, June Hatchett's Indian name

Wa-can-ja-gu-wem-ga:	Coming Back Thunder, Pat Hatchett's Indian name
Wa-can-ja-goo-ga:	Rolling Thunder, Ed Hatchett's Indian name
Wa-can-ja-penga:	Good Thunder, Kathryn Hatchett's Indian name
Wa-can-ja-wega:	White Thunder, Wilma Hatchett's Indian name
Wa-can-ja-zen-ga:	Yellow Thunder, Maxine Hatchett's Indian name
Wa-da-shoh-ttohch:	hominy soup
Wa-sha:	corn soup
Wy-skop:	bread
Y-shop da-xay-ttay:	fried bread or fry bread
Y-Sape:	(Black Robe) religious white man
Xu Kagle Gle:	Buffaloes Sitting in a Circle, Alan Walker's Indian name

REFERENCES

Adams, David
Education for Extinction: American Indians and the Boarding School Experience 1875–1928
1995
University Press of Kansas

Bureau of Indian Affairs
Statement by then assistant secretary Kevin Gover
2000
Indian Boarding Schools

Child, Brenda J.
Boarding School Seasons: American Indian Families, 1900–1940
2000
University of Nebraska Press, Lincoln and London

Child, Brenda J., and Lomawaima Tsianina
Away from Home: American Indian Boarding School Experiences
2000
Heard Museum, Phoenix, Arizona

Churchill, Ward
Kill the Indian, Save the Man
2004
City Lights Books

Fort Atkinson, Iowa
Research on the Neutral Ground, 1830–1846
2006
Fort Atkinson, Iowa

Genoa U.S. Indian School Foundation
Research on Edward L. Hatchett
2006
Genoa, Nebraska

Kearns, Richard
Personal interview
2005
Winnebago, Nebraska

Lewis, Henry M. G.
Phone interview, Hatchett history
2005
Layton, Utah

Mullin, June (née Hatchett) We-can-je-cho-wega (Blue Thunder)
Phone interview, Hatchett history
2007
San Jose, California

National Archives and Records
Research on Edward Hatchett
Winnebago Agency records on heir-ship
2006
Kansas City, Missouri

Nebraska State Historical Society
2006
Omaha Creek flood of June 1940
Lincoln, Nebraska

Porter, Kathryn J. (née Hatchett) Wa-can-ja-penga (Good Thunder)
Personal interview, Hatchett history
2005
Fairview, Michigan

Radin, Paul
The Winnebago Tribe
1990
University of Nebraska, Lincoln and London

Smith, David L.
Little Priest
The Last of the Breed
2003
Winnebago, Nebraska

Smith, Dave
Personal interview
2007
Santa Ynez, California

Smith, William, retired lieutenant colonel USMC
Personal interview
2006
Thousand Oaks, California

Tallmadge, Annie (née Sine)
Interview, Ho-Chunk history and language
2008
Wisconsin Dells, Wisconsin

Thurston County Clerk's Office
Records
2006
Pender, Nebraska

Walker, Michael R. (brother)
Personal interview
2008
Clearfield, Utah

Walker, Winifred P. (née Hatchett) Wa-can-Ja-wem-ga (Coming Back Thunder)
Personal interview, Hatchett history
2002
Winnebago, Nebraska

Walker, Terry W. (brother)
Personal interview
2008
Aberdeen, South Dakota

Winnebago Language Department
Harold Cleveland
Research
2008
Winnebago, Nebraska

Woodruff, Mark
Foxtrot Ridge: A Battle Remembered
2002
Vandamere Press

Yellowthunder, Ralph
Interview, Ho-Chunk history and language
2004
Fairchild, Wisconsin